Service-Dominant Logic

In 2004, Robert F. Lusch and Stephen L. Vargo published their ground-breaking article on the evolution of marketing theory and practice toward "service-dominant (S-D) logic," describing the shift from a product-centered view of markets to a service-led model. Now, in this keenly anticipated book, the authors present a thorough primer on the principles and applications of S-D logic. They describe a clear alternative to the dominant worldview of the heavily planned, production-oriented, profit-maximizing firm, presenting a coherent, organizing framework based on ten foundational premises. The foundational premises of S-D logic have much wider implications beyond marketing for the future of the firm, transcending different industries and contexts, and will provide readers with a deeper sense of why the exchange of service is the fundamental basis of all social and economic exchange. This accessible book will appeal to students, as well as to researchers and practitioners.

Robert F. Lusch is the James and Pamela Muzzy Chair in Entrepreneurship, and Professor of Marketing at the Eller College of Management, University of Arizona. He is past editor of the *Journal of Marketing* and chairperson of the American Marketing Association. Professor Lusch's research focuses on marketing strategy and theory with a major focus on the service-dominant logic of marketing. He is the recipient of many awards including the 2013 AMA/Irwin Distinguished Marketing Educator Award.

Stephen L. Vargo is a Shidler Distinguished Professor and Professor of Marketing at the University of Hawai'i at Manoa. Prior to entering academia, he had a career in entrepreneurial business and consulted with many corporations and governmental agencies. Professor Vargo's primary areas of research are marketing theory and thought, and consumers' evaluative reference scales. He has been awarded honorary professorships and has held visiting positions at many leading universities worldwide and is the recipient of major awards for his contributions to marketing theory and thought.

"Lusch and Vargo's new volume is a radical innovation in marketing thinking. The volume brilliantly advances and consolidates the S-D logic initial research proposal, intriguingly suggesting an interdisciplinary scientific paradigm which will engage numerous scholars across various knowledge domains."

Sergio Barile, Full Professor of Business Management,
University of Rome "La Sapienza"

"In *Service-Dominant Logic: Premises, Perspectives, Possibilities*, Bob Lusch and Steve Vargo bring us to an elevated understanding of *service* as the foundation of value and exchange in modern society. The book provides in one place a compendium of existing S-D logic knowledge and, at the same time, takes us to new levels of possibilities achievable through adopting a service mindset. The book should be required reading for all students of business and society, old and young. Bravo!"

Mary Jo Bitner, Professor and Executive Director, Center for Services Leadership,
W. P. Carey School of Business, Arizona State University; Editor of the *Journal of Service Research*

"If you are a business practitioner or academic who has been following, either casually or carefully, the development of service-dominant (S-D) logic, you should read this book, for it pulls together the foundations, structure, and implications of S-D logic for business practice and theory. If you have not been following the development of S-D logic, you should *definitely* read this book, for it will alert you to a transformational framework for thinking about economic activity."

Shelby D. Hunt, The Jerry S. Rawls and P.W. Horn Professor of Marketing,
Rawls College of Business Administration,
Texas Tech University

"This is the most seminal contribution to management and economic thinking that I have encountered during the whole of my career. Lusch and Vargo offer theory and concepts that unite the exponentially growing volume of data and research fragments from our complex modern society. Still, it is not the hard sell of yet another magic management bullet. The book should be read by everyone in management and economic disciplines: students, practitioners and politicians."

Evert Gummesson, Emeritus Professor, Stockholm University, Sweden

"Ten years ago, Lusch and Vargo turned upside down more than 200 years of economic thought, advancing the view that capabilities rather than goods are fundamental to economic exchange, and setting the stage for the emergence of a new science of service. Now they have distilled their argument to its essence in a remarkable new book that is sure to become required reading for service scientists everywhere."

Paul P. Maglio, Professor of Technology Management at the University of California, Merced and Editor-in-Chief, *Service Science*

"*Service-Dominant Logic: Premises, Perspectives, Possibilities* draws together nearly two decades of pioneering work and thought leadership by the authors. This scholarly and provocative text provides a penetrating analysis of the new discipline of service science. It combines groundbreaking research, deep insight and practical models and is an essential read for both reflective practitioners and students."

Adrian Payne, Professor of Marketing, Australia School of Business,
University of New South Wales

"Two thirds of the world's population still live on less than two dollars per day. To start changing this, we need to understand this huge segment of society not as passive aid recipients and consumers (Goods Dominant Logic), but as innovative entrepreneurs constantly co-creating solutions to survive in their daily life (Service-Dominant Logic). The *base of the pyramid* is a rich, living laboratory where actor-to-actor collaboration integrating scarce resources for value co-creation in complex subsistence ecosystems is rooted and practiced every day; where people are *SDL Natives*. This definitive book by Lusch and Vargo provides us with the ultimate platform to better understand the complexities and opportunities of a service-dominant culture."

Professor Javier Reynoso, Service Management Research Chair,
EGADE Business School, Mexico

"Service-dominant logic has been widely accepted as a leading theory and thinking framework for service sciences and engineering. It is now entering the consciousness of business leaders and practitioners: in multiple disciplines in business research and technology development, service-dominant logic is becoming part of the standard vocabulary and its relevance to practice is even more prominent as the data- and analytics-driven economy is emerging. Written by the pioneers who defined and framed the theory and applications of service-dominant logic, this monograph is a must read for researchers and practitioners alike."

Daniel Dajun Zeng, Professor in Management Information Systems,
Eller College of Management, University of Arizona;
Research Faculty, Chinese Academy of Sciences; Editor-in-Chief of *IEEE Intelligent Systems*

SERVICE-DOMINANT LOGIC

PREMISES, PERSPECTIVES, POSSIBILITIES

Robert F. Lusch
University of Arizona

and

Stephen L. Vargo
University of Hawai'i

CAMBRIDGE
UNIVERSITY PRESS

CAMBRIDGE
UNIVERSITY PRESS

University Printing House, Cambridge CB2 8BS, United Kingdom

One Liberty Plaza, 20th Floor, New York, NY 10006, USA

477 Williamstown Road, Port Melbourne, VIC 3207, Australia

314-321, 3rd Floor, Plot 3, Splendor Forum, Jasola District Centre, New Delhi-110025, India

79 Anson Road, #06-04/06, Singapore 079906

Cambridge University Press is part of the University of Cambridge.

It furthers the University's mission by disseminating knowledge in the pursuit of
education, learning and research at the highest international levels of excellence.

www.cambridge.org
Information on this title: www.cambridge.org/9780521124324

First published 2014

A catalogue record for this publication is available from the British Library

Library of Congress Cataloging in Publication data
Lusch, Robert F.
Service-dominant logic : premises, perspectives, possibilities / Robert F. Lusch,
University of Arizona and Stephen L. Vargo, University of Hawaii.
   pages   cm
Includes bibliographical references and index.
ISBN 978-0-521-19567-6 (alk. paper)
1. Customer relations – Philosophy.   2. Customer services – Philosophy.
3. Service industries – Philsophy.   I. Vargo, Stephen L., 1945–   II. Title.
HF5415.5.L85   2014
658.8′12–dc23

2013045870

ISBN 978-0-521-19567-6 Hardback
ISBN 978-0-521-12432-4 Paperback

To Mark and Stephen Lusch for their assistance, encouragement, and lively debates.

Robert F. Lusch

To my students, past, present, and future.

Stephen L. Vargo

CONTENTS

PART I
PREMISES

PART III
POSSIBILITIES

EXHIBITS

FOREWORD

Service-dominant (S-D) logic has rapidly become an essential new way to see and think about our world today, its history, and possible futures.

Why S-D logic?

The two-decade collaboration of Lusch and Vargo reflects the influence of thinkers across the ages, integrating elements from Aristotle, Bastiat, Clark, Gummesson, Hunt, Kotler, Levitt, McLuhan, Normann, Penrose, Romer, Smith, Williamson, Zimmermann, and many others, yet nevertheless manages to succinctly tell a unique and compelling story for today's researchers, practitioners, leaders, and innovators. I first heard the story when Lusch visited IBM Almaden in the fall of 2004, and then again in conversations with Vargo at the Frontiers in Service Conference in 2005. These were exciting conversations, providing fresh perspective on a subject of great economic importance and scientific significance, and conversations have continued to this day as S-D logic has evolved.

This latest book more than any other work brings us all along on their journey together, and invites us to contribute as well. After all, cocreation of value is at the heart of service-for-service exchange and S-D logic. Hundreds have already contributed to this rapidly growing body of knowledge and practice, and this book will invite hundreds, if not thousands, more to contribute in the years to come. This book is a wonderful invitation to cocreate the future together; by first understanding what constrains our thinking today and historically how we got here.

The way we see and understand our world of human activities, economic exchanges, and social interactions, matters a great deal. Think of how intellectually important and economically significant Newton's view on mass and gravity or Hooke and Pasteur's views on cells and bacteria were and have become, and quite quickly one comes to appreciate the way we see and understand our world matters a great deal.

Also, these earlier stories of scientific progress reinforce that much of what matters to people is invisible, and only with new tools can we appreciate what is real, and what is really going on all around us. By the end of this decade smart phones will not only be much smarter, but perhaps half of the world's growing population will keep one close-at-hand as they live their daily life. New tools for seeing the big data of economic exchanges and social interactions are already clearly on the horizon.

The way we talk about our world matters too. To explain S-D logic, Lusch and Vargo meet head on the challenge of working with the existing lexicon. The S-D logic foundational premises interconnect and move old words and new concepts forward step by step in the direction demanded by our times. Terms like "service ecosystem," "resource integrators," and of course "cocreating value" have become well-established S-D logic vocabulary.

In fact, this book provides a primer for S-D logic newcomers and a compact summary for established S-D logic collaborators. For readers unfamiliar with the attempts of economists to throw off the deeply rooted neoclassical economic worldview and move towards evolutionary economics, new institutional economics, and experimental economics, S-D logic is to many a much more accessible starting point, laying out goods-dominant (G-D) logic versus service-dominant (S-D) logic as the fundamental dichotomy to grasp.

Practitioners in search of ways to apply S-D logic to enhance their firm's transformation from a producer of output for customers to a cocreator of outcomes with stakeholders will also find this book invaluable. In an interconnected world where insights derived from human activities in context matter most, we are all increasingly indistinguishably simultaneously customers and providers of service. In short, we as individuals, our firms, and our government institutions as well, are resource integrators cocreating value in a service ecosystem. Service science terms these resource integrators "service system entities" and studies their evolution in a nested, networked service ecology. S-D logic is the foundation on which service science is being built.

"Jot down ideas and discuss"

The best way to read and benefit from this book is to follow the authors' advice, and to jot down notes and discuss them with a colleague.

There is no better time to do this than when you read and study the ideas and concepts in this book. Jot down ideas as they occur that relate to your situation and then revisit those as you read more and engage with others in a discussion around these ideas.

As I read the book for the first time, I extracted over ten pages of quotes that sparked ideas in my head, and to share just a few, I would like to highlight the following ten, one from each chapter.

Chapter 1 introduces the notions of the institutionalization and performativity of logics, the way we see and think about our world, illustrated compellingly by G-D logic and S-D logic. I was most struck by this statement to which I subscribe:

In this more dynamic, actor-centric view of the economy, it follows that there are no fixed, preexisting markets; rather, the market is more a representation of the continual quest of human actors for well-being in an ever-changing context.

Actors create markets to push the limits. The quest to improve quality of life drives generation after generation of innovators to challenge and then transcend limits, to raise the ceiling (improve the strongest link) and the floor (improve the weakest link). It is not just about reducing costs (e.g., resource specialization); it is also about improving the capabilities of actors (e.g., resource integration) – pushing beyond all limits.

Chapter 2 has such depth and breadth of connections, exposing the intricate roots and heritage of S-D logic, it is hard to settle on just one quote to highlight. However, practitioners with less interest in the evolution of academic thought should not miss this nugget:

Translated into a normative, managerial approach, S-D logic becomes something like:
- Identify or develop core competences, the fundamental knowledge and skills of an economic and social actor that represent potential competitive advantage.
- Identify other actors (potential customers) that could benefit from these competences.
- Cultivate relationships that involve the customers in developing customized, competitively compelling value propositions to meet specific needs.
- Gauge the success of your value proposition by obtaining economic and non-economic feedback and use it to improve your value proposition and your performance.
- Involve customers collaboratively in value creation – that is, cocreate value.

This normative approach more than hints at the importance of co-elevation of competences that should accompany actors cocreating value, while they actively compete for collaborators in the service ecosystem. Fundamentally, competing for collaborators drives the upward spiral of capabilities in the service ecosystems.

Chapter 3 presents the lexicon, axioms, and foundational premises of S-D logic:

Resource integration can also be used to describe the process of innovation.

More than anything else, what makes learning the lexicon, axioms, and foundational premises of S-D logic essential today is the way it can change conversations about innovation. Using examples from Brian Arthur to explain the nature of technology and its evolution, they demonstrate that resource integration is unbounded. S-D logic opens the doors wide for rethinking technology, value propositions, business models, institutions, stakeholder roles, and the process of innovation.

Chapter 4 addresses perhaps one of the most telling and fundamental questions from critics of S-D logic:

"Why 'service'?"

Why not "knowledge" or "value" or "actors" or "resources" or "capabilities" or "networks" or "relationships" or "interaction" or "progress" or "change" or "context" or "outcomes" or "cooperation" or any of a thousand other important words and concepts associated with the evolution of markets, economies, and society? The six reasons Lusch and Vargo provide are worth the price of this book. The application of knowledge by actors to create change that is mutually beneficial is both profoundly simple and profoundly integrating.

Chapter 5 delves into the nature of actors, ranging from individuals to businesses to nations:

Viewing actors generically allows the development of a logic of human exchange systems that includes the economy and society and transcends academic disciplines. We argue that it also allows for an academic discipline that has robust, practical application.

S-D logic encourages an A2A, or actor-to-actor view of the world, which subsumes business-to-consumer (B2C), business-to-business (B2B), customer-to-customer (C2C), government-to-citizen (G2C), and much more. Individuals augmented with tools and organizations deserve a great deal more study, as we enter the age of cognitive computing and our tools and systems become much smarter. A transdiscipline, such as service science, borrows from many disciplines, without replacing any. However, S-D logic helps us to better appreciate the institutional logics we use even when we aspire to be more transdisciplinary T-shaped thinkers, with depth and breadth, across disciplines, sectors, and cultures.

Chapter 6 in many ways is the most challenging, and deals with resources. According to Erich Zimmermann:

Resources are not, they become.

The improvisational nature of actors as they struggle for viability, sometimes grasping at straws and managing to do the improbable, is hard to explain. Because it is one of the most challenging chapters in the book, I jotted down more ideas from this one than from any other. This is one I plan to go back and read several times more.

Chapter 7 addresses collaboration and normalizing practices such as language, standards, and information technology.

Modular architecture can be thought of as a normalizing practice. Modularization is a means of parts and job standardization.

Information technology as a meta-force simultaneously reducing transaction costs and expanded capabilities is explored here. This chapter provokes many ideas about the fundamentally nested, networked structure of the world's systems, and hierarchical complexity.

Chapter 8 delves deeply into service ecosystems:

With the emergence and growth of service science, interest has arisen in studying major service systems in society, often a geopolitical area such as a city.

Over the coming decades, governments, businesses, academics, and entrepreneurs will increasingly need to apply S-D logic to rethink cities.

Chapter 9 explains service-dominant strategy:

Service-dominant (S-D) strategy focuses on increasing the effectiveness of the firm's roles as an integrator of resources and a cocreator of value, through service exchange, in complex, dynamic systems.

Society is in the early stages of understanding how to dynamically reconfigure resources in direct and indirect service–for–service exchanges. Business model innovations and platform innovations, especially information technology enabled platforms, are often successful because they allow actors to dynamically reconfigure resources better.

Chapter 10 both summarizes and sets the stage for several future considerations. The notion of S-D logic as a meta-idea is advanced:

Paul Romer refers to a meta-idea as one that helps to support the creation and transfer of other ideas. However, meta-ideas can also provide a transcending worldview, a fertile and robust platform for the creation and application of other, more specific ideas.

Romer's own meta-idea in the context of Charter Cities, where people can experiment with rule systems as easily as they can experiment with technology systems, is all about accelerating the unlocking of human potential trapped in institutional logics that do not serve them well. The links between S-D logic and Charter Cities are one of many important areas touched on in this book ripe for further exploration.

Where to from here?

In sum, as Paul Maglio and I have written frequently, S-D logic provides the logic and deep philosophical foundation for service science. In fact, Lusch and Vargo correctly note that IBM's focus on service science, management, and engineering (SSME) is a direct reflection of the two-decade transformation journey of one whole firm from G-D logic toward S-D logic. Furthermore, everyone in the service science community can most certainly benefit from a deeper appreciation of S-D logic, as that community works together to build the body of knowledge and tools (service appliances) that will help us to better understand service systems and value cocreation phenomena. I thank Bob and Steve for their inspiring spirit of adventure, insatiable curiosity about the world, and inviting us all along on this exciting journey.

JIM SPOHRER
SAN JOSE, CA
2013

PREFACE

For nearly two decades we have collaborated on developing a more unifying and transcending view of business and, more broadly, economic and social organization. It began, more modestly, as an exercise in sense-making for ourselves, concerned with intractable issues such as the distinction between goods and services – and the related implication that goods marketing and services marketing are different – and the notion that service only becomes economically important after industrialization.

Over the past decade, it has grown to more encompassing concerns. For example, we were struck by alternative and competing views and frameworks, for managing business and marketing effort, as represented by the various subdisciplines and research streams in marketing – B2B marketing, international marketing, industrial marketing, consumer marketing, services marketing, retail marketing, tourism marketing, high-technology marketing, social marketing, macromarketing, and so on – that were, for the most part, seemingly irreconcilable. However, it became apparent that all of these had a common driver: the inadequacy of the logic of the underlying model of economic exchange, what we now call "goods-dominant (G-D) logic." We also sensed that there were similarities in the perspectives of not only these research traditions, but in many business practices in general (as evidenced in the popular, trade press): a move toward understanding business in terms of intangibilities and human experiences, interactions and collaborations, the evolution and integration of resources, and so on. In short, we saw business thought moving toward a convergence that has now become known as "service-dominant (S-D) logic."

The scope and purpose of our collaboration have broadened from curious sense-making to the facilitation of the development of a more transcending, unifying, and robust framework for thinking about economic and social activity. Not only has the scope of our collaboration expanded, so has the number of participants, to the point where it now involves, in varying degrees, hundreds of academics and practitioners around the world. Increasingly, we are sensing the need for our writing to be accessible to a wider audience, especially students and thoughtful and seasoned practitioners.

Although it took us a decade to publish our first work, which appeared in early 2004 in the *Journal of Marketing* and was titled "Evolving to a New Dominant Logic for Marketing," the next decade witnessed many more articles by us and hundreds by others. Throughout the past decade we found the central ideas and concepts of S-D logic seeping into areas that went well beyond marketing. Importantly, it became viewed by many as the foundation upon which the new discipline of service science was being assembled and we witnessed rising interest in design thinking and science, business strategy, and information technology, as well as other fields. Not surprisingly, we thus began to realize we were not just presenting a new dominant logic for marketing (as our initial article suggested) but, more importantly, a new dominant logic for creating the wealth (and viability) of a nation, city, enterprise, or simply a household or any other economic and social organization.

A key challenge we have faced in developing and communicating S-D logic is the precision of its lexicon. We soon realized how important words and language are in framing our view and conceptualization of the world and, hence, how it influences our actions or behavior. We found subtle yet important distinctions between terms such as "services" versus "service," "customers" versus "consumers," static and tangible resources and dynamic and intangible resources. Thus, much of what is to be learned from this book concerns how to uncompact new and/or revised meanings for old terms – for example, what are a resource, cocreation, and value? But we also found it necessary to develop new "concepts" and language, which we will introduce and explain here. These include "service ecosystems," "resource integration," "resourceness," and "value-in-context." We believe that, although it will take some effort to develop an understanding of the lexicon, most readers will find it worthwhile.

In this book we wish to accomplish three goals. First, due to requests of scholars, consultants, and enterprise leaders, we hope to provide a basic primer on S-D logic that is accessible and can, if needed, replace reading our numerous writings on this topic. Second, our intent is to provide a sufficient grounding in S-D logic to allow the reader to begin to question old practices that are overly bound to a neoclassical economics view of the firm as producing units of output and attempting the maximization of a single profit outcome. We actually refer to this as goods-dominant (G-D) logic. In brief, our goal is to help rid the reader of his or her G-D logic thinking and mindset. Third, we hope this book will provide the knowledge to develop more innovative service offerings and compelling value propositions. Much of this will come not from strategies for competitive advantage but rather from collaborative advantage through cocreation to design the future of the enterprise.

Enterprise and industry groups, doctoral students, and others often ask us to "teach" the basics of S-D logic. From the outset, we try to be clear, and wish also to make the message clear in this book: "S-D logic cannot be taught but S-D logic can be learned." Certainly this book and our lectures can be teaching vehicles but, for the reader to understand and embrace S-D logic, he or she has to be an active and engaged learner. We also often receive the related request, "Tell us how to apply S-D logic." Once again, it is necessary to adopt the mindset and perspective that S-D logic offers and determine for the enterprise or other entity how to apply these ideas to its unique context. There is no better time to do this than when reading and studying the ideas and concepts in this book. We recommend that readers jot down ideas as they occur that relate to their situation and then revisit these as they read more and engage with others in a discussion about these ideas.

The book comprises three parts. Part I, "Premises," offers an introduction to the premises of S-D logic and is organized into four chapters. Chapter 1, "The service-dominant mindset," provides the necessary concepts and ideas behind S-D logic to allow the reader to begin to view and think about social and economic organization in terms of the exchange of service among human actors. Chapter 2, "Roots and heritage," explains how political and economic thought developed over hundreds of years around the concept of the production and export of surplus tangible goods as the key to national wealth and, subsequently, to the major paradigm for firm management, through profitable production. It also illustrates how repeated attempts to patch up G-D logic, due to its incongruities, has led to the development of, and deep interest in and acceptance of, S-D logic. Chapter 3, "Axioms and foundational premises," offers a more in-depth discussion and explanation of the ten foundational premises of S-D logic and how they can be summarized in four axioms. "Service as a guiding frame-work" is the focus of Chapter 4. Often we are challenged on why service should be the guiding framework for social and economic organization and thus in this chapter we provide a more complete response and explanation about why service is the "right" frame of reference.

Part II, "Perspectives," enables the reader to begin to view the world around him or her differently. We begin with Chapter 5, "It's all actor-to-actor (A2A)," which provides a perspective based on ending the practice of dividing actors into groups of buyers and sellers or producers and consumers and argues for viewing the social and economic organization as an actor-to-actor network and/or system. In Chapter 6, "The nature, scope, and integration of resources," we offer a broadened perspective of resources that will expand how resource man-agement is viewed. It also discusses and explains how social and economic actors, when viewed as resource-integrating actors, become the key to unleashing innovation in the enterprise and in society. "Collaboration" is the focus of Chapter 7. S-D logic is viewed as seeking strategic advantage not through competitive advantage but via collaborative advantage. This lens allows one to see many more possibilities for mutualistic service exchanges. Finally, in Chapter 8, "Service ecosystems," a framework is presented that enables viewing the most micro service-for-service exchanges between actors, as well as the meso structures that these micro exchanges create and, in turn, the more stable and longer-term macro structures. Thus, this facilitates an understanding of micro- and macromarketing systems, not as separate domains but as part of a unified and coherent system that the enterprise needs to navigate.

Possibilities are the focus of Part III, which comprises two chapters. Chapter 9, "Strategic thinking," places special emphasis upon expanding enterprise possibilities by developing strategic directions around service ecosystems, design thinking, collaboration, rebundling resources, and value propositions. Chapter 10, "Conclusions and considerations," discusses how S-D logic is resulting in a convergence of many lines of thought that are creating an emergence of a more unified theory of business and society. We explore the idea of S-D logic as a meta-idea that positions S-D logic as an idea platform upon which enterprises and governments can more easily create specific ideas and strategies to enhance system viability. We conclude with an appeal for more work to be done on the role of institutions in the development of S-D logic and also we echo the need for more mid-range theory.

ACKNOWLEDGMENTS

Cocreation is a good term to describe this book. Although we are the authors, many of the ideas presented come from scholars and writers over at least 200 years and in some cases longer. We have tried to cite the most central to the development of S-D logic but the list is not exhaustive.

Many colleagues both on our respective campuses and throughout the world have been friendly and sometimes appropriately harsh critics that have collectively served to sharpen our thinking and writing. These individuals go well beyond our home discipline of marketing and significantly beyond North America and beyond academia. In this regard we are especially grateful to: Robert Aiken, Tor Andreassen, Melissa Archpru Akaka, Eric Arnould, David Ballantyne, Mary Jo Bitner, Ruth Bolton, Rod Brodie, Stephen W. Brown, James Carver, Jennifer Chandler, Elizabeth Davidson, George Day, John Deighton, Beth DuFault, Amber Epp, Michael Etgar, Bo Edvardson, Daniel Flint, Pennie Frow, Bob Greer, David Griffith, Christian Grönroos, Evert Gummesson, Anders Gustafsson, Stephen Haeckel, Michael Harvey, Anu Helkkula, Tomas Hult, Shelby D. Hunt, Keith Joiner, Hans Kjellberg, Michael Kleinaltenkamp, Ajay Kohli, Gene Laczniak, Doug Lambert, Roger Layton, Sidney Levy, Helge Lobler, Paul Maglio, Naresh Maholtra, Alan Malter, Matthew Mars, Cristina Mele, Michael Merz, Stefan Michel, Fred Morgan, Patrick Murphy, Satish Nambisan, Ange Nawaswari, Suvi Nenonen, Irene Ng, Matthew O'Brien, Amy Ostrom, Adrian Payne, Jacquie Pels, Lisa Penaloza, Francesco Polese, Linda Price, Wesley Randall, Roland Rust, Mohanbir Sawhney, Hope Schau, Lisa Scheer, David Schmidtz, Ainslie Schultz, Ray Serpkenci, Clifford J. Shultz II, Jaakko Siltaloppi, Shelia Slaughter, Kaj Sorbacka, Jim Spohrer, David Stewart, Mohan Tanniru, Marja Toivonen, Bard Trönvoll, Rajan Varadarajan, Richard Varey, Sangeetha Venkataramani, Jameson Watts, Frederick Webster, Heiko Weiland, Michelle Weinberger, William Wilkie, Ian Wilkinson, Daniel Wren, Christopher Wu, Valarie Zeithamal, Jurui Zhang.

Finally, we would also like to acknowledge and thank Paula Parish, our editor at Cambridge University Press, Claire Poole (Assistant Editor), and Jessica Ann Murphy (Production Editor).

Robert F. Lusch, Tucson, Arizona
Stephen L. Vargo, Honolulu, Hawai'i
2013

Part I
Premises

1 The service-dominant mindset

> Once destiny was an honest game of cards which followed certain conventions, with a limited number of cards and values. Now the player realizes in amazement that the hand of his future contains cards never seen before and that the rules of the game are modified by each play.
>
> Paul Valéry

Introduction

Part of our nature as humans is to develop belief systems that become handy ways for seeing and understanding the world around us and for ordering our reality. We can refer to these mechanisms as institutional logics.[1] Institutional logics become normative and play a key role in guiding and determining our behavior. Many of these institutional logics arise from our training and education and thus the ordered view of the world from the perspective of an economist is different from that of an accountant, mechanic, sociologist, physicist, fire fighter, or moral philosopher. Regardless, they enable viewing a complex world in what promises to be coherent terms and provide a lens for perceptually separating noise from signal. Thus, they contribute to comfort, understanding, and sense-making.

Just because we are comfortable with our institutional logics does not suggest these logics are always correct or appropriate or do not need to change or evolve. In fact, some institutional logics become so strongly held across individuals that they become paradigmatic and very difficult to shift.[2] It has been found repeatedly throughout history that these paradigms can restrict vision and under-standing and scientific advancement. Of course, in business, there are many such "worlds" that need to be understood: cultural, ecological, economic, social, physical, political, technological, and many others. The primary purpose of this book is to contribute to the understanding of the world of economic and social exchange among human actors, both individually and in groups, by proposing an alternative view or perspective, what we call "service-dominant logic" (S-D logic), to the traditional "goods-dominant logic" (G-D logic).

Specialization and exchange

Humans specialize and exchange because they have limited but often advanta-geous individual abilities. It is noteworthy that it takes more than specialization, since the specialization of one actor must be advantageous to another actor for exchange to occur. By specializing, humans can enhance their abilities but in turn need to exchange their abilities with other actors. This results in systemic interdependencies. Society and, along with it, many institutions, such as lan-guage, norms, industries, markets, and organizations (e.g., firms, or enterprises) are created to facilitate this exchange system for efficiency and coordination purposes. While systems of human actors and institutions[3] are complex, theories of marketing, business, and society that deal with them need to be appropriately simple if they are to be broadly generalizable. At the same time, these theories need to be sufficiently representative of the complexity of the world of exchange to serve as the basis of useful, normative applications that they are intended to facilitate.

Problems emerge immediately when constructing simple theories of exchange, business, and society. Arguably, the most difficult of these problems is the dominance of an institutional logic with serious limitations, which is deeply rooted in a discipline and thus monopolizes associated thought processes. One such worldview is G-D logic. This logic frames the world of exchange in terms of *units of output* (goods). Others have referred to it as "old enterprise logic," "manufacturing logic," and other, similarly descriptive tags.

G-D logic views the production and exchange of goods as the central compo-nents of business and economics. That is, it frames the purpose of the firm and the function of economic exchange in terms of making and distributing products – units of output, usually tangible. It is closely aligned with neoclassical econom-ics, which views actors as rational, firms as profit-maximizing, customers as utility-maximizing, information and resources as flowing easily among economic actors, and markets as equilibrium-seeking – scholars within and outside economics have challenged all these perspectives. For instance, Penrose conceived of the firm as a group of physical and human resources that were deployed in many ways to provide productive services.[4] Richardson, also an economist, built on this idea and introduced the concept of "capabilities" to economics.[5] But the holding power of G-D logic was largely too strong to overcome.

In later chapters, we explain that G-D logic has additional aspects that make it an inappropriate logic for viewing human exchange systems but, for now, we will focus on how G-D logic creates problems for those trying to apply it normatively to the management of firms or public policy. Throughout the book, we propose that a more general and useful understanding of social and economic exchange among human actors, both individually and organizationally, is needed. We offer S-D logic as an alternative.

Goods-dominant logic centricities

There are many problems with G-D logic but some of the most important relate to where it focuses attention. Therefore, before we propose a more useful and robust framework for understanding economic (and, more generally, social) exchange, a brief review of several of the problematic "centricities" of G-D logic and how they misguide academic and practical thought and action, is useful. These centricities are illustrated in Exhibit 1.1 and briefly reviewed in the following sections.

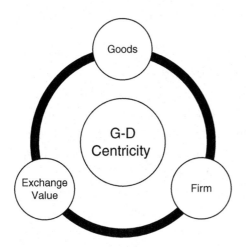

Exhibit 1.1 G-D logic centricities

Goods centricity

Perhaps not surprisingly, the major problem with G-D logic is that it fosters *goods centricity*. As Theodore Levitt suggested fifty years ago, firms produce products but that is not what customers buy.[6] In his vivid examples of the railroad and motion picture industry he proclaims that customers actually want or need transportation and entertainment services, rather than the products – railroad freight and passenger cars and theater seats – that firms often see themselves selling. In brief, customers seek solutions and experiences, not products. To this day, marketing myopia continues; we submit that this is largely attributed to a deeply embedded G-D logic, which has institutionalized it. As we will argue, goods are just vehicles for service provision, usually enabling self-service. They provide a means, rather than represent an "end-product."

Firm centricity

With the G-D model, the firm is central to economic exchange because the firm is seen as the proactive actor: it is viewed as the innovator, developer, producer, distributer, and promoter of goods, and thus is seen as representing the heart of markets and exchange. It also is viewed as central in its role of making major financial commitments, hiring other actors as workers, taking risks, and making a myriad of other decisions. All of this, under the rubric of managerial decision-making, is intended to minimize risks and maximize profitability for the firm, through markets. Markets, on the other hand, are seen as almost passively (i.e., waiting, with unfilled demand) "out there" (i.e., preexisting), and comprising "customers and consumers" from whom the firm profits by producing, selling, and distributing goods.

But just as goods in and of themselves are not the central purpose of exchange, so too firms are not the central actors. Organizations and firms are inventions to help humans solve the problems associated with the exchange of their individual advantageous abilities. Humans are the key actors in the cocreation of their well-being by combining resources from various market-facing (organizations and other actors), private (themselves, friends, family, etc.), and public (government and community institutions, etc.) sources, to continually resolve issues in the context of their own lives. This does not imply or suggest that human actors are not influenced by organizations and other structures. Humans create organizations and structures that in turn influence and control them.

Also, any particular exchange or human action is part of a continuing process that is stitched to other processes and actors that unfolds over time. In this regard, human actors are not end-users at all. Rather they, in turn, contribute both positively and negatively to the well-being of other actors through ongoing market, public, and private exchange. In this more dynamic, actor-centric view of the economy, it follows that there are no fixed, preexisting markets; rather, the "market" is more a representation of the continual quest of human actors for well-being in an ever-changing context. This shift in centrality in no way diminishes the role of the firm in the aggregate, just in the creation of value for other actors. As a result, how the firm thinks about its role in value creation must shift.

Exchange-value centricity

G-D logic is also problematic because of its implicit promotion of *exchange-value centricity*. Scholars have been debating the role of *exchange-value* – what something is worth in exchange – in comparison to *use-value* – the extent to which the use of something contributes to the well-being of some actor – at least since the fourth century BCE, when Aristotle distinguished between the two and discussed them. Generally, they have come down on the side of the primacy and centrality of use-value. For example, the medieval Schoolmen clearly advocated this position in their economic philosophy, based on their views that exchange is motivated by human needs.[7] However, with the development of a more formal economic philosophy, beginning with the work of the "father of economics," Adam Smith, and later extended in the development of economic science, the focus on use value largely diminished, at least temporarily.

Importantly, as discussed in the next chapter, Adam Smith did not set out to be the father of economics; rather his focus was on determining how England could become wealthy through international trade at the time[8] – the early part of the Industrial Revolution. He concluded that the key source of national wealth was the production and the export of surplus tangible goods and reserved the word "productive" only for those activities that contributed to this production and export. Though he acknowledged value-in-use as "real value," given his limited purpose, he used exchange-value as a surrogate, because he felt it was both easier to understand and provided a standardized measurement of wealth. There were several attempts to shift the emphasis back to value-in-use by the economic philosophers who followed Smith, such as Say's introduction of "utility."[9] But, as we will explain in Chapter 2, even that word morphed back into an exchange-value meaning.

The meaning of exchange-value was amplified and institutionalized as economic thought transformed from philosophy to science at a time that "science" meant Newtonian Mechanics – a model that viewed matter as embedded with properties – and thus provided for an easy translation to the concept of a product, or "good," embedded with "utilities" (exchange-value). This, in turn, paved the ground for marginal utility theory,[10] which became the basis of the neoclassical model of economics that, in time, was adopted by other business disciplines.

The early scholars, including Smith in his original analysis of economic exchange, had it right all along: value is created at the point of what we have been calling "consumption" and, more recently, "experience", rather than during production. This latter point is worth pondering. If your house is burning down and you can take one thing (not another person) what would it be? It is likely not something that has a high economic value but something that has meaning to you outside of value-in-exchange. It is something that will be useful to you in continuing experiences that you perceive as valuable. Although the value may not be in exchange, it is also not in the thing *per se* but how you evaluate your connection to or experiences with that thing.

Recap

These centricities, focused on goods, the firm, and exchange-value, are important because, again perhaps ironically, they point firms attempting to "go to market" in the wrong normative directions by blinding them to the purpose and nature of the market, value creation, and the mutual roles of the various actors. They suggest that the firm is the prime mover, that producing goods is its primary purpose, and that this production process embedded goods with value – that goods have intrinsic value. Of course, if this were true, there would be no sales events focused on price reduction and no inventory write-downs. But, even more important, they direct attention away from both the real meaning of value and the way it is created, interactively, in concert with a whole host of actors, singly and collectively (e.g., through organizations, firms), contributing resources that are eventually integrated by other actors to provide service. In short, *value is cocreated.* They also direct attention away from the most important resources being integrated and doing the integration – human actors with their skills, knowledge, and innovative and entrepreneurial abilities. What is needed is a logic that, rather than abandoning goods logic, transcends it, by recognizing the *primacy of human resources applied for the benefit of others* (and ourselves) – *service.*

Toward transcendence

It is difficult to escape the paradigmatic pull of G-D logic to develop a broad and general view of social and economic exchange. However, it can be helpful to use a sort of "linguistic telescope" to zoom out to a broader view of economic and social exchange for more clarity. Through this telescopic view, we can see social and economic actors exchanging in many different contexts but, as we will argue throughout this book, they are fundamentally always doing three common things: (1) integrating resources from various sources, (2) exchanging service for service, and (3) cocreating value. However, to clearly see this and to fully appreciate its significance and power requires refocusing away from firms and customers to an actor-to-actor (A2A) framework.

The actor-to-actor (A2A) perspective

Arguably, one of the most detrimental conceptualizations of G-D logic is the associated "producer–consumer" distinction. Consider what this implies: some actors (e.g., firms) "produce" (create) value, whereas others (e.g., customers) "consume" (destroy) that value. Exhibit 1.2 illustrates the goods-dominant view of producers and consumers. Let's explore whether that accurately describes what goes on.

We suggest that, to the extent that "production" and "consumption" are appropriately descriptive, they apply to all actors. Consider a professor who

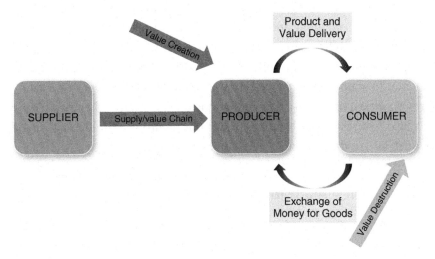

Exhibit 1.2 G-D lens

uses a car, gas, and so on, to go to the university to teach students; is he or she a producer or a consumer? Likewise, consider the students, who take notes so that the professor's insights can be used in their jobs; are they producers or consumers? How about one of the students who is an employee of the car company that makes the car driven by the professor, which, in turn, pays tuition, which provides the university with the resources to pay the professor? Are they producers or consumers? The answer to all of these is "both" and "neither." On the one hand, all economic actors both "produce and consume"; on the other hand, at best, these characterizations do not inform us about anything useful concerning the actors, and, at worst, mislead us about their role in economic exchange in ways that misinform attempts to engage them economically.

For this reason, which will be elaborated on in subsequent chapters, we believe it is important to think about and refer to economic (and social) actors as just that, generic "actors," without introducing (referential) confusion. Fundamentally, all actors (e.g., business firms, nonprofit and government organizations, individuals, and households) have a common purpose: *value cocreation through resource integration and service-for-service exchange.* Therefore, throughout this book, we generally avoid the terms "consumers" and "producers" (except in citations of others) and, wherever possible, the terms "customers" and "firms" (except where needed for relative reference). We use "firm" and "customer" when we need to distinguish between actors, with the firm referring to the provider of direct service or indirect service through a good and the customer referring to the provider of service indirectly, through money. However, we will generally be using an "actor-to-actor" (A2A) notation, replacing "business-to-business" (B2B), "business-to-consumer" (B2C), and "consumer-to-consumer" (C2C)[11] notations, by transcending them. We suggest that economic and social exchange, viewed from a perspective of actors interacting with other actors, as opposed to business exchanging with other businesses or consumers or any combination of these differentiated actors, opens the investigator to a more revealing and transcendent view of the world. An actor-centric versus a firm-, producer-, household-, customer-, or any other role-centric labeling is also less restrictive because it does not predispose differential, single activities, such as "production" and "consumption."

Service-for-service exchange

Just as it is helpful to refocus on the nature of the actors doing the exchanging, it is essential to refocus on what is being exchanged. We often use a discussion of a fisherman and a farmer in our teaching to illustrate alternative conceptualizations.

The discussion starts by reminding the students that the necessary resources for life, such as protein in the form of fish and carbohydrates in the form of wheat, are unevenly distributed, as are the skills and abilities necessary to obtain them. Thus, specialization and exchange become dual and reinforcing sources of advantage for actors. The students are asked to consider a farmer and fisherman, each specializing in his (or her) respective skills. The fisherman has become very proficient at harvesting fish from the sea, by developing his physical skills as well as his mental skills – the knowhow concerning when and where to fish. He has also developed tools to assist him, such as nets, hooks, and spears. Similarly, the farmer has developed the physical and mental skills necessary to grow and harvest grain and innovatively develop tools to assist.

Predictably, the students quickly grasp the essential roles of specialization and exchange. At this point the students are asked a simple question: "When the fisherman and farmer exchange, what are they exchanging?" Asking this question often results in a long pause, because the students believe we must be trying to trick them; the answer seems obvious: "They are exchanging fish for grain." This answer reflects both individual and collective views that the world is primarily about the outputs produced and exchanged by actors. This "obvious answer" is grounded in G-D logic. We argue it is wrong.

We suggest that, more accurately, or at least more generally, what the two actors are exchanging is the *application* of protein-provisioning *competences* for the application of carbohydrate-provisioning competences. That is, they are exchanging *fishing services* for *farming services*. Students often reply: "Okay, we get it but why is the distinction important?" The answers, which become apparent in the discussion that follows, are several. First, this service-oriented interpretation focuses attention on the only resource the actors really possess to take to market: their own knowledge and skills, rather than the byproducts of their application (fish and wheat). Thus, the service (application of competences) focus is more general and transcending, since it applies to exchange situations, involving different types of goods, and also in situations where there are no intermediate products (i.e., direct service provision).

In short, service is the transcending, and thus the unifying, concept for understanding economic exchange in all economies (and all businesses). Perhaps more subtle, but arguably much more important, is that, extrapolating from fishing and farming to business in general, there is a fundamental difference in how the business process is informed between understanding the purpose as *selling things* to people and understanding it to be *serving the exchange partner's needs*. This difference is a key difference between G-D logic and S-D logic.

A broadened view of service

Given the dominance of G-D logic, at least for the past several hundred years, definitions of service(s) have been couched in terms of *what goods are not* or, more apparently linked, as *intangible goods* – "all of those *nonphysical things* for which we spend money."[12] Thus, they were conceptualized as anything that *was not* defined in terms of manufactured, mined, or grown. Interestingly, this same "definition by exclusion" was (is) used for manufacturing – what is not extracted (mined or grown) – resulting in a sequential view of economic development in which the "extractive" sector is seen as primary, the "manufacturing" sector is viewed as secondary, and what remained, typically considered to be the "services" sector, is seen as "tertiary." However, all of these "sectors" can easily be translated into service, since, at the core, all of them are driven by human ingenuity used for the benefit of others, which, in turn, reciprocally benefits the servicing party – that is, through *service-for-service exchange.*

"Service" versus "services"

We will discuss the long, historical struggle for words to capture the "service(s)" phenomena in Chapter 2. Here, we raise the question of whether the nature of service(s) is (are) adequately captured by historical definitions – a residual, or what goods are not. Part of the problem is revealed in the use of the word *services* (plural), which we suggest implies *units of output – intangible goods.* More directly, though perhaps ironically, we argue that "services" is a G-D logic term. It suggests that an airline produces seat miles, rather than provide transportation, a bank sells quantities of loans, rather than provide financial service, a hotel produces units of lodging (bed nights), rather than provide lodging experiences, and so on.

On the other hand, we suggest that *service* (singular) implies a *process* of one actor doing something for another – a beneficiary. The process of serving requires the application of knowledge and skills – competences, as discussed. Thus, we more formally define "service" as the "application of competences (knowledge and skills) for the benefit of another entity or the entity itself."[13]

Role of goods

From this definition of service, it follows that goods also provide service. Goods began with some individual(s) applying their competences (knowledge and skills) to invent and/or manufacture the good. The good is then used by other individual (s) and in this sense goods are *appliances that act as intermediaries in service delivery.* This is probably obvious in some settings, such as the kitchen, where they clearly assist cooks in the process of meal service. However, it is just as true in the factory, where equipment and machinery function as appliances for manufacturing service, when combined with labor (another resource) and materials (another resource), or in everyday life, where automobiles serve as transportation appliances. In fact, it is actually quite common for computers and related equipment to be referred to as "information appliances."

Most people quickly get the idea that a refrigerator and toaster, and even a bathtub and shower, are appliances. However, often when it comes to a glass of wine or bowl of cereal, they have difficulty viewing this as an appliance. But, if the product is viewed as a resource (something to draw upon for support) then the relationship between a good and appliance and the role of the good in service provision is clearer. A glass of wine is a resource to help one relax, enhance food taste and digestion, and perhaps even facilitate health and, in many cases, it also communicates something about the drinker – refinement, frugality, social status, and so on. In all of these functions, then, it is, in a very true sense, an appliance, created by the winemaker, who has embedded in it both competences and market knowledge through the design, production, and distribution process. Likewise, a bowl of cereal can be seen as a nutritional and dietary service appliance in its displacement of physical and mental skills and time resources that would otherwise be required to prepare and serve a full breakfast meal.

A broadened view of resources

Broadly, there are two types of resources: operand and operant. *Operand resources* are generally static resources that require some action to be performed on them before they can provide value. A natural resource, such as gold (which must be found, extracted, refined, formed, and used) is an example. Goods (appliances) are also operand resources. *Operant resources*, by comparison, are resources capable of acting on other resources to create value (given appropriate circumstances). The most obvious example of operant resources is human competence – knowledge and skills that can be used in value-creating acts, such as the abilities of finding, extracting, refining, forming, and using gold. In the case of goods, it should be clear that they require operant resources both *to make them and to use them* before the intended value is created. This essential role of operant resource in all value creation makes them primary. However, they are not treated that way on balance sheets, which typically list only operand resources such as supplies, plant, equipment, finished goods, and other tangibles.

Managers and executives, almost always trained and educated with a G-D logic curriculum, learn how to manage inventory, production facilities, capital budgets, and other primarily operand resources; that is, they learn to manage balance-sheet assets. However, although not trained or educated in S-D logic, it is interesting to note that when executives are asked by us to list their firm's three most important resources they virtually never mention balance-sheet assets or operand resources, natural or man-made. Most often, they list the firm's employees (operant resources) and intangibles, such as culture, brands, alliances with other organizations, intellectual property, and reputation. Sometimes they mention the positive business climate.

Similarly, if older individuals are asked what they most value in life, they inevitably mention their relationships with family and friends and the things they have done in their careers; they seldom mention owning and driving their sports car or sailing their yacht or their association with other operand resources. More generally, the most valuable resources are often operant – in business, such things as employee abilities, business climate, and corporate culture; yet, our models of business are often centered on operand resources.

In summary, over hundreds of years the logic that actors had to confront static natural resources gave way to the view that dynamic operant resources were pivotal to well-being and wealth creation. In this renewed thinking, knowledge and the development of specialized competences serve the role of operant resources and enable human actors to expand the *usable* stockpile of natural and other static (operand) resources. Applied and specialized knowledge and skills are developed and refined through specialization, which in turn necessitates exchange and dependency on other actors. Stated alternatively, service-for-service exchange drives the expansion and not depletion of the total resources humans can draw on for support. From this service–for-service exchange, the economic and social pie has the potential to expand almost unbounded.

The four "axioms" of S-D logic

During the first few years of S-D logic's development, we focused on the historical unfolding of the events and contexts that led to the development of the foundations of economic science, which we now refer to in terms of G-D logic.[14]

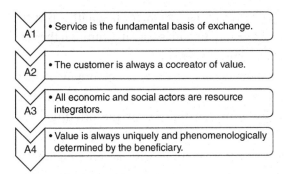

Exhibit 1.3 Axioms of S-D logic

We found that many of the assumptions on which the standard, G-D logic-based model of economic thought had been based were being increasingly questioned and that an alternative, service-based model seemed to be emerging. To capture the essence of this emerging model, we identified eight foundational premises (FPs); later, these were expanded to ten. These are discussed in later chapters. However, there are four FPs in particular that capture the essence of S-D logic, and from these the other FPs could arguably be derived. Thus, these four FPs might be considered the axioms of S-D logic. They are listed in Exhibit 1.3 and are briefly introduced here.

Service is the fundamental basis of exchange is the first axiom. This axiom is based on the previously introduced definition of service: the application of operant resources (knowledge and skill) for the benefit of another actor. As was discussed in relation to the story of the farmer and fisherman, it is always fundamentally service, rather than goods, *per se*, that actors exchange as they strive to become better off. In other words, *service is exchanged for service* and, as noted and discussed later in more detail, this implies that (1) *goods are appliances for service provision*, (2) *all businesses are service businesses*, and (3) *all economies are service economies*. It follows that *money*, when it is involved in exchanges, represents *rights to future service*. It also suggests that the essence of society and what holds together the actors that comprise it is service exchange.

The customer is always a cocreator of value is the second axiom. This axiom contradicts G-D logic, which views the firm as the producer, the creator, of value; rather, it suggests that value is something that is always cocreated through the interaction of actors, either directly or through goods.[15] Thus, a physician providing medical service to a patient is cocreating value with the patient, never independently, and, if the physician gives the patient medicine (a good), it is seen as an appliance for aiding the service provision. In both cases, it is through the use of this physician-provided service that value is cocreated.

Also, this axiom enables one to see more clearly that the service-oriented view is inherently relational because value does not arise from firm or producer internal processes. Rather, value arises through the use of the offering in a particular context, in conjunction with resources provided by other service providers and this value unfolding extends over time with a consequence of continuing social and economic exchange, implicit contracts, and relational norms.

All social and economic actors are resource integrators is the third axiom. Integrable resources come from a variety of sources, including *private sources* (e.g., self, friends, family), *market sources* (i.e., from other actors, through barter or economic exchange), or from *public sources* (i.e., collective access from communal and governmental sources), or, most likely, through the service provision of all of these, often simultaneously. It is through the integration of these resources in its many possible explicit and implicit combinations, facets, and intricacies that value is cocreated. This resource integration not only occurs with the resources directly available to actors involved in an exchange, but also indirectly with the resources and actors that provide these resources in a network of other resource-integrating actors.

Value is always uniquely and phenomenologically determined by the beneficiary is the fourth axiom of S-D logic. Here the term beneficiary reflects the generic nature of actors. This axiom reinforces that *value is experiential*. We paid particular attention to choosing the word *phenomenological*, rather than "experiential," however, because the latter often invokes connotations of something like a Disneyworld event – always positive, entertaining, and so on. Some may prefer the word experiential, viewing it as more appropriate, and certainly there is considerable talk about customer experiences and even the suggestion we are entering an "experience economy."[16] We have no issue with the use of the term experience, at least in its broader sense. However, we take exception to the idea that we are somehow entering an experience economy; on the contrary, we would argue that all economies are experience economies. Ponder this for a moment: can you think of a consumption situation that was not experiential? More importantly, the key message of this axiom is that all market offerings, all service provisioning, all goods, and all value propositions are perceived and integrated differently by each unique actor and, thus, value is also uniquely experienced and determined.

Having illustrated a broadened view of service and resources and the four axioms of S-D logic, it is possible to provide a glimpse of what marketing, or what we call *market-ing* (calling attention to both the market and marketing), is like with S-D logic and how it differs from a G-D logic perspective. It should become obvious as this discussion progresses why a G-D logic mindset is difficult to overcome.

Market-ing with S-D logic: the counterintuitive nature of S-D logic

The S-D logic meaning of marketing is different from that usually associated with G-D logic in a number of ways. Perhaps most importantly, in S-D logic, market-ing is not so much a function of the marketing department as it is a *primary function of the enterprise.* In G-D logic, an enterprise is a relatively finite, closed entity and the purpose of the enterprise is to produce and sell value-laden goods to existing markets made up of consumers with demand. More recently, this purpose has been seen to include the production and selling of "services" (intangible goods), since we are now supposedly entering a "services economy." It follows that it is the task of the marketing department to understand consumers so that it can promote and sell these goods and services.

In S-D logic, the fundamental purpose of the enterprise is *to serve itself by serving others.* This is done by integrating internal resources and the resources it has available to it through various public and market sources to create new resources that it can apply for the benefit of other enterprises (individuals, family, firms, etc.). Since the resources available to both the serving and the beneficial actors are continually changing, so too are service opportunities. For providing this service, the beneficial enterprises provide reciprocal service, often through money (service rights), rather than directly. Thus, in S-D logic, rather than marketing being a responsibility of the marketing department, it is a primary function of the enterprise – connecting with and serving other enterprises in an ever-changing market. In short, it is market-*ing.*

It is normal for managers, business analysts, journalists, and others to act and speak as if there is an economy, comprising a number of existing markets, composed of consumers for whom distinct and separate producers create and distribute goods and services and that this economy is becoming increasingly services based. However, fully locking onto S-D logic and market-ing requires the acceptance of several mental models that, given the dominance of G-D logic, are counterintuitive at best and which some view as blasphemous. These are: (1) there is no new services economy, (2) there are no "services," (3) there are no "producers" and "consumers," (4) enterprises cannot create value independently, (5) enterprises are relatively unbounded, and (6) markets do not exist.

Totally grasping and accepting these counterintuitive tenets of S-D logic can be difficult because of two related human practices regarding the development of dominant logics: institutionalization and performativity. *Institutionalization* refers to the shared acceptance of concepts, meanings, and normative behaviors – it allows coordination by providing *rules of the game*. It also allows human actors to "think," communicate, and act without taxing their limited calculative capacity. A dominant logic is a set of related, institutionalized conceptualizations concerning some activity or object – in the case of G-D logic, economic exchange.

Performativity relates to *acting in accordance with an institutionalized logic* and thus implies at least a partial self-fulfillment. For instance, if society agrees that femininity or masculinity is differentiated in terms of interests, abilities, and proper actions and related to gender, then young boys or girls are treated accordingly (i.e., are socialized), and they begin to think and act at least somewhat in accordance with the institutionalized conceptualizations. This happens regardless of whether there is a direct link between gender and these thoughts and actions.

To paraphrase Michel Callon, performativity also relates to the common conception of markets and economies: the economy is a function of economics.[17] Similarly, in the marketing discipline "market orientation" is defined as gathering and disseminating market information in the firm in order to develop market offerings, develop marketing communications, appropriately pricing offerings, and distributing them to the market. Thus marketing managers, based on this conception of market orientation, think and act in accordance. In brief, actors perform based on institutionalized logic and, hence, the logics appear to be at least partially true.

Some of the counterintuitive conceptualizations of S-D logic have been discussed or at least implied above but, given the resistance often associated with ideas that run counter to the dominant thinking, all are worth (re)emphasizing here.

There is no new services economy

How can one say that there is no new services economy? Very simply, what all actors exchange is the application of their physical and mental skills and knowledge – "service" in S-D logic terms – and, thus, *all economies are service economies.* This applies to hunting and gathering, agricultural and mining, and industrial or manufacturing and post-industrial eras. Over time, changes among relative proportions and types of mental and physical skills have occurred. However, in all cases, service is the common denominator for all of these "economies." In short, ever since human actors began to specialize and exchange, they have been dependent on the service of others and have provided service to others with service needs, and, thus, the economy always has been service based.

Despite this argument, the performative nature of G-D logic makes it appear that there is something like a "new services economy" as illustrated in Exhibit 1.4. Using standard government accounting and classification demonstrates this. Given the use of a classification system that views "services" as any activities that do not result in the extraction and processing of natural resources (fishing, mining, forestry), agriculture, or in the production of a good (i.e., manufacturing), then if an auto manufacturer employs people with specialized skills and competences to create an in-house, company-operated cafeteria, then employment in the manufacturing sector rises but if it decides to have an outside enterprise that specializes in food preparation and provisioning to provide cafeteria services (i.e., it outsources) then employment in the services sector of the economy rises. But has anything really changed in the composition of the workforce? National accounting systems reinforce the idea that we are entering a services economy by pronouncements that 70–80 percent of the economy (in developed countries) is service based. This sets up a rather ironic situation, since manufacturing (goods production) is seen as preferable (at least since industrialization) and services are seen as somewhat inferior forms of goods (because they are intangible, heterogeneous, inseparable from production and perishable[18] – that is, what are sometimes called the "IHIP" characteristics) it follows that advanced economies are defined by their production of

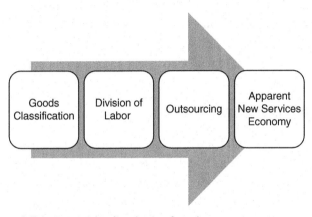

Exhibit 1.4 Misleading logic of services economy

inferior goods, and the related prominence of inferior jobs. Furthermore, because government and industry leaders believe they are in a new services economy, they act as such and thus engage in a variety of practices that they believe reflect the new services economy mindset, such as trying to produce "added value" through the addition of more services, conducting surveys of perceived service quality, hiring chief experience officers, and so on. But these moves miss the critical, underlying issue that the common denominator, the purpose, of exchange is mutual service provision, rather than the creation and addition of more "services."

There are no services

S-D logic proffers the counterintuitive claim that there are no "services." But if we have always been in a service economy, how can that be? The answer lies in the subtle but critically important distinction between the plural "services" and the singular "service," at least in S-D logic. As mentioned, the traditional conceptualization of "services" is a derivative of G-D logic and implies that economies should be focused on units of output. During the Industrial Revolution, the focal units were manufactured products. It followed, then, that, as attention shifted toward exchange in which manufactured goods were not involved, it was conceptualized in terms of "intangible goods" – "services." Thus, providing lodging service becomes producing and selling bed-nights; providing transportation service becomes producing and selling passenger-miles, and so on. By contrast, in S-D logic "service" (singular) implies the act of helping another actor through the application of available resources (knowledge and skills) for that actor's benefit. In this situation, the hotel would view service as the full range of activities performed in the process of assisting guests with their comfort and security (and other) needs while away from home. *"Services" is a noun* (e.g., bed-nights), whereas *"service" is a verb* (helping and assisting guests). "Services" is a G-D logic term and inconsistent with S-D logic.

There are no producers and consumers

Previously, we introduced the rationale for viewing economic and social agents as generic "actors," rather than "producers" and "consumers." Here, in this discussion of the counterintuitive (to G-D logic) nature of S-D logic, we want to take another opportunity to emphasize this point. Economic science is grounded in the concept of the supply of valuable products that are demanded, in which the firm is viewed as producer and supplier of a quantity desired and the customer is viewed as the demander and consumer of some desired quantity. If one considers this a bit more closely, it is easy to challenge the idea that supply is a unique, one-sided firm characteristic and demand is a unique, one-sided customer characteristic. For instance, whereas firms might supply particular resources, they also have a demand for (and expect) customers' resources; in fact, that is why they engage in marketing activities – in order to engage in exchange with customers. At the same time, whereas a customer might have demand, it also is a very important part of the exchange process and is an active supplier or provider. This might happen through money – financial resources or what, in S-D logic, are called service rights – but it also can happen through codesign, self-service, providing positive word-of-mouth, cocreating a brand community, and so on. In addition, if all actors are cocreators of value through the integration of firm resources with other market, public, and private resources, then they must be performing "production," as well as "consumption" functions. But is *consumption* really the right word? It implies *using something up* so that it has no more value, but is education consumed? Are books? Is entertainment? Or are they simply used in future "production"? The point of all of this is that the "producer–consumer" divide offers us nothing in the quest to understand economic exchange; on the contrary, the whole notion of a one-way flow of production to consumption masks the very nature of exchange and value creation. For these reasons, it is best to view all actors as resource-integrating, service-exchanging, value-cocreating enterprising actors. And, thus, producers and consumers do not exist, at least as actors with separate functions.

Enterprises cannot independently create value

The message of this inversion is partially implied by the last one. It rests on the S-D logic tenet that, in markets, value is something that is cocreated through the exchange, integration, and use of resources in the context of other resources, associated with multiple actors. For the same reason, neither can it provide *added value*. Undoubtedly, it can add economic costs but value is something uniquely and phenomenologically determined by the actor as beneficiary. This value is not only a function of the resources the firm exchanges with another actor but also a function of how this actor integrates other resources with this resource offering. The best that a firm can do is to provide a value proposition, followed by the application of its resources, through service, in a manner that makes integration of the offering possible, if the proposition is accepted.

Enterprises are relatively unbounded

G-D logic suggests that the firm is bounded by economic transactions with other actors, most notably suppliers and customers.[19] In this view, suppliers include employees, credit grantors, and suppliers of direct materials entering a particular production process, as well as actors who provide materials and other inputs indirectly through market exchange. Therefore, there are boundaries to the market and to the firm delineated through economic exchange. However, a broadened view suggests the firm, like the customer, integrates a variety of resources (both tangible and intangible) from private, market, and public sources. In this way, an enterprise cocreates value with all of its stakeholders, including those with whom they are not directly engaged in economic exchange. Therefore, the enterprise is relatively unbounded or part of an open system because it cannot separate itself from the society within which it is embedded. The reason this matters is that managing a closed system is different from "managing" an open system. The latter is more of an iterative, effectual process, in which actors operating in an open system riddled with uncertainty cannot predict the future but can take actions that effect it, a step or two at a time. Incidentally, the household, for the same reason, is relatively unbounded. The notion that the enterprise (and household) are relatively unbounded does not mean that there is not often substantial variation in their ability to access and integrate resources and hence their relative advantage or well-being over time.

Markets do not exist

Conventional thinking in marketing is that markets exist "out there," consisting of waiting, demanding customers and, thus, firms need to be "market driven." That requires (1) analysis of consumer needs, wants, and preferences and (2) then responding to those with market offerings. We suggest that markets, like value, are continually being cocreated by actors seeking solutions or experiences and other actors with offerings captured in value propositions. As Theodore Levitt shared over fifty years ago in "Marketing myopia,": "In truth, there is no such thing as a growth industry, I believe. There are only companies organized and operated to create and capitalize on growth opportunities."[20] At the extreme, this suggests that not only are there no growth markets (industries) but also that markets and industries do not exist *per se*. Rather, markets are continually created by enterprising actors that can read the signals properly and integrate the resources needed to serve other actors, who are similarly integrating resources to cocreate value for themselves and others, through offering a relatively compelling value proposition.[21]

The contextual nature of value creation: the structurated world of S-D logic

The application of operant resources is dynamic and, when coupled with the networked nature of value creation, implies the primacy of value-in-use versus value-in-exchange, as discussed. However, it also implies that even the term "value-in-use" might not adequately reflect the contextual nature of value creation. It is for this reason that we have more recently been referring to "value-in-context."[22] *Value-in-context* suggests that value is not only always cocreated; it is contingent on the integration of other resources and actors and thus is contextually specific.[23] Consider, for example, children playing with a toy alone or with other children or grandparents. The play could be done at a friend's house, at the child's house, or at a grandparent's house. Furthermore, the play could be while also watching television or listening to music. In each of these contexts, the value co-creation is different.

It also resonates with the axiomatic contentions of S-D logic that all social and economic actors are resource integrators and that the value perception is always uniquely and phenomenologically determined by the beneficiary. Thus, value creation needs to be viewed in the context of social systems in which value is created and evaluated, idiosyncratically. This idiosyncrasy, however, should not be confused with randomness. Rather, social network structures (and the actors they comprise) display apparently purposeful, systemic, autopoetic behaviors driven not only by connections between (potential) resources but also by rules that govern their exchange, combination and, to some extent, the determination of the value of some kinds of resource integration (i.e., values). Giddens refers to this interplay between actors and the structures, comprising rules and resources, within which they act as "structuration."[24]

The duality of structuration

Structuration theory posits a duality: human actors act within the social rules (institutions), norms, and collective meanings that are part of the structure within which they exist; however, the structures are formed and reformed by these same actors as they enact practices that enhance and modify these structures in the process of creating value for themselves and others. Essentially, the micro actions of actors and actor-to-actor interactions help to create the environment that is the playing field for their future actions. Thus, structures both enable and constrain actors and actors both act within and create structures.

To capture these dualistic, dynamic, resource-integrating (through service exchange), enabling, and constraining value-(co-)creating structures, we use the term "service ecosystems."[25] A *service ecosystem* is a relatively self-contained, self-adjusting system of resource-integrating actors that are connected by shared institutional logics and mutual value creation through service exchange. By including shared institutional logics we point towards a link between S-D logic and structuration theory which describes human actions within social systems as enabled and constrained by social structures – that is, as contextual and contingent.

This position, that structures can be conceptualized as both the medium and the outcome of human practices, represents a major departure from the G-D logic-motivated models (e.g., the traditional marketing management model), in which the legal, ethical, political, social, technological, and competitive structures are usually viewed as exogenous, uncontrollable environmental factors that define the constraining conditions of business. In that world, a central premise is that an actor (i.e., firm) targets another actor (i.e., customer) and "positions" its offering by mixing its controllable, marketing resources – the marketing mix (the "four Ps") – within the constraints of this external environment, including a predefined market. In this world, the firm is pretty much limited to "build a better mousetrap" approaches.

In the structurated world of S-D logic, however, the "environment" is the venue for innovation and structural transformation is often the means. Value creation occurs by changing rules and resource relationships. For example, the Internet, and the businesses and organizations that emerged out of it and drew upon it, has effectively and drastically changed many of the rules and resources (structures) that customers use to exchange. In addition to connecting potential buyers and sellers, it provided further resources that actively encouraged changes in the "rules of shopping" by creating a rating system to overcome the lack of direct relationship governance between parties, providing safe ways to transfer money online, and offering a neutral system for conflict resolution. This, in turn, recasts the role of eBay from merchant to platform-support role by creating a new business model by providing rules and resources that assist individual actors in their own value-creation activities, through exchange. We argue that under-standing social structures in this way is an important component of understand-ing the contextual value cocreation and resource integration in social systems. The potential rewards for these service-driven insights are enormous because they suggest that the *strategic advantage* of a firm can be recast from a logic that focuses *on making better products to increase market share in existing markets* to one of *redefining existing markets for strategic advantage or defining and thus creating new markets.*

It is important to recognize that structures and *ecosystems are multilayered* and often *nested*. That is, they can be seen at a *micro level*, such as centered on exchange among a small number of actors (e.g., car dealer and customers), or at a *meso level*, involving a diverse set of actors organized around a particular approach to solving some problem. For instance, the "automobile market" gets stitched together and includes a retail network of auto dealers, auto repair and parts establishments and supporting wholesale distribution, and customers, as well as supporting actors such as insurance and fuel providers, and public resources to include roadways, traffic laws, and regulations, and tax incentives for various types of automobiles. In turn these help to stitch together the more *macro-level* structures, such as cultures or societies built around the personal mobility that the automobile provides. Complicating this even further, though also providing a rich field for innovation, is the fact that actors are characteristi-cally members of multiple, overlapping structures associated with work groups, social groups, families, sub-cultures, and so on.

All of this dynamic complexity could imply a somewhat impossible playing field for actors trying to acquire and integrate needed resources through service exchange, if it were not for the *commonality of socially constructed and shared institutions* – "rules of the game" – such as language, norms, and practices. Because of structuration, these institutions are shared across structures, reducing variability, and, through performativity, the outcome for at least some practices becomes quasi predictable. One particular type of institution is a *market*, a generally agreed upon solution to a common problem – for example, the auto-mobile market.

Solving problems under uncertainty

Even allowing for the idea of *markets as institutionalized solutions* to common human problems, S-D logic's consideration of systemic interaction among multi-ple actors with varying and changing viewpoints on what constitutes value implies a high level of uncertainty. This is particularly the case in actors' inability to accurately assess what will be considered valuable to other actors in the future. Thus, it is relatively impossible to be sufficiently insightful to be rational, optimizing, or maximizing actors, as suggested by G-D logic. Except to the limited extent made possible because of shared institutional logics, including the institutionalized solutions (markets), this implies the need for "non-predictive" approaches to the market and management in general to include the management of innovation.

Effectuation theory[26] is helpful in this regard because it stands in sharp contrast to causal models of decision-making. As we have suggested, traditional decision-making models often focus on a set of independent variables that help to predict some dependent variable in an attempt to control and manipulate the independent or causal variables to create a maximum outcome. This is the standard, G-D logic-based marketing management framework taught in virtually all MBA programs around the world. In brief, mix the four Ps (the "marketing mix": product, promotion, price, and place) and aim for the optimal combination to maximize firm profitability.

Effectuation takes the view that actors operating under uncertainty cannot predict the future but that actors can take actions that effect it, a step or two at a time. In essence, actors are constantly adapting and learning as they go along and making adjustments to actions they can control. The effectual actor starts with knowing *who they are*, *what they know*, and *whom they know*, and from this they decide *what they can do* in the constrained and unpredictable world they experience. This process unfolds to reveal new goals and opportunities that then are pursued using the prior steps and this is done incrementally, through time, to produce effects, including the creation of new markets.

S-D logic and effectuation theory have a strong synergy for a pair of reasons. First, S-D logic views actors as operating in an uncertain world but one in which they are learning through their actions and partially creating their own new environments in the process. However, they can never totally create their own new environments because, in line with structuration theory, structures both enable and constrain actors. Second, S-D logic puts a strong focus on coproduction and cocreation of value, which involves collaborations with other actors as does effectuation theory, with its focus on who I know and how to work with these other actors to create effects. Before concluding this brief introductory chapter we outline what to expect in the remainder of the book.

Outline of the book

Organizationally, the book consists of ten chapters separated into three major parts that align with the title of the book, *Service-Dominant Logic: Premises, Perspectives, Possibilities*. Consequently, Part I consists of four chapters on premises of S-D logic, Part II comprises four chapters on perspectives offered by S-D logic, and Part III includes two chapters on possibilities for further development of S-D logic.

Part I on premises begins with the present chapter, "The service-dominant mindset," which provides special attention to how S-D logic is distinct from G-D logic and how an S-D mindset opens up new possibilities for viewing and thinking about economic and social exchange and the role of marketing in these processes. Particularly important is the move in S-D logic to generic actors versus producers and consumers and toward systems and network perspectives. In preparation for a better understanding of subsequent chapters, four axioms of S-D logic are introduced. A discussion is also provided of market-ing with S-D logic. Chapter 2, "Roots and reritage," provides an important grounding in the history of political, philosophical, and economic thought that places S-D logic into a proper historical context. We also review how a divergence from G-D logic began to converge toward S-D logic. In Chapter 3, "Axioms and foundational premises," the basic lexicon of S-D logic is presented, followed by a detailed presentation and discussion of the ten foundational premises of S-D logic. Collectively, an understanding of the ten FPs provides the social scientist and business person with a refreshing and integrative view of social and economic exchange. Finally, Part I concludes with Chapter 4, "Service as a guiding frame-work." This chapter provides detailed discussion of what has been a continuing question about S-D logic and that is "why service" as an organizing concept?

Part II on perspectives begins with Chapter 5, "It's all actor-to-actor (A2A)." Here a description is given of how prior conceptions of business or producers versus buyers or consumers are biasing and misleading and how generic resource–integrating, enterprising actor to generic resource-integrating, enter-prising actor or simply actor-to-actor is more transcending and appropriate. We discuss the general types of exchange (restricted, generalized, and complex) and the common exchange institutions (reciprocity, redistribution, market, and hybrid). Next, Chapter 6, "The nature, scope, and integration of resources," discusses the nature, scope, and integration of resources. We discuss how resour-ces are not innately resources, but come about through human appraisal and overcoming resistances. The operand and operant nature of resources is explained as well as the concepts of resourceness, accessness and density. We also discuss the perspective of viewing actors as enterprising resource-integrating actors. This perspective offers a way of thinking not only about micro economies and society but also macro economies and society. Chapter 7, "Collaboration," addresses the important topic of collaboration and the concepts of coproduction and cocreation of value. It also introduces a set of three practices that are intertwined and are vital to the collaborative cocreation of value and systems. These practices are representational, normalizing, and integrative. Attention is focused on the pervasive influence of communication and IT systems and how these can be used to develop platforms for cocreation and coproduction. In this chapter it is suggested that collaborative advantage is becoming more important to enterprise success. The service ecosystem is the topic of Chapter 8, "Service ecosystems." Here a discussion is provided of how old concepts such as supply chain and marketing channel do not capture the dynamic self-adjusting, value-proposing activities of actors in a broader ecosystem setting. The ecosystem perspective provides new insights into institutions, value propositions, externalities, and value centricity. In addition, although ecosystems cannot be fully managed or designed the actor can make certain strategic choices about which other actors to interface with and thus can influence, to some extent, the structure it confronts. As the above suggests, service ecosystems go beyond micro-level interactions and create meso and macro systems (structures). Next, how a service ecosystem is a system of interlinked processes is discussed. Finally, we return to biological ecosystems to discuss ecosystem services.

The book ends with two chapters, which suggest possibilities for S-D logic. Chapter 9 is about "Strategic thinking" and contrasts a G-D strategy with S-D strategy. Briefly, a G-D strategy versus S-D strategy focuses on value chains versus value networks or service ecosystems, prediction versus control (learning), choice versus design, competing versus collaboration, and value-added versus value propositions. Chapter 10, "Conclusions and considerations," discusses how S-D logic is resulting in a convergence of multiple lines of thought that are creating an emergence of a more unified theory of business and society. We explore the idea of S-D logic as a meta-idea which positions S-D logic as an idea platform upon which enterprises and governments can more easily create specific ideas and strategies to enhance system viability. We conclude with the statement that S-D logic can be characterized as a meta-idea, which is an idea that supports the creation and transfer of other ideas. For instance, S-D logic supports the primacy of entrepreneurship over management, market-ing over manufacturing, the process of innovation versus inventing, and effectiveness over efficiency. We also conclude by suggesting the need for more research and theorizing on the role of institutions and we call for more mid-range theory in the development of S-D logic.

NOTES

1. Roger Friedland and Robert R. Alford, "Bringing society back in: symbols, practices, and institutional contradictions," in Walter W. Powell and Paul J. DiMaggio (eds.), *The New Institutionalism in Organizational Analysis* (University of Chicago Press, 1991), pp. 232–266.
2. T. S. Kuhn, *The Structure of Scientific Revolutions* (University of Chicago Press, 1962).
3. An insightful treatment of institutions in economics and how many of the optimization techniques in economics are not very useful is provided by Brian Loasby, *Knowledge, Institutions and Evolution in Economics* (New York: Routledge, 1999).
4. Edith Tilton Penrose, *The Theory of the Growth of the Firm* (Oxford: Basil Blackwell, 1959), pp. 24–25.
5. G. B. Richardson, "The organisation of industry," *Economic Journal*, 82 (September 1972), 883–96.
6. Theodore Levitt, Theodore (1960), "Marketing myopia," *Harvard Business Review*, 38 (July–August 1960), 26–44, 173–181.
7. Donald F. Dixon, "Marketing as production: the development of a concept," *Journal of the Academy of Marketing Science* 18 (Fall 1990), 337–343.
8. Stephen L. Vargo and Fred W. Morgan, "Services in society and academic thought: an historical analysis," *Journal of Macromarketing*, 25 (June 2005), 42–53.
9. Jean-Baptiste Say, *A Treatise on the Political Economy* (Boston: Wells & Lilly, 1821).
10. Alfred Marshall, *Principles of Economics* (London: Macmillan, 1927 [1890]); L. Walras, *Elements of the Political Economy* (Homewood, IL: Richard D. Irwin, 1984 [1954]); Stephen L. Vargo, Paul P. Maglio, and Melissa Archpru Akaka, "On value and value co-creation: a service systems and service logic perspective," *European Management Journal*, 26 (June 2008), 145–152.
11. Stephen L. Vargo and Robert F. Lusch, "It's all B2B . . . and beyond: toward a systems perspective of the market," *Industrial Marketing Management*, 40:2 (2011), 181–187.
12. Paul D. Converse, *Essentials of Distribution* (New York: Prentice-Hall, 1936), p. 492.
13. Stephen L. Vargo and Robert F. Lusch, "Evolving to a new dominant logic for marketing," *Journal of Marketing*, 68 (January 2004), 1–17.
14. The first few years of effort on what led to S-D logic was by Steve Vargo in his historical study of the treatment of services in the economy and society and independent work by Robert Lusch on operand and operant resources and marketing support systems.
15. Management as a discipline is beginning to recognize that value creation through consumer involvement is an important and often neglected area with profound implications for management strategy; see Richard L. Priem, "A consumer perspective on value creation," *Academy of Management Review*, 32:1 (2007), 219–235.

16. Joseph Pine and James H. Gilmore, *The Experience Economy: Work is Theater and Every Business a Stage* (Boston: Harvard Business School Press, 1999).
17. Michel Callon, *The Laws of Markets* (Oxford, UK: Blackwell, 1998).
18. See Stephen L. Vargo and Robert F. Lusch, "The four services marketing myths: remnants from a manufacturing model," *Journal of Service Research*, 6 (May 2004), 324–335.
19. Ronald H. Coase, "The nature of the firm," *Economica*, 4 (November 1937), 386–405.
20. Levitt, "Marketing myopia," p. 47.
21. A variety of scholars have begun to address the idea that, rather than being market driven, firms drive markets. See, for example, N. Kumar, L. Scheer, and P. Kotler, "From market driven to market driving," *European Management Journal*, 18:2 (2000), 129–42.
22. Stephen L. Vargo and Robert F. Lusch, "Service-dominant logic: continuing the evolution," *Journal of the Academy of Marketing Science*, 36:1 (2008), 1–10. See also Jennifer Chandler and Stephen L. Vargo, "Contextualization: network intersections, value-in-context, and the co-creation of markets," *Marketing Theory*, 11:1 (2011), 35–49.
23. Stephen L. Vargo, Robert F. Lusch, Melissa Akaka, and Yi He, "Service-dominant logic: a review and assessment," *Review of Marketing Research*, 6 (2010), 125–167.
24. Anthony Giddens, *The Constitution of Society* (Berkeley: University of California Press, 1984).
25. Stephen L. Vargo and Robert F. Lusch, "It's all B2B . . ."
26. Saras D. Sarasvathy, *Effectuation: Elements of Entrepreneurial Expertise* (Northampton, MA: Edward Elgar, 2008).

2   Roots and heritage

> The great economic law is this: Services are exchanged for services ... It is trivial, very commonplace; it is nonetheless, the beginning, the middle, and the end of economic science ...
>
> Frédéric Bastiat

Introduction

Tracing the history of how a concept has been conceptualized, understood, and approached helps to uncover the roots and pathways that lead to its nuanced meanings today. These pathways diverge and converge as a function of the purposes of the times. A historic account of the development of economics and how it viewed service reveals a divergence in the understanding of value and value creation. This historic account points toward the development of an economic paradigm focused on tangible, transportable, and quantifiable value, with service seen as something left over, less valuable, and tertiary in economic development.

The traditional, dominant "worldview" developed from the idea that tangible goods could have (possess) utility (value) and be transported and exchanged for other goods, also possessing utility, thus increasing the wealth of both parties. We call this paradigm "goods-dominant" (G-D) logic. Arguably, it has become the most pervasive and foundational of the paradigms available for understanding business and economic exchange. Briefly stated, G-D logic postulates:

- The purpose of economic activity is to make and distribute things that can be sold.
- To be sold, these things must be embedded with utility (value) during the production and distribution processes and must offer to the consumer superior value in relation to competitors' offerings.
- The firm should set all decision variables at a level that enables it to maximize the profit from the sale of output.
- For both maximum production control and efficiency, the good should be standardized and produced away from the market.
- The good can then be inventoried until it is demanded and then delivered to the consumer at a profit.

G-D logic is depicted in Exhibit 1.2 in Chapter 1. It is a simple but powerful image, in which the "producer" is central and the value creator and the customer is the value recipient and destroyer ("consumer"). It is also linear and unidirectional, except for the flow of money.

G-D logic is so compelling that it is normally unquestioned. However, it is not so much a logic that came from the systematic study of business and economic exchange phenomena as it is the *artifact* of purposeful thinking about a subset of related phenomena – international trade – in a specific, restricted context, which, in turn, set up a path-dependent course that made G-D logic perhaps inevitable. This is not to suggest that G-D logic is mistaken, but rather that it is somewhat myopic, particularly for dealing with today's complex, technologically driven world.

The development of the G-D logic paradigm largely ignored exchange phenomena related to intangibles, later categorized as "services." Thus, when services began receiving attention by academics as well as practitioners, they were treated as either intangible add-ons to goods (e.g., customer service) or a special type of good – "immaterial." Arguably, this view caused initial problems for the business disciplines, such as marketing and management, as they tried to deal with these intangibles, resulting in the creation of associated subdisciplines (e.g., service marketing and service management).

Recently, however, seemingly disparate views appear to be converging on a more comprehensive and integrative logic of exchange, one that is, perhaps ironically, centered on the same phenomenon that had been largely ignored – service. As noted in Chapter 1, in contrast to the traditional, G-D logic paradigm, this alternative logic is called "service-dominant" (S-D) logic. It sees (1) service – defined as the application of resources for the benefit of another actor – as the basis for economic exchange; (2) goods as mechanisms for service provision; (3) value as always cocreated by a service provider and a beneficiary (and others); and (4) value as always uniquely determined by the beneficiary.

This chapter provides an overview of the primary divergences and convergences that contributed to the development of the G-D logic paradigm and subsequent emergence of S-D logic. This historical account explores the bifurcations of goods and services, productive and unproductive activities, value-in-use and value-in-exchange, product orientations and customer orientation, and transactions and relationships.

Foundations of economics

The beginning of modern economic thought is usually considered to coincide with the publication of Adam Smith's *Wealth of Nations*.[1] Although Smith is often recognized as the "father of economics," he did not invent economics. He did, however, explicate and integrate the dominant "worldviews" of the time and provided a synthesized explanation that later served as the foundation of economics. These views on the market and exchange came from a variety of perspectives.[2] Some focused on concerns dating back to Aristotle about how human activities contribute to well-being for other humans, whereas others focused on more recent concerns of identifying the activities, other than agriculture, that created value for individuals and nations. He tried to reconcile these views with the role of the industrial production of surplus tangible goods as a value-creating activity.

Smith's work integrated and was integrated into these various perspectives. His political-economic views focused on the efficiency of the "division of labor" that was increasingly evident during the Industrial Revolution. Smith noted that this division of labor not only pointed toward the necessity of exchange but extended its scope – the market. For Smith, labor was the "fund which originally supplies (the nation) with all the necessities and conveniences of life which it annually consumes."[3] By labor, Smith did not mean physical work so much as the application of specialized knowledge and skills. Thus, he established the application of mental and physical skills, actors doing things for other actors (what in S-D logic is identified as "service"),[4] as the foundation for economic exchange.

Distinguishing productive and unproductive service(s)

Although Smith, somewhat incidentally, provided an explanation for the foundation of exchange and value creation, his work was actually focused more
narrowly on an explanation of how to increase the economic wealth of
England (or other countries) – hence, *The Wealth of Nations*. That is, he sought
to explain how some services (types of labor) *contributed to national well-being*
through export and trade. Given the plausible conditions and methods of economic exchange, particularly world trade, at the time and the limitations on
international communications and travel, Smith focused on services that were
required for the production and distribution of exportable, tangible goods.

This narrowed focus can be seen in Smith's discussion of "productive" and
"unproductive" services – a discussion on which he is frequently misquoted.
Smith is credited with the view that services are not valuable. This attribution
is usually grounded in some portion of the following statement:

The labor of some of the most respectable orders in society is . . . unproductive of any
value, and does not fix or realize itself in any permanent subject, or venerable commodity
which endures after that labor is past, and for which an equal quantity of labor could
afterwards be produced. The sovereign, for example, . . . produces nothing for which an
equal quantity of service can be afterwards procured.[5]

The phrase "for which an equal quantity of labor could afterwards be produced" is
an especially important distinction. If a barber, for instance, shaves and cuts the
hair of a person, that person cannot take this service, however valuable, and trade
it for another item (tangible or intangible). However, if a person exchanges and
receives a tangible product he or she can then take that product and exchange it
for something else. Thus the notion developed that the good was embedded with
transportable and transferrable value.

Although Smith focused his discussion of national wealth creation on tangible
items that could be exported, he defined *real value* as the labor required to afford
the "necessities, conveniences, and amusements of human life" through the labor
of others.[6] However, having established that labor (or what we identify as service)
was the fundamental source of value when applied to providing the "necessities,
conveniences, and amusements of human life" – contemporarily referred to as
customer needs – he moved his attention to *nominal value* – the price paid in the
market. Smith believed that it was easier to quantify and measure the exchange-
value (nominal value) of things rather than labor and thus focused on the former,
even though it did not represent real value. Smith's selection of exchange-value

as a surrogate for real value, even with the caveat that he recognized that value was actually determined phenomenologically by the beneficiary, rather than in production or through trade, established a path that would limit the generalizability of the economic philosophy and science that followed.

Those who followed Smith did not always agree with his productive–unproductive standards. For instance, Say viewed production as the *creation of utility* (a term intended to point back to value-in-use), not as a physical form of matter.[7] Thus, he defined services as those activities that are "consumed at the time of production itself" and described them as "immaterial products." Like Say, Mill also disagreed with the classification of labor as unproductive unless it resulted in some material object.[8] He also argued that the production of objects was really a *rearrangement of matter* (i.e., not really produced – created), because "no human being can produce one particle of matter."[9] He believed that the value of production was not found in an object itself, but in the usefulness of that object. Thus, labor was "not creative of objects, but of utilities."[10] In fact, Mill asked, "Why should not all labor which produces utility be accounted productive," including labor "consisting of a mere service rendered?"[11]

In spite of their objections regarding Smith's productive–unproductive classifications, most economic philosophers acquiesced to the emerging dominant logic of "productive," referring to only those types of labor that contributed to the creation of utilities embedded in material objects for which there was customer demand. Eventually, this productive–unproductive distinction became reflected in, if not morphed into, the good-service classification. Attempts to break free from the developing production-centered paradigm were largely unsuccessful.

One scholar who maintained his opposition to the dominant thinking of the time was Frédéric Bastiat, who argued against the political economists' position on value and their primary focus on tangible objects. Bastiat explained that people have "wants" and attain "satisfaction" through (1) "gratuitous utilities," which are provided by Providence, and (2) "onerous utilities," which must be purchased with effort.[12] Satisfaction was associated with a particular individual, whereas the necessary effort associated with the onerous utility was seen often to reside with other individuals. Bastiat argued that "it is in fact to this faculty ... to work the one for the other; it is this transmission of efforts, this exchange of services, with all the infinite and involved combinations to which it gives rise, through time and through space, it is *this* precisely which constitutes Economic Science, points out its origin and determines its limits."[13] Thus, value was viewed as "comparative appreciation of reciprocal services" exchanged to obtain utility.

Like Mill, Bastiat suggested that humans transformed matter, rather than created it, through service, into a state in which satisfaction could be obtained from the matter. Bastiat summarized his perspective:

The great economic law is this: Services are exchanged for services ... It is trivial, very commonplace; it is nonetheless, the beginning, the middle, and the end of economic science ... Once this axiom is clearly understood, what becomes of such subtle distinctions as use-value and exchange-value, material products and immaterial products, productive classes and unproductive classes? ... Now since these reciprocal services alone are commensurate with one another, it is in them alone that value resides, and not in the gratuitous raw materials and in the gratuitous natural resources that they put to work.[14]

Other economists noted Bastiat's work but, given that his views diverged from the popular thinking at the time, the idea that service was the basis of exchange was largely ignored and not considered true economic theory.[15]

In Exhibit 2.1 we explain how performativity resulted in the eventual institutionalization and reification of an emerging logic of goods production. This led to goods produced and delivered at market prices so as to maximize profits for the firm. It further led to the creation of surplus goods production for export that became the primal source of national wealth. In brief, the goods logic that emerged from the Industrial Revolution became the dominant logic.

Economic science

Say's concept of utility took hold as the primary unit of analysis by the middle of the nineteenth century, albeit arguably as more of an *embedded property of matter* than as a measure of *usefulness*, as he had intended. With this focus, the issue regarding differences in use-value and exchange-value could be ignored; value-in-use became essentially equivalent to value-in-exchange. That is, the price a customer was willing to pay for a good could be considered equivalent to value as perceived by the customer, which could, in turn, be represented by *utility, as a property of the thing being exchanged* (i.e., the perceived *usefulness* of a hammer to an individual in a particular situation represented by the *utility* of the hammer, as captured by *price*). This abstracted conceptualization of utility provided the foundation for the development of economic science, based on the Newtonian tradition – a model of matter with properties.

Perhaps the person most responsible for moving economics from a philosophy to a science was Leon Walras, who considered the function of pure economics as

Nothing in the above or in what follows should be interpreted as a suggestion that the economic philosophers or the economic scientist who followed did not have an awareness of and some appreciation for customers and their responses (e.g., demand, satisfaction). As noted, Smith explicitly tied real value to value-in-use and offered early insight into the role of demand (especially effectual demand – demand accompanied by ability to pay) on market price. Additionally, Say objected to the term "productive" except to refer to activities that resulted in exportable commodities because he felt other activities played equally useful roles as perceived by customers and society as a whole. Likewise, as will be indicated below, economic scientists like Walras and Marshall were keenly aware of customers, as well as the fact that their own economic models often assumed away much of the richness of customers. In fact, in some cases, they issued cautiousness in interpretation. However, having made these observations, they typically went on about the business of philosophy and science building, necessarily ignoring at least some of their own insights.

This is the nature of sense-making. It is not about accounting for everything that plays a role, but rather it is about accounting for as little as possible to deal reasonably with phenomena of interest, *given some purpose*. It is a process of building simplified models that parsimoniously emulate *some aspect* of the world of interest. But these models, in spite of the cautions and more comprehensive insights of their framers, because of their very useful simplicity, are an excellent example of *performativity* as introduced in Chapter 1. Simplified models of the world that offer to make sense of the world can become institutionalized, if not reified. They form paradigmatic foundations for thinking about related (and often relatively unrelated) phenomena. In the case of economic models, scholars, journalists, business people, and public policy makers use their concepts to talk about business; they use their categories to create classifications (e.g., labor and industrial) for mapping changes in the phenomena of interest; and they use their implied assumptions to evaluate relative contribution of activities, such as manufacturing and service provision. These concepts and categories in turn influence the formation of business models and the political institutions that govern them. That is, somewhat paradoxically, as sociologists advise us, because actors approach the phenomena from the orientation of the models, the models shape the phenomena with which they

Exhibit 2.1 A necessary digression on performativity

deal: in short, in the present discussion, the *economy is a function of economics.*[16]

None of this is intended as an indictment or meant to disparage the philosophers and scientists involved for not building models that accounted for all of their observations and causations. Rather, it is simply to point out that, to some extent, the dominant models of economic philosophy and science and their impact must be understood somewhat apart from the more general observations of their framers. Indeed, S-D logic, at least in part, reclaims many of the insights of the early economists that were left behind given more immediate purposes, especially the transformation of economic philosophy into economic science – at a time when "science" was epitomized by Newtonian Mechanics.

Exhibit 2.1 (cont.)

the theoretical determination of price.[17] Interestingly, Walras saw services as the source of all production and separated "services of capital goods" into "consumer services" that possess direct utility and "producer services" that have indirect utility. His primary goal, however, was the development of a pure theory of economics, which he envisioned as "a physio-mathematical science like mechanics and hydraulics and its practitioners should not fear to employ the methods and language of mathematics."[18]

Walras' equilibrium theory was based on a mathematical relationship between supply, demand, and price, centered on the then well-established "ideal-type" concept of utility which was treated as an abstracted quantifiable property and thus susceptible to mathematical manipulation. With equilibrium theory, Walras believed that economic thought had finally caught up with the Newtonian model of a mechanistic, deterministic, rational, and certain world; hence, economics could be deemed a legitimate "science."

However, most of the credit for the advancement of equilibrium theory has been attributed to Alfred Marshall.[19] Nevertheless, Marshall was cautious about equilibrium theory.[20] He recognized that only "tendencies" toward the equilibrium were discernable through the science of economics and could only be written as normative "laws," if the caveats of perfect information, perfectly rational buyers, perfectly accessible competition, and so on were applied.

It has been suggested that, toward the end of the nineteenth century, there were somewhat parallel models of economic activity, sometimes proffered by the same economics scholars, to represent economic activity.[21] One perspective intimated a service-dominant model of exchange, which reflected economic activity in terms of discrete and collective relationships between specialized service providers exchanging services with other specialized service providers. This view reflected Smith's initial discussion on the division of labor and real value (value-in-use). However, Smith, along with many of the other political economists and economic scientists (except for Bastiat) of the time, acknowledged and then abandoned the service-dominant model and opted for a model that focused on utility embedded in tangible goods, arguably more for its elegance and simplicity than for its emulation of real-world events.

The alternative, goods-dominant model emphasized (the demand and supply of) "goods," with an abstracted property of utility. A demand function for a good represented the total demand (quantity demanded) of consumers for that particular good. A supply function for the good represented the total supply (quantity produced). Price moderated the relationship, establishing equilibrium. In this model, the "good" was the common denominator in exchange.

This goods-dominant view of economic activity aligned the popular views of political economists and their focus on virtues of international trade of materialistic goods and those of economic scientists' desire to be "scientific" in accordance with the mathematical prerequisite of the natural sciences. With the goal of developing a respectable science in the Newtonian tradition, the emphasis on goods flourished and the service-centered view was relegated to a footnote status in economic science, at least temporarily.

The impact of a goods-dominant paradigm

Economic science established the foundation for thinking about the exchange and the market and, subsequently, provided the underlying theories and models for the development of business disciplines, such as marketing and management, as well as accounting and finance. As production shifted from the household to the factory, the "producer" and "consumer" were seen to be separated. The firm's role was to create value in the market through the efficient production and sale of goods. The customer's role, then, was to "consume" the firm's output – to use up and destroy the value created by the firm – and then to return to the market for more firm-created value. In Chapter 1 we introduced the generic actor and actor-to-actor exchange, networks, and systems but for economic science once it turned to a G-D orientation the central economic actor in society became the company or firm – that is, the producer. The well-being of the nation (and firm) were seen to flow from this producer of wealth.

Guided by the economic paradigm described above, the firm was focused on producing tangible goods beyond local demand that could be transported to customers across wide geographical areas. Over time, the gains made during the Industrial Revolution resulted in firms being able to produce higher and higher quantities of tangible goods. That is, these excess goods posed a problem for firms: management science had resolved issues related to production efficiency but production efficiencies created new problems of distribution and oversupply. Thus, one of the major efforts of the firm was to connect the supply of its offerings with additional demand. From this need, marketing, as a discipline, was born.

The publication of the first scholarly article in marketing is usually credited to Shaw,[22] who focused his early scholarly efforts on the role of marketing in value creation. Both the goods-centered and Newtonian Mechanics perspective of economics was evident in his contention that "industry is concerned with the application of motion to matter to change its form and place. The change in form we term production; the change in place, distribution."[23] Similarly, Weld considered marketing as part of the division of labor in the *function of production*, which he saw as the "creation of utilities," specifically form, time, place, and possession utility, with marketing contributing to the last three.[24] Weld, an economist, felt that marketing's distributive activities were mistrusted because of the absence of a body of knowledge about its role in creating utility in economic systems.

Nonetheless, the questions regarding the contribution of marketing to value creation lingered. Thus, early marketing scholars continued to try to deal with issues regarding the identification of the functions or services provided by marketers and the value-adding roles of marketing services. However, the goods-dominant paradigm remained and the related attitudes that goods have value through production and that distribution (marketing) added costs and thus economic waste prevailed. This generally negative view toward marketing also extended to services as a whole. Following the development of economic thought and science, the consideration of services as wasteful was deeply ingrained in the thinking of the day.

The shift toward consumer orientation

Several overlapping events began to unravel about a quarter of the way through the twentieth century, which significantly impacted the evolution of economic thought regarding exchange. The economic expansion of the 1920s increased levels of specialization. Many activities that were traditionally performed internally to the firm and thus classified as part of manufacturing – for example, design, promotion, accounting – became increasingly outsourced and then classified as services. The worldwide depression era followed by World War II had also amplified government activities, accelerating what was conventionally thought of as the service sector.

Partly in response to these apparent increases in service activities, Fisher differentiated among the roles of primary (agriculture), secondary (manufacturing), and tertiary stages or sectors in the development of economies.[25] However, contrary to what is often claimed, he *did not* equate services with the tertiary sector. Rather, he argued that *some of Smith's unproductive activities* could be considered *productive* – that is, useful to societies that have advanced beyond basic agriculture and manufacturing.

The economic expansion that followed World War II also increased demand, as well as production and competition. With this shift in the market, scholars became increasingly concerned with customer choice and satisfaction during the exchange process rather than just aggregate national well-being analyses.[26] Evidence of this shift can be found in the emergence of two new "schools of thought": "consumer behavior," which was concerned with buyer judgment and decision-making processes, and "marketing management," which was concerned with how the firm influenced these processes. Additionally, the "marketing concept" – the belief that markets are energized by consumers' desires and thus firms should be customer oriented, that firm profits are driven by customer satisfaction, and that all activities (production, marketing, management, finance, etc.) of the firm should be directed toward satisfying customers – developed as the foundation for both schools. This move to a *consumer orientation* and emphasis on customer satisfaction marked the beginning of a major reorientation that resulted in a shift in the meaning of "quality" from being understood in terms of *manufactured quality* to the *customer's perception of quality* as the major determinant of exchange.

At first glance, this refocus on the customer appears to represent a significant departure from traditional economic thought. However, a second and perhaps more reflective glance raises a subtle but critically important issue: do these shifts actually correct the foundational economic models that preceded them or are they more superficial fixes that serve to mask deeper, more fundamental issues associated with the process of economic exchange?

In part, this issue was captured in a conversation during the middle of the twentieth century between Wroe Alderson, whom many consider to be the most insightful marketing scholar to date, and Theodore Beckman, known for his advancement of the idea of "value-added." Both argued against trying to identify some particular type of utility associated with marketing. However, Beckman advocated what would later be identified as a "value-in-exchange" view of various parties directed at *increasing the selling value* of products,[27] whereas Alderson advocated a "value-in-use position," leading him to suggest: "What is needed is not an interpretation of the utility created by marketing, but a marketing interpretation of the whole process of creating utility."[28] That is, rather than make an adjustment to our foundational, economic model, the discipline of marketing, and more generally business, needs to rethink the foundation.

At the same time, Peter Drucker, whom many consider to be the most insightful overall business scholar of the past century, was rejecting standard management theories that focused on production, labor, and government policy, and identifying marketing – not as a functional-division activity but as a primary firm activity – as the catalyst in economic development and "*the process through which economy is integrated into society to serve human needs.*"[29]

Although the stage was at least partially set for a shift in the orientation for understanding economic activity, the traditional, G-D logic orientation persisted, though parts of what might be considered a service orientation were evident. However, it would take further bifurcation in the business disciplines before a service orientation would begin to "break free" from the paradigmatic grips of G-D logic. Business scholars would have to discover new foundational concepts and models through the development of, and further investigations within, its subdisciplines, especially service marketing and service management and operations.

The rise and evolution of service(s) thought

The shift in emphasis toward the customer orientation had a major impact on the study of exchange, particularly in the field of marketing. But the impact was not sufficiently transformative to prevent the subdiscipline of service marketing from slowly emerging in the following context:

(1) the consumer behavior movement and the related, increasing recognition that consumer choice was more than just a function of the utilitarian benefits of goods and the motivation to maximize utility;

(2) the apparent increased salience of services in society and exchange and the related view that economies evolve into service economies;

(3) the realization that marketing was concerned with the process of exchange, which could not be adequately understood from the economic science perspective of goods with exchange-value; and

(4) the idea that the customer and producer could not necessarily be separated and viewed as distinct entities but were involved in cocreating value.

Early scholars focused on conceptually separating "services" from "goods" and understanding how to manage the marketing of intangibles. Even in its separation from traditional "goods" marketing, the influence of the G-D logic paradigm is evident in the way in which service was initially defined, residually, as what goods are not.[30] To be sure, there were some attempts at more positive definitions through inclusion of terms such as "performance,"[31] and "interactive experience"[32] to describe the role of the customer. However, generally, services continued to be defined by exclusion from goods.

These goods-centered conceptualizations of service were also evident in the characteristics used to distinguish services from goods. The four commonly cited classifiers of service are (1) intangibility – lacking the physical or concrete quality of goods, (2) heterogeneity – the relative difficulty of standardizing services in comparison to goods, (3) inseparability – the inability to separate production from consumption, and (4) perishability – relative inability to inventory services as compared to goods.[33] Importantly, these characteristics were generally considered to be negative aspects or *disadvantages of services*, thus requiring strategic adjustments to make them align with the management and marketing of goods provision.[34]

Although many conceptualize services in relation to goods, other scholars have questioned the definition of service based on these four characteristics. Evert Gummesson, a service marketing and management pioneer, argued that using physical products as a definitional foundation "presupposes that there is a fairly unambiguous definition of goods" and it "forces services to exist on goods' conditions instead of allowing them to exist on their own conditions."[35] Beaven and Scotti suggested that common descriptors fail "to differentiate between these two production processes and [confuse] outputs with outcomes" and "[inhibit] the development of services as a truly distinct subdiscipline."[36]

Lynn Shostack, an early service practitioner and scholar who is often credited with the crystallization of service thinking, emphasized the dominance of good-centered thinking in marketing and explained, "The classical 'marketing mix,' the seminal literature, and the language of marketing all derive from the manufacture of physical-goods." She urged services to "break free from product marketing."[37]

As the goods versus services debate went on, services marketing scholars also discussed more substantive issues. In the United States, Zeithaml, Parasuraman, and Berry,[38] three pioneer service academics, proposed a conceptual model and standardized instrument for assessing perceptions of *service quality* and Len Berry coined the term *relationship marketing.*[39]

At the same time, scholars in Europe, particularly in the Nordic countries, were rethinking concepts of service quality[40] and relationships. This work was done independently from, but essentially simultaneously with, similar work being done in the United States. Some European service marketing scholars also extended the notion of relationship to the construction of an interactive logic of "service management."[41]

Concepts such as service quality, relationship marketing, and service management were intended to provide viewpoints for understanding service and service marketing. The development of these perspectives was necessitated by the inadequacies of their goods-centered counterparts. *Service quality* moved the focus of the firm from *engineering specifications* of goods production to the *perceived evaluations* of the customer. *Relationship marketing* shifted the focus of exchange from the *discrete transaction* to *ongoing interactivity. Service management* shifted the focus from Taylor's *scientific management* perspective[42] – the highly structured standardization of economies of scale – to the "teamwork, *interfunctional collaboration, and interorganizational partnership*"[43] perspective necessary for "service firms."

These service conceptualizations that began in the confines of the emerging subdiscipline of service marketing and management began to displace, or at least subordinate, their G-D logic counterparts. Rather than explicating service qualities as different from goods, as originally intended, these conceptualizations became unifying perspectives for understanding all "services" as well as "goods" exchanges. They were eventually applied by marketers who did not identify themselves as having a service focus and are now reshaping the logic of mainstream marketing and business more generally.

This emphasis on service-centered models of exchange seems to support the notion that services marketing was indeed "breaking free from products marketing," as was advocated by Lynn Shostack over thirty years ago.[44] However, more significantly, a more general breaking free was beginning to take place. A latent service orientation for economic activity, parts of which can be found throughout the history of economic thought, was beginning to loosen the constraints of its dominant, goods-centered paradigm.

Divergence from the goods-dominant paradigm

Simultaneous with management and marketing adopting service subdisciplines, other, related, signs of transition in thinking about market exchange were also becoming evident. For example, some academics argued that the new frontier of competition was moving from commoditized, standardized output based on mass production to more "mass-customized," offerings, especially as production techniques advanced.[45] Others began shifting the focus of value creation away from the firm and toward the customer, with the notion that value was collaborative, partly based on the recognition of the customer's role in service provision.[46] Some academics suggested that a movement was occurring not only towards a service economy, but beyond to an "experience economy".[47] Alternatively, that value is created through complex experiences involving input from many sources, rather than simply and singly through firm output. Increasingly, this experiences interpretation was seen to be applicable regardless of whether firm output was tangible or intangible.

The view of the nature of firm resources was also being examined. For example, C. K. Prahalad and Gary Hamel and others championed the concept of core competency theory (collective learning in the organization) as a primary means for competitive advantage.[48] Similarly, Shelby Hunt, a marketing scholar, proposed a resource-advantage view of the firm and competition as a framework for a more general theory of market competition while specifically identifying problems with the microeconomic model, in which much of marketing thought was grounded.[49] Zuboff and Maxmin suggested a new relational logic in which value originates with the individual and the role of the firm is to provide support, to replace what they called the "old enterprise logic" (essentially what is now called G-D logic).[50] Others argued for a "change in focus from value exchanged to value-creation relationships,"[51] pointing to "partnering relationships."[52]

Along with the relational approach to marketing, management, and strategy that developed in conjunction with the service subdisciplines, a relational approach also developed, largely independently, in B2B marketing, particularly by the Industrial Marketing and Purchasing (IMP) Group in Sweden, under the rubric of the "network approach." This network orientation had impact in more traditional schools of thought; for example, Achrol and Kotler – the latter name almost synonymous with traditional marketing models – advocated a network perspective by suggesting, "The very nature of network organization, the kinds of theories useful to its understanding, and the potential impact on the organization of consumption all suggest that a paradigm shift for marketing may not be far over the horizon."[53] Many of these ideas regarding networks were also discussed under the headings of supply and value-chain management or value constellations.[54] This dynamic approach was a substantial shift away from the standard integrated logistics management model of moving "matter" to market in a linear and unidirectional fashion.[55]

Toward the end of the twentieth century, Fred Webster explained, "The historical marketing management function, based on the microeconomic maximization paradigm, must be critically examined for its relevance to theory and practice."[56] Similarly, other marketing scholars proclaimed the logic of the "four Ps" – the long-taught "marketing mix" comprising product, price, promotion, and place (distribution) – as "merely a handy framework."[57] Others suggested that "an alternative paradigm of marketing is needed, a paradigm that can account for the continuous nature of relationships among marketing actors."[58]

Parallel shifts away from traditional economic perspectives were also found beyond the marketing and management literature and often by economists that departed from tradition. Resource-based views of the firm had been developing for some time.[59] Even within economics, some scholars challenged "orthodox" economic theory and proposed a model of evolutionary economics based on capability-driven organizational "routines."[60] Like Hunt, Teece and Pisano argued that "the competitive advantage of firms stems from dynamic capabilities rooted in high performance routines operating inside the firm, embedded in the firm's processes, and conditioned by its history."[61]

The collective divergences from conventional thinking and calls for new models, theories, and paradigms can be interpreted as either an increasing fragmentation of exchange-related thinking or a convergence on a more integrative and encompassing logic of exchange and related phenomena. To many observers, the latter is occurring with increased frequency and seemingly diverse transitions in thinking about market exchange are actually converging toward a new dominant logic.

Convergence toward service-dominant logic

Various transitions are occurring in conceptualizing economic exchange that intersect and converge to weave the foundations of a new, service-dominant logic. This logic arises out of the following shifts in thought:

(1) What actors exchange is less well characterized as "goods" than as applied specialized resources.
(2) Most critical resources are often not tangible but rather intangible resources like actor (human) knowledge and skills (competences).
(3) Value creation cannot occur in factories or through distribution but rather through the interactions of the actors sharing and using these resources – that is, through service provision.
(4) Business and economics are less about units of output than about the process of sharing the application of resources among actors.
(5) Actors in their role as customers are not static resources to be targeted or marketed to but active and creative resources to be collaborated and marketed with.
(6) Competitive advantage is a function of applied resources that are better able to provide service for some portion of the market.
(7) Value is cocreated and ultimately can only be evaluated and hence determined by the beneficiary.
(8) Markets do not exist *per se*; rather, entrepreneurial actors are able to sense opportunities for value cocreation that provide the basis for creating growth markets and industries.
(9) When goods are involved, they are tools for the delivery and application of resources – that is, service.
(10) Systems of exchange or what some refer to as markets (at least, free markets) are not characterized by states of equilibrium but rather by constant

disequilibrium, caused by effectual actors continually creating new resources and their competitive application for others' benefit in a dynamic, changing context.

These commonalities of new and emerging perspectives of the market and exchange point toward service as the basis of exchange. Translated into a normative, managerial approach, S-D logic becomes something like:

- Identify or develop core competences, the fundamental knowledge and skills of an economic and social actor that represent potential strategic advantage.
- Identify other actors (potential customers) that could benefit from these competences.
- Cultivate relationships that involve the customers in developing customized, compelling value propositions to meet specific needs.
- Gauge the success of your value proposition by obtaining economic and non-economic feedback and use it to improve your value proposition and your performance.
- Involve customers collaboratively in value creation – that is, cocreate value.

Moving forward

Perhaps serving as partial confirmation of the service focus of S-D logic, there has been a similar shift among businesses from thinking about themselves as manufacturing firms to thinking about themselves as service firms. Perhaps most notable, because of their size and traditions, are IBM and GE. IBM has also been at the forefront of establishing a new service-focused discipline, tentatively called service science management and engineering (SSME) or, service science (SS) for short. The SS initiative has now moved far beyond IBM and has been adopted by a host of other companies and supported by hundreds of universities worldwide. The very existence of this initiative is telling. The widespread support is even more so. It implies that, even after over 200 years of formal economic thought and 40-plus years of academic work focused on service, the concepts and models for understanding and dealing with service exchange do not exist. Some argue that this is because just now a "service economy" is emerging and becoming visible. S-D logic, however, suggests that a service economy has always existed but has been understood from the confines of a G-D logic model and its related classification system for economic activity. That is, given a goods-based, manufacturing classification, in which services were what was left over, as more and more specializations (accounting, production design and engineering, advertising, etc.) that were once performed inside firms (or all types, including manufacturing) become outsourced, the service category appears to grow, relative to manufacturing (see Exhibit 1.4). Regardless of the orientation, the bottom line is that, at a minimum, there is an emerging consensus that an adequate and workable understanding of service phenomena is non-existent. It is important and significant that the initiators of the SS movement have indicated that S-D logic is foundational to the development of a science of service.[62]

S-D logic represents the convergence of contemporary thinking regarding market and economic exchange. Importantly, this view represents a view of exchange that has been developed by marketing and related disciplines, rather than inherited from the historical foundations of economics and industrialization. It could be that this new, emerging logic is what Alderson had in mind when he made the call for "a marketing interpretation of the whole process of creating utility."[63] Although S-D logic remains consistent with the logic of exchange from which economic models were derived, it broadens the scope of the logic by shifting focus from goods (and services) to a transcending conceptualization of service. Thus, it is suggested that S-D logic represents a transcending convergence, one that provides a better foundation for understanding exchange phenomena, both in economic activity and, more generally, in society.

NOTES

1. Adam Smith, *An Inquiry into the Nature and Causes of the Wealth of Nations* (London: Printed for W. Strahan and T. Cadell, 1904 [1776]).
2. J. B. Bell, *A History of Economic Thought* (New York: Ronald Press, 1953); Jean-Claude Delaunay and Jean Gadrey, *Services in Economic Thought* (Boston: Kluwer Academic Press, 1992); Joseph Schumpeter, *History of Economic Analysis* (New York: Oxford University Press, 1954); Stephen L. Vargo, Robert F. Lusch, and Fred W. Morgan "Historical perspectives on service-dominant logic," in R. F. Lusch and S. L. Vargo (eds.), *The Service Dominant Logic of Marketing: Dialog, Debate, and Directions* (Armonk, NY: M. E. Sharpe, 2006), pp. 29–42.
3. Smith, *Wealth of Nations*, p. 1.
4. Stephen L. Vargo and Robert F. Lusch, "Evolving to a new dominant logic for marketing," *Journal of Marketing*, 68 (January 2004), 1–17.
5. Smith, *Wealth of Nations*, p. 314.
6. Smith, *Wealth of Nations*, pp. 30–31.
7. Jean-Baptiste Say, *A Treatise on the Political Economy* (Boston: Wells & Lilly, 1821).
8. John Stuart Mill, *Principles of Political Economy* (London: J. P. Parker, 1848).

9. Mill, *Principles of Political Economy*, p. 45.
10. Mill, *Principles of Political Economy*, pp. 45–46.
11. Mill, *Principles of Political Economy*, pp. 45–46.
12. Frédéric Bastiat, *Harmonies of Political Economy*, trans. Patrick S. Sterling (London: J. Murray, 1860), p. 40.
13. Bastiat, *Harmonies of Political Economy*, p. 43, emphasis in original.
14. Frédéric Bastiat, *Selected Essays on Political Economy*, trans. S. Cain, ed. G. B. de Huszar (Princeton, NJ: D. Van Nordstrand, 1964 [1848]), p. 162.
15. Schumpeter, *History of Economic Analysis*.
16. Michel Callon, *The Laws of the Markets* (Oxford, UK: Blackwell, 1998).
17. Leon Walras, *Elements of the Political Economy* (Homestead, IL: Richard D. Irwin, 1954 [1894]).
18. Walras, *Elements of the Political Economy*, pp. 29–30.
19. Schumpeter, *History of Economic Analysis*.
20. Alfred Marshall, *Principles of Economics* (London: Macmillan, 1927 [1890]).
21. Jean-Claude Delaunay and Jean Gadrey, *Services in Economic Thought* (Boston: Kluwer Academic Press, 1992).
22. Arch W. Shaw, "Some problems in market distribution," *Quarterly Journal of Economics*, 26 (August 1912), 706–65; Jagdish N. Sheth and Barbara L. Gross "Parallel development of marketing and consumer behavior: a historical perspective," in T. Nevett and R. A. Fullerton (eds.), *Historical Perspectives in Marketing* (Lexington, MA: Lexington Books, 1988), pp. 9–33.
23. Shaw, "Some problems in market distribution," p. 12; Eric Shaw, "The utility of the four utilities concept," in Jagdish Sheth and Ronald Ferguson (eds.), *Research in Marketing* (Greenwich, CT: JAI Press, 1994), pp. 47–66.
24. Louis D. H. Weld, *The Marketing of Farm Products* (New York: Macmillan, 1916).
25. Allan G. B. Fisher, *The Class of Progress and Society* (New York: Augustus M. Kelley Publishers, 1935).
26. Wroe Alderson, *Marketing Behavior and Executive Action: A Functionalist Approach to Marketing Theory* (Homewood, IL: Richard D. Irwin, 1957); W. J. McInnis "A conceptual approach to marketing," in Reavis CoxWroe Alderson, and Stanley Shapiro (eds.), *Theory in Marketing* (Homewood, IL: Richard D. Irwin, 1964), pp. 51–67.
27. Donald F. Dixon, "Marketing as production: the development of a concept," *Journal of the Academy of Marketing Science*, 18:4 (1990), 337–343.
28. Alderson, *Marketing Behavior and Executive Action*, p. 69.
29. Peter F. Drucker, "Marketing and economic development," *Journal of Marketing*, 22 (1958), 252–259, pp. 253, 255, emphasis added.
30. Robert C. Judd, "The case for redefining services," *Journal of Marketing*, 18 (1964), 58–59; John M. Rathmell, 'What Is Meant by Services?' *Journal of Marketing*, 30 (1966), 32–36.
31. Christopher H. Lovelock, "Classifying services to gain strategic marketing insights," *Journal of Marketing*, 47:3 (1983), 9–20, p. 13; see also Michael R. Solomon, Carol F. Surprenant, John A. Czepiel, and Evelyn G. Gutman, "A role theory perspective on dyadic interactions," *Journal of Marketing*, 49:1 (1985), 99–111.
32. John E. G. Bateson, *Managing Services Marketing* (Fort Worth, TX: Dryden, 1991), p. 7.

33. Valerie A. Zeithaml, A. Parasuraman, and Leonard L. Berry, "Problems and strategies in services marketing," *Journal of Marketing*, 49:2 (1985), 33–46.
34. Zeithaml, Parasuraman, and Berry, "Problems and strategies in services marketing."
35. Evert Gummesson, *Quality Management in Service Organization* (New York: International Service Quality Association, 1993), p. 32.
36. Mary H. Beaven, and Dennis J. Scotti, "Service-oriented thinking and its implications for the marketing mix," *Journal of Services Marketing*, 4:4 (1990), 5–19, pp. 7–8.
37. G. Lynn Shostack, "Breaking free from product marketing," *Journal of Marketing*, 41:2 (1977), 73–80, p. 73.
38. Zeithaml, Parasuraman, and Berry, "Problems and strategies in services marketing."
39. Leonard L. Berry, "Relationship marketing," in L. L. Berry, G. L. Shostack, and G. D. Upah (eds.), *Emerging Perspectives in Services Marketing* (Chicago: American Marketing Association, 1983), pp. 25–38.
40. E.g., Christian Grönroos, "From scientific management to service management," *International Journal of Service Industry Management*, 5:1 (1994), 5–20.
41. Christian Grönroos, "Relationship marketing: the Nordic school perspective," in Jagdish N. Sheth and Atul Parvatiyar (eds.), *Handbook of Relationship Marketing* (Thousand Oaks, CA: Sage Publications, 2000), pp. 95–117; Richard Normann, *Service Management: Strategy and Leadership in Service Business* (New York: John Wiley & Sons, 1988).
42. Frederick W. Taylor, *Scientific Management* (London: Harper & Row, 1947).
43. Grönroos, "From scientific management to service management," p. 5, emphasis added.
44. Shostack, "Breaking free from product marketing."
45. E.g., Joseph B. Pine, *Mass Customization: New Frontiers in Business Competition* (Cambridge, MA: Harvard Business School Press, 1993).
46. E.g., C. K. Prahalad and Venkatram Ramaswamy, "Co-opting customer competence," *Harvard Business Review*, 78:1 (2000), 79–87.
47. Joseph B. Pine and James H. Gilmore, *The Experience Economy: Work as Theater and Every Business a Stage* (Cambridge, MA: Harvard University Press, 1999).
48. C. K. Prahalad and Gary Hamel, "The core competence of the corporation," *Harvard Business Review*, 68 (1990), 79–91; George Day, "The capabilities of market-driven organization," *Journal of Marketing*, 58 (October 1994), 37–52.
49. Shelby D. Hunt, *Foundations of Marketing Theory: Toward a General Theory of Marketing* (Thousand Oaks, CA: Sage Publications, 2002).
50. Shoshana Zuboff and James Maxmin, *The Support Economy: Why Corporations Are Failing Individuals and the Next Episode of Capitalism* (New York: Viking Press, 2002), p. 323.
51. Jagdish N. Sheth and A. Parvatiyar, "Relationship marketing in consumer markets: antecedents and consequences," in Jagdish Sheth and A. Parvatiyar (eds.), *Handbook of Relationship Marketing* (Thousand Oaks, CA: Sage Publications, 2000), p. 126.
52. James A. Constantin and Robert F. Lusch, *Understanding Resource Management* (Oxford, OH: The Planning Forum, 1994).
53. Ravi S. Achrol and Philip Kotler, "Marketing in the network economy," *Journal of Marketing*, 63 (special issue) (1999), 146–163, p. 162.

54. Richard Normann and Rafael Ramirez, "From value chain to value constellation: designing interactive strategy," *Harvard Business Review*, 71:4 (1993), 65–77.
55. Robert F. Lusch, "Reframing supply chain management: a service-dominant logic perspective," *Journal of Supply Chain Management*, 47:1 (2011), 14–18.
56. Frederick E. Webster, Jr., "The changing role of marketing in the corporation," *Journal of Marketing*, 56:4 (1992), 1–17, p. 1.
57. George Day and David Montgomery, "Charting new directions for marketing," *Journal of Marketing*, 63 (special issue) (1999), 3–13, p. 3.
58. Sheth and Parvatiyar, "Relationship marketing in consumer markets," p. 140.
59. Edith Tilton Penrose, *The Theory of the Growth of the Firm* (Oxford: Basil Blackwell, 1959).
60. Richard Nelson and Sidney G. Winter, *An Evolutionary Theory of Economic Change* (Cambridge, MA: Belknap Press, 1982).
61. David Teece and Gary Pisano, "The dynamic capabilities of firms: an introduction," *Industrial and Corporate Change*, 3 (1994), 537–556, p. 537.
62. James Spohrer and Paul Maglio, "Fundamentals of service science," *Journal of the Academy of Marketing Science*, 36 (2008), 18–20.
63. Alderson, *Marketing Behavior and Executive Action*, p. 69.

3 Axioms and foundational premises

Production is not the application of tools to materials, but logic to work.

Peter F. Drucker

Introduction

All logics are based on premises and assumptions. Often these are not explicit or spoken but are implicit and unspoken. Logics can be observed in everyday practices and language. In the development of service-dominant (S-D) logic we have attempted to be explicit about its premises, assumptions, and language (or what we call its lexicon).

Four axioms form the foundation of S-D logic, as briefly reviewed in Chapter 1. These four axioms serve as a platform for a half-dozen additional foundational premises that, in addition to the four axioms, form the ten foundational premises (FPs) that comprise the underlying structure of S-D logic. These are illustrated in Exhibit 3.1.

As noted in Exhibit 3.1, under axiom 1 (FP1), "service is the fundamental basis of exchange," we have four derivative FPs: FP2, "indirect exchange masks the fundamental basis of exchange"; FP3, "goods are distribution mechanisms for service provision"; FP4, "operant resources are the fundamental source of competitive advantage"; FP5, "all economies are service economies." Under axiom 2 (FP6), "the customer is always a cocreator of value," there are two derivative FPs: FP7, "the enterprise cannot deliver value, but only offer value propositions; and FP8, "a service-centered view is inherently customer oriented

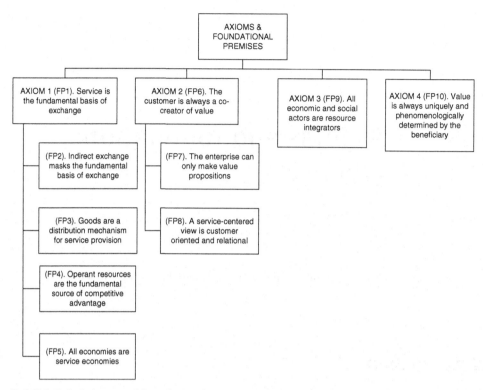

Exhibit 3.1 Axioms and foundational premises of S-D logic

and relational." Axiom 3 (FP9), "all economic and social actors are resource integrators," and axiom 4 (FP10), "value is always uniquely and phenomenologically determined by the beneficiary," stand alone without direct derivative FPs. The structure and the order of the FPs under the four axioms are used primarily for pedagogical purposes.[1] As you become more familiar with the FPs and all of their intricacies you will begin to see how all of the FPs relate to each other but with the four axioms as the most foundational. In brief, six FPs are nested under four axioms.

All logics also have a lexicon developed by the community that supports and uses the logic. The lexicon comprises the terms and concepts, represented through words or symbols, which communicate meaning and help to coordinate thought among the community. To understand S-D logic, its axioms, and FPs, it is critical to become familiar with its lexicon. This can be difficult because some of the language is similar to the language of G-D logic, albeit with nuanced meanings. We begin with a review of the essential parts of this lexicon.

The lexicon of service-dominant logic

Theories and models are abstractions of reality. Language and words are used to develop abstractions, and these abstractions are then related to each other in order to describe or explain the phenomena of interest. The goal is to be parsimonious, while still being as isomorphic as possible. This implies using as few concepts as necessary to describe and explain the phenomena of interest; while, at the same time, striving for correspondence between the theory or model and real-world phenomena. Predictably, it is very difficult to be both parsimonious and isomorphic with the same theory, model, or logic. We suggest that S-D logic strikes a reasonably good balance between these two objectives.

As noted, we believe S-D logic is reasonably parsimonious in its lexicon. In fact, it deals with only four core, foundational concepts (actors, service, resources, value), and from these we derive ten additional concepts. Exhibit 3.2 presents the S-D logic lexicon.[2] Let us now further explain the concepts that compose the lexicon of S-D logic.

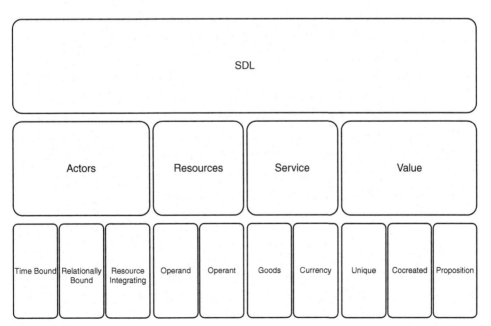

Exhibit 3.2 The S-D logic lexicon

Actors

Actors are entities that have agency, the ability to act purposefully. But they also act within structures, such as norms and experientially and socially acquired attitudes, and other institutions that constrain these purposeful actions. The relative degree to which agency versus structure determines any given action has been debated for hundreds, if not thousands, of years.[3]

We will not try to resolve that debate here but will suggest that, most likely, at least some of what appears to be agency probably results from multiple, overlapping structures. In fact, it might be that agency actually represents the *individual's reconciliation* of these sometimes-conflicting structures. The important point is that agency and structure are intertwined. That is, given the limits of the human mind,[4] without the structure that makes bounded rationality possible, meaningful actions would not be possible and, without some degree of agency, there would be no structure. In the following chapters, we will explore some of this interplay in our discussion of the interplay of practices, institutions, and context as they relate to value cocreation, through service-for-service exchange.

Actors are also time bound in several ways. First, all actors have a unique past that influences their beliefs, values, and ideology in general. Actors also sit in the present and are enveloped in a habitus that characterizes their everyday existence and, as we will learn later, much of this involves practices. Finally, actors are able to project themselves into the future and establish goals and future desired states that in turn influence their actions and exchanges in the present.

As illustrated in Exhibit 3.2, actors are relationally bound to other actors but also are relationally bound to society or other communities through shared institutions; these shared institutions are central to service ecosystems, as we will discuss in Chapter 8. In addition, all actors are resource integrating. As we will discuss, they integrate resources to enhance the viability of a relevant system. Viability consists of multiple characteristics of a system to include adaptability, flexibility, resiliency, and well-being. The relevant system can be the individual actor or any assemblage of actors that comprise a system.

Service

Service is defined as the application of resources for the benefit of another actor or oneself. It can be provided directly (e.g., a haircut) to other actors or indirectly, either through a good (e.g., personal transportation service through a car), with the good serving as an appliance or distribution mechanism for service, or through a currency. Currency, in turn, can be economic currency most commonly thought of in terms of money, which provides a right to future service, or social currency – that is, social capital, created through the obligation for future service.

Resources

Resources are anything that an actor can draw on for support. Often this is for value creation. *Operand resources* are (potential) resources that require other resources to act on them to provide benefit. They are static and often tangible, such as natural resources. *Operant resources* are resources that are capable of acting on other (potential) resources to create benefit; they are often intangible and dynamic. Common examples of operant resources are human skills and capabilities. Operand and operant resources are almost always interlinked. Generally, for operand resources to provide benefit, actors need to know how to act on them. This can be as simple as knowing how to gather and cut wood and start a fire to create warmth, or it can be as complex as knowing how to take silica and turn it into a microprocessor. Thus, the application of operant resources to operand resources is what creates benefit for humans.

Value

Value is *benefit*, an *increase in the well-being* of a particular actor. Because it is actor specific and every instance of its creation is contextually distinct, every occurrence is unique. It is also holistically and phenomenologically determined, implying that it is an experiential concept, rather than being tied to the service of a single actor or to a particular resource. In fact, we argue that value is cocreated because resources from multiple sources are always integrated to create value. Since it is always *cocreated and phenomenological*, value cannot be provided by one actor to another; rather, it can only be proposed. A *value proposition* is a representation of how an actor proposes to positively participate in value creation with a beneficial actor.

The lexicon can be used to further develop and elaborate the ten FPs, as illustrated in Exhibit 3.1.

Axiom 1 and foundational premise 1: service is the fundamental basis of exchange

Actors have two basic operant resources: physical and mental skills. These resources are "operant" because actors use them to create beneficial effects by acting on other resources (operant or operand). Actors develop and apply these resources and exchange their application with other actors to enhance their system viability. This is necessary because these physical and mental skills are unequally distributed in the population; thus, each actor's skills are not necessarily sufficient for his or her system viability. This exchange for mutual benefit requires the development of social contracts and complex social systems for governance.

Largely because actors specialize in particular skills and competences, they achieve scale and learning effects. Specialization requires exchange; this is true today and has been true ever since human actors recognized that they could live more satisfactorily by serving each other than simply being self-servers.[5] With improved skills and competences and associated scale and learning effects the economic actors find increasing advantage to exchange and being of service to each other. However, as argued in Chapter 1, when discussing the fisherman and farmer, the view of what is exchanged can vary dramatically depending on perspective – that is, from a goods-centered or a service-centered vantage point. Under the goods-centered view, it is believed that the *output* from the performance of specialized activities is being exchanged. On the other hand, the service-centered view suggests that the *performance of the specialized activities* (i.e., the application of operant resources) is being exchanged.

What does this first axiom (and FP1) of S-D logic suggest for actors? Essentially, it suggests that all actors, whether they are individuals, households, firms, non-profit or governmental agencies, or even nations, should recognize the primary nature of what they are offering in exchange with other actors. All economic actors thus need to get relatively good at some combination of mental and physical skills and use these to develop specialized advantageous service offerings.

Foundational premise 2: indirect exchange masks the fundamental basis of exchange

If service is the fundamental basis of exchange, as suggested in the first axiom, and if, as Frédéric Bastiat argued, the essence of economic activity is service-for-service exchange, then the world of economic exchange should be fairly simple to understand. Exchange of service, however, is seldom as direct as it might appear. In Exhibit 3.3 we portray how intermediaries can mask the service-for-service nature of exchange.

In contemporary society and economy, one-to-one trading of specialized skills is largely a historical artifact. In its place has arisen the indirect exchange of skills

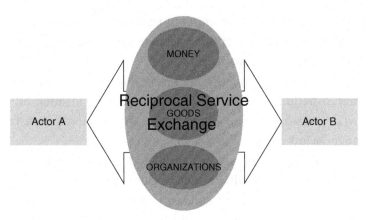

Exhibit 3.3 Intermediaries mask the service-for-service nature of exchange

facilitated by money as a common medium of exchange in which one actor offers money to another actor in return for direct service, such as when an actor pays a personal fitness trainer for his or her service. The fitness trainer now has money that he or she can exchange for service he or she may need or want – for example, automobile insurance. Of course, money is also often exchanged for a good, such as when an actor purchases a vitamin supplement. Here the good provides nutritional service; however, it also substitutes for an actor going out and gathering plants and extracting from them vitamins that could be consumed. However, once again, the exchange of service for service is not direct but indirect. The organization receiving the money in return for the nutritional service received (through a pill) can use the money for a variety of services; perhaps it uses the funds to pay the rent on its facility.

Service can also be masked because there can be many service exchanges that occur within an organization. As Coase and Williamson have suggested, organizations are substitutes for market exchange and thus service exchange in the organization is not directly market facing.[6] For instance, the personal trainer with whom the actor exchanged money for fitness service probably works for a fitness club and the actor was actually paying the fitness club. The fitness club also employs accountants, janitors, sales personnel, managers, and so on who are each providing service that helps to support the fitness advisor that is serving the actor directly. In fact the organization can be viewed as a habitat for micro-specialized actors that perform service in return for a wage or economic compensation paid by the firm, rather than by the service beneficiary. Unfortunately, often when these micro-specialized actors perform service, but not in direct exchange for service, they can lose sight of the service-for-service nature of exchange. It is likely that the accountant and janitor often do not realize that they are also involved in (indirect) service-for-service exchange with the actor that is exchanging money for personal fitness service.

Indirect exchange and its tendency to mask the service basis of exchange is something that appears to be universal across different societies. In brief, all civilizations move toward creating goods, organizations, and money to assist them in service exchange. Below we explain why this occurs.

Human actors, as we have suggested, are not very good at calculating and being able to rationally plan and coordinate their actions with other actors. Human actors are, however, very clever at solving problems. Some of their solutions are generalizable and adopted by others and thus the solution becomes institutionalized. Institutions assist humans in solving recurring problems related to planning, calculating, and coordinating. With direct service-for-service exchange it is difficult for actors to calculate the availability and location of other actors that have a need for the service offering that another actor could provide. Even if the actor was able to calculate where other actors were located and the time they would desire to exchange, these might not match up well with where the actor himself or herself was located and the time he or she would need the service. Let us now illustrate how actors have solved this problem by indirect exchange through money, goods, and organizations. In this illustration we also demonstrate how money, goods, and organizations have become institutionalized.

To explain the rationale for indirect exchange, we will revisit the farmer and fisherman example from Chapter 1. If the society developed the institution of money as a medium of exchange, then an actor (let us call them a merchant) could begin to specialize in acquiring the fish the fisherman did not need and the grain the farmer did not need. The farmer and fisherman would then have a storehouse of economic value (money or service rights) that they received from exchanging the application of their fishing skills or the application of their farming skills with the merchant. In turn, the merchant would not only hold an inventory of money (service rights) but it would also store or inventory fish and wheat. In fact the merchant might speculate about when and where the farmer and fisherman might need the protein and carbohydrate service the fish and grain provide. If the merchant succeeded at making a living performing the services described above, then others would copy and thus the merchant becomes a generic intermediary, through institutionalization. Note that we now have two institutions that are helping humans solve their calculating, coordination, and planning problems: a monetary system and intermediaries as facilitators of exchange.

Next consider that the farmer and fisherman in the development of their skills and competences develop tools (goods) to assist them or to leverage their physical and mental efforts. The tools or goods are operand resources and the physical and mental efforts are operant resources. For the fisherman the tools or goods include hooks and nets and sailing vessels. For the farmer these could include hoes and sickles. In fact, another actor could begin to specialize in the development and refinement of these tools (just as the merchant specialized in trading). What do these tools provide? One could present several answers but one primary answer is that they allow the actors to be more productive in applying their skills and capabilities. If they did not have these tools then they would either need to work longer hours and days or recruit other actors to assist them. Without the tools the actors are more dependent on their physical and mental skills and thus they would need to do more computation, coordination, and planning. This is because all tools institutionalize how tasks are performed. Thus, in addition to the institutions of money and merchants, we now have tools and goods which are also emerging as institutions. In brief, the fishing net and fish hook, as well as the hoe and sickle, once they are demonstrated to solve problems for humans, become institutionalized. Stated alternatively, generic product forms become institutionalized solutions to recurring human problems.

Money, goods, and organizations proliferated as institutions over time but especially during the Industrial Revolution. During the Industrial Revolution we witnessed the acceleration of the division of labor and the extent of the market economy, which brought forth considerable economic efficiency. More and more capital (tools) were substituted for labor, the market economy proliferated, more and more commodification of offerings occurred, and large bureaucratic hierarchical organizations ascended in prominence to calculate, coordinate, and plan the use of resources. However, this economic efficiency came at the cost of no longer having direct interaction. Without direct interaction, it is difficult to gain information and knowledge about the beneficiary actors that the organization is serving.

Ultimately, when an actor does not interact directly with the actor he or she is serving, it is not easy to hear the voice of the intended beneficiary. When the voice is heard, it is often faint and distorted. Before long, actors in their role as employees, focus on the units of output they produce (i.e., they adopt a G-D logic lens) and lose a sense of the purpose of their service provision to the ultimate beneficiary of the organization. Actors performing micro-specialized functions deep within the organization have internal beneficiaries. One actor performs a micro-specialized task and then passes the work product on to another actor, who performs an activity; this process continues throughout a service chain. The actors along the chain do not pay one another; however, they may engage in other forms of reciprocal exchange such as communication. Nevertheless, they do not typically interact or exchange directly with external beneficiary actors. All of this sets up a system in which the actor tends to ignore quality. To correct for this problem that is rooted in G-D logic, a variety of management techniques developed under the rubric of "total quality management."[7] The techniques were intended to reestablish the focus of actors in the organization on both internal and external beneficiary actors who could be the arbiters of quality.

The preceding problem of actors not paying attention to, or even knowing of, the service-purpose of their work is not uniquely a manufacturing problem. Just because a company is not a manufacturer and provides primarily intangibles does not alter the masking of service exchange by indirect exchange. Banks, airlines, phone providers, colleges and universities, and health care organizations are not necessarily more focused on the beneficiary actor. In fact, many non-goods-producing organizations, especially large bureaucracies, are just as subject as goods-producing institutions to the masking effect of indirect exchange. This is because they provide services through organized micro-specializations that are focused on minute and isolated aspects of service provision and they never interface with the external actors a firm engages in exchange.

It should be kept in mind that not only do workers specialize, but also entire organizations can specialize. For instance, a firm that makes bumpers for automobiles and trucks needs to view itself not as producing units of output (bumpers) but providing the service of accident shock absorbing and/or damage protection. They need to look beyond the firm they sell their bumpers to and look to the service that the ultimate beneficiary is receiving.

Regardless of the type of organization, the fundamental process does not change; actors still exchange their often collective and distributed specialized skills for the individual and collective skills of others in often market-based, monetized exchange. Actors still exchange their service for other service. Money, goods, and organizations are only the exchange vehicles or intermediaries.

Foundational premise 3: goods are distribution mechanisms for service provision

Service-dominant logic's challenge of goods-dominant logic does not and should not be taken as downplaying the role of goods. Undeniably, goods play a vital role in economic exchange and in the advancement of human civilization. Perhaps ironically, we argue that this critical role can be seen more clearly from an S-D logic perspective than from a G-D logic perspective.

Traditionally, tangible products have been viewed as the fundamental components of economic exchange. This is understandable; when basic subsistence and survival are of paramount concern, one cannot ignore the importance of tangibles such as food and shelter and tools. Our concern, however, is that the focus on tangible goods became the primary focus not only of firms but also nations in the pursuit of economic wealth. As discussed in FP2, when service exchange becomes masked through indirect exchange, one can lose sight of the underlying service-provision processes. Even when it comes to goods innovation and production, the key message throughout human civilization is the remarkable role of humans in acquiring the knowledge and skills to alter natural resources to form and shape tools (or, more generally, goods) and to use these goods to deliver service.

Service provision can be provided directly or indirectly. The direct transfer occurs when actors exchange their knowledge and skills directly. For instance, an actor may not have the knowledge (or time) to perform some function such as medical treatment. Thus, the actor in need of medical service may enter into an exchange with another actor. Of course, medical service can also be provided through education and/or training, which enables the actors to provide for their own medical care. A second option for providing medical service occurs when it is provided via a tangible good such as a pharmaceutical, which serves as a distribution mechanism or appliance for service provision or the transfer of knowledge and skills. Of course, in health care and medicine both knowledge transfer options can be used simultaneously. For instance, a heart surgeon performing open heart surgery on a patient (1) uses his or her knowledge of medicine directly and provides the patient with pre- and post-surgery education about proper diet and lifestyle so that the patient can perform self-service; (2) uses a variety of goods, such as surgical tools, tables and linens, pharmaceuticals, computers and robotic equipment. It is useful to view these goods as service appliances that other actors used their knowledge and skills to create.

The entanglement of goods and knowledge is often characterized as products being "frozen activities"[8] or "informed" with embodied knowledge.[9] Think of it as the infusion of matter with structure or information, which provides the good with the capacity for self-service by another actor. Viewed in this fashion, one can see the Industrial Revolution as, in part, fostered by wheels, pulleys, conveyor belts, and engines, all of them embodied knowledge or "informed" matter.

In all cases, from the tools developed for the factories of the Industrial Revolution to the appliances in the household kitchen, the properly informed matter becomes the distribution mechanism for applied skills (i.e., service). As Kotler has noted, "the importance of physical products lies not so much in owning them as in obtaining the service they render."[10]

Viewing goods as embodied knowledge or informed matter and as being used as a distribution mechanism for service provision, or more simply as appliances, allows a product designer or an entrepreneur to see new opportunities for innovation. Consider the evolution of the early automobile from the late 1800s to today and how a large number of innovative, tangible components were introduced or modified to provide better service or, essentially, to offer a more compelling value proposition. Here is a short list: windshield wipers, automatic self starter, glove box, automatic transmission, power steering, power brakes, tubeless tires, cigarette lighter, ash tray, cargo hold-down straps, adjustable and heated seats, drinking cup holder, seat belts, air conditioning, radio, automatic windows and door locks, air bags, skid control, navigation system, and so on. Some of these innovations *relieve* the human of tasks, such as the automatic transmission relieving the human of gear shifting and thus lessening the need for developing skills and knowledge of gear shifting; other innovations are *enabling* because they allow human actors to do things not possible before, such as listening to music while driving.

Goods not only provide service; they can also meet higher-order needs.[11] A pair of athletics shoes, automobile, or tablet computer meets needs beyond functionality – for example, the need for recognition, prestige, and status. Prahalad and Ramaswamy refer to appliances as "artifacts around which customers have experiences."[12] Essentially, the good can serve as a means of reaching valued end states.[13]

Foundational premise 4: operant resources are the fundamental source of competitive advantage

Operand resources are important and S-D logic recognizes the role of the tangible good and other operand resources. However, without knowledge and skills of the appropriate type, which allow the actor to draw on and use an operand resource, it is not useful. Consider, for instance, Saudi Arabia with its substantial petroleum reserves. It was not until actors developed knowledge of oil extraction and oil use that they were able to transform the petroleum gunk into a resource. Before then, it was, at best, neutral matter.[14] This would also be true of an actor who has in his or her pantry the ingredients to cook a nutritious meal but doesn't have the knowledge to draw on the ingredients in the proper way to create it.

In both of these cases, what is illustrated is that only if an actor has operant resources and knows how to apply resources does he or she gain advantage. Although FP4 focuses on the notion of competitive advantage, mostly because markets as usually experienced involve firms competing with other firms and seeking ways to gain competitive advantage, it is a bit of a myopic term. Perhaps a more neutral term that would work better with a generic A2A framework is "strategic advantage." Importantly, when actors innovate and discover novel ways of integrating existing resources with new resources, such as when the knowledge and skills of computational science and technology are integrated with silica to create a microprocessor, the actors are able to create new markets and/or expand existing markets.

Since service is the application of resources to benefit another actor or oneself, only those resources that can produce effects can serve as the fundamental source of competitive or strategic advantage and those resources are never solely static operand resources. Clearly, in the short run, any actor, either an individual, organization, or nation, may have a large stockpile of tangible operand resources but these static resources are relatively unimportant over the long run because they can be used up or easily transferred.[15] Without the ability to replenish and grow these operand resources, they cannot be a sustainable source of advantage.

However, even growing operand resources will not be a source of *sustainable* strategic advantage if the focus is on the market, as it exists. S-D logic takes a view of strategic advantage in terms of helping actors solve tomorrow's problems or doing tomorrow's "jobs." For instance, consider the prior example about petroleum and the knowledge and skills to find, refine, and distribute petroleum fuel. The job faced tomorrow is how to create, develop, and distribute non-carbon-based energy or to develop market offerings that require less energy. Or consider the example about having the knowledge to take food from your food pantry and to prepare a nutritious meal. Tomorrow the job may be how to integrate food both at home and outside the home with mental and physical fitness. Enterprises in the traditional petroleum industry and packaged food industry that respond and shape these jobs to be done tomorrow will face boundless market-ing.

In a real sense, then, strategic advantage is not about gaining market share by "beating" the competition in today's market; it is about fostering and developing "sustainable market creation." Stated alternatively, it is not about viewing markets or market potential as bounded but as unbounded, since the jobs to be done constantly change and expand.

Sustainable market creation will never solely be the result of the operand resources on the balance sheet that represents the assets and liabilities and equity of an organization. An organization can have plenty of static matter, such as cash, inventory, buildings, and equipment, or rights to physical matter (leases) listed on it. However, all of this "valuable" static stuff on the balance sheet is never a source of sustainable market creation. What are especially valuable are the dynamic and largely intangible resources, such as the managerial competences to use the cash to make the proper strategic acquisitions or investments in research and development and personnel. As enterprises increasingly become part of a network of actors that work collaboratively to cocreate value, the need arises for the entire network or community of actors to be a knowledge-generating and knowledge-using mechanism for sustainable market creation.

Foundational premise 5: all economies are service economies

From the first axiom, that service is the fundamental basis of exchange, the fifth foundational premise, that all economies are service economies, is derived. Economists have taught us to think about economic development in terms of "eras" or "economies," such as hunter-gatherer, agricultural, and industrial. Formal economic thought developed during one of these eras, the "industrial economy," and it has tended to describe economies in terms of the types of output (game, agricultural products, manufactured products), associated with markets that were expanding rapidly at the time. However, the "economies" might more accurately be viewed as macro-specializations, each characterized by the expansion and refinement of some particular type of competence that could be exchanged. The hunter-gatherer macro-specialization was characterized by the refinement and application of foraging and hunting knowledge and skills; the agricultural macro-specialization by development and refinement of cultivation knowledge and skills; the industrial economy by the refinement of knowledge and skills for mass production and organizational management; and the information economies by the refinement and use of knowledge and skills about information and its exchange.

The fundamental economic exchange process pertains to the application of mental and physical skills (service provision), and manufactured goods are mechanisms for service provision. Nonetheless, economic science, as well as most classifications of economic exchange that are based on it, is grounded in Adam Smith's narrowed concern with manufactured output (see Chapter 2). Consequently, as mentioned in chapters 1 and 2, services have traditionally been defined as anything that does not result in manufactured (or extractive – mining, forestry, fishing, and agricultural) output. It doesn't take much of a leap to conclude that only recently (the past fifty years) have most nations entered into a non-manufacturing and thus services economy.

Transitioning out of a manufacturing economy does not imply entering a service economy. Return for the moment to the notion that specialization breeds micro-specialization. Throughout history, actors have been moving toward more specific specialties. The same tends to be the case for organizations. Activities and processes that were once routinely performed internally by a single economic actor become separate specializations which are then often outsourced, further expanding the market. Consider, for instance, a manufacturer that outsources the employee cafeteria, the human resources recordkeeping and payroll system, information technology, or legal or marketing research. When this occurs the enterprises that take on performing these activities through market exchange are clearly classified by most governments as non-manufacturing or "services" firms and employment in these "sectors" rises. At the same time, since the manufacturer does not perform these activities it appears that manufacturing employment is declining. However, the "real nature" of the economic activity has not changed.

Distortions in statistics are the result of a national economic accounting system that is based on the type of output (e.g., agricultural, mining, manufacturing, wholesaling, retailing, intangibles). Although governments around the world continue to abide by output-focused classification schemata they are often aware of the distortions created. For instance, the US Bureau of Economic Analysis states:

[O]ne in the same activity, such as painting, may be classified as goods or service production depending purely on the organization of the overall process of production . . . If the painting is done by employees within the producer unit [that] makes the good, it will be treated as [part of] the goods production, whereas if it is done by an outside painting company, it will be classified as an intermediate input of services. Thus, when a service previously performed in a manufacturing establishment is contracted out, to a specialized services firm, data will show an increase in services production in the economy even though the total activity of "painting," may be unchanged.[16]

Not only can one see how the move to outsourcing in manufacturing enterprises results in a perceived and statistically government-certified move to a services economy, it can also be witnessed in the typical household in a developed nation. Here, more and more shifts between internal or household provision of service to external provisioning of service can be seen. For instance, when a household eats more meals outside the home, the parents send the children to school, hire workers to clean the house or landscape the exterior, or go to a movie theater or sporting event for entertainment what is occurring is the growth of what appears to be a services economy. But one hundred years ago and more these activities were performed, service provided, by household members or extended family members. Service is universal and arises as more and more specialization occurs among actors and often this specialization goes beyond the boundaries of the enterprise (business or household) and thus results in more exchange of service.

In both the classification of economic activity and the economic eras, the common denominator is the increased refinement and exchange of specialized knowledge and skills, or operant resources. Virtually all the activities performed today have always been performed in some manner; however, they have become increasingly separated into specialties and exchanged in the market.

All this may seem to be an argument that traditional classificatory systems underestimate the historical role and rise of services. In a sense, it is. It is not that service(s) is only now becoming important, but that only now is it becoming more apparent in the economy as specialization increases and as less of what is exchanged fits the dominant manufactured-output classification system of economic activity. Service and the operant resources they represent have always characterized the essence of economic activity.

Axiom 2 and foundational premise 6: the customer is always a cocreator of value

Nowhere is the idea that enterprises make and deliver value more evident than in the concept of "value added." Value added has been a term used to describe the process of firms transforming matter to change its form, and its time, place, and possession. Predictably, these transformations require effort and thus costs, and these costs became labeled "value added" and often identified as a source of "utility." However, offerings (tangible or intangible) are not embedded with value (value-in-exchange) or utility but rather value occurs when the offering is used.

Accountants might believe that an unsold good has value but this is economic value; value creation from an actor-centric and service-dominant vantage point is only possible when market and other offerings are used – that is, when they contribute to the well-being of some actor in the context of his or her life.

With G-D logic, the value is embedded during production and distribution/marketing without the involvement of the actor who will become the beneficiary of the enterprise's offering. Early scholars in the area of services marketing succinctly identified the problem with G-D logic. For example, Gummesson argued: "if the consumer is the focal point of marketing, value creation is only possible when a good or service is consumed. An unsold good has no value, and a service provider without customers cannot produce anything."[17] Similarly, Grönroos stated:

Value for customers is created throughout the relationship by the customer, partly in interactions between the customer and the supplier or service provider. The focus is not on products but on the customers' value-creating processes where value emerges for customers and is perceived by them ... the focus of marketing is value creation rather than value distribution, and facilitation and support of value-creating processes rather than simply distributing ready-made value to customers.[18]

Because firms grounded in G-D logic believed that value was created and added during production and distribution/marketing activities they had to be taught or instructed to develop a customer orientation.[19]

In Chapter 1, a brief rationale for thinking of exchange partners as generic actors was offered and the adoption of actor-to-actor or A2A terminology was suggested. However, as is well known, economic science and the various business disciplines did not develop around such a generic actor-to-actor conceptual framework. It developed around differentiated, often-opposing, roles of firms versus customers, producers versus consumers, sellers versus buyers, employers versus employees, as well as a host of other distinctively labeled actors.

The emergence, adoption, and proliferation of terminology related to actors in their various roles undoubtedly had consequences – some of them rather profound – in shaping the development and progress of the science(s) of economics, marketing, and business. A lexicon has a way of orienting actor thinking and his or her worldview. Consider, for instance, the common association of the firm with the "producer" label and the household with the "consumer" label.

In the myopic, categorical view, a mindset develops around firms that produce value and customers ("consumers") that destroy value.[20] From this thought it is natural to conclude that the customer may get in the way and interfere with the value-production activities of the firm. Thus, a consequence becomes the dominant practice of firms and customers being separated in order to maximize manufacturing or production efficiency. With the huge gains in economic efficiency brought about by the Industrial Revolution it took a long time for firms to learn that manufacturing efficiency obtained via separating the producer and consumer often comes at the cost of marketing effectiveness. Viewing customers as cocreators of value helps to overcome the G-D logic of firms as producers of value and customers as recipients of this value.

Service-centered thinking orients one to examine the entire process of what had been thought of as production through consumption in G-D logic. From this longer and more holistic view it can be seen that production of tangible or intangible market offerings exchanged for money or service rights only reflects economic value (value-in-exchange). However, the value-creation process does not end with the sale and distribution of the product offering to the actor as beneficiary; rather, the beneficiary actor continues the process of "producing." Stated alternatively, production does not end with manufacturing and distribution; rather, these are intermediary processes. As has been noted, goods are appliances that provide service for and in conjunction with the beneficiary actor. However, for this service to be delivered, the beneficiary still must learn to use, maintain, repair, and adapt the appliance to his or her unique needs, usage situation, and behaviors. In summary, in using a product, the beneficiary is continuing the marketing, value-creation, and delivery process. Cocreation of value thus recognizes that value is always created in the use and integration of resources.

With the adoption of the generic actor and A2A framework, it becomes easier to recognize that all actors are cocreators of value. What the actors in an A2A network are doing is attempting to enhance the viability, the well-being, of what they define as their relevant system. That relevant system could include themselves and a small set of resources they can draw on for support including other actors (e.g., family), or it could include a much larger set of resources and other actors (e.g., community). Consider a simple example, in which the actor needs to be mobile so he or she can travel to work, shop, and transport children to school and events. Transport is of course related to where one has a house or apartment, and also where schools, retail stores, and places of work are located. Thus, if one actor alters any one of these, it has an effect on other actors. If the actor works in the center of the city but decides to live in the distant suburbs he or she needs to spend more time and use more of his or her service rights (money) in exchange for transport service. Thus the actor has less time to spend with his or her children and partner and to provide service to them and others. This may cause the actor to use some of his or her service rights for timesaving appliances such as quick preparation meals or home meal replacements. It becomes evident then that the value of the quick preparation meal or home meal replacement is cocreated with other actors and resources and hence the value is cocreated.

In the above simple example, the relevant system is never the isolated human actor because to be human is to be part of a network of other human actors, which involves connection to other resources that can spill over and connect the actor to other actors. In the connection to other resources it will be elaborated shortly (in FP9) that the actors are always resource integrators. Consequently, at a high level of abstraction, the cocreation of value is the process actors go through of increasing the viability of a system via the development of specialized and applied knowledge and skills, service exchange, and resource integration. System viability is a broader concept than well-being and includes system adaptability, flexibility, and resiliency, in addition to well-being.

From the second axiom, that the customer is always a cocreator of value, two additional foundational premises can be derived. Foundational premise 7 states that the enterprise cannot deliver value, but can only offer value propositions, and FP8 states that a service-centered view is inherently customer oriented and relational. Each is now reviewed.

Foundational premise 7: the enterprise cannot deliver value, but can only offer value propositions

What the preceding section is intended to illustrate is that value, from an actor-centric perspective, is not something that a firm can produce and deliver to other actors. As FP7 clearly suggests, business enterprises or any other actor cannot deliver value to other actors; they can only offer a value proposition.[21] A value proposition can be thought of as an invitation to engage with the firm for benefit. The value proposition is often viewed as a set of promised benefits in relation to expected costs; and these do not necessarily need to be put into economic terms. What traditionally is viewed as the marketing mix is directly or indirectly part of a firm's value proposition. This includes product, price, marketing communications (promotion), distribution (place), and branding. Regardless, all of these elements should be focused on the jobs to be done by the beneficiary actor. Stated alternatively, how can a firm's offering help the beneficiary actor get a job done? Looked at from the beneficiary perspective they hire a firm and its offering to get a job done.[22]

All of the preceding aspects and factors that comprise a value proposition are cocreated with a community of other actors such as a firm's brand community, supply chain partners, and even government. For instance, a firm's brand community may, through social media and other communication, significantly influence the firm's brand image. At the same time, how suppliers focus on quality and support, allow co-branding, set their prices, and provide warranties also influence the firm's value proposition. Government can also influence the firm's value proposition by taxing certain offerings and the profits of enterprises but also by controlling the market exchange of certain offerings or regulating advertising, product form and content, or the market segments with which the firm can exchange. In fact, most governments have hundreds, if not thousands, of laws and regulations that shape a firm's value proposition.

Therefore, a value proposition under S-D logic is how an actor co-proposes to positively affect another actor. This recognizes that value is obtained when an actor experiences through engagement with the firm the unfolding of the interactive market offering.[23] Stated alternatively, firms and other actors can offer potential value through value propositions; however, they *cannot create value* but only cocreate it.

Value propositions are therefore promises but they must be fulfilled. Firms and actors, in general in developing exchange relationships, should view their role as offering more compelling value propositions than other competing actors but then making sure, to the extent possible, that actual value as experienced by the beneficiary meets or exceeds promised value.

Foundational premise 8: a service-centered view is inherently customer oriented and relational

A logical derivation from axiom 2, that the customer is always a cocreator of value, is the eighth foundational premise: *a service-centered view is inherently customer oriented and relational*. The concepts of customer orientation and relationship marketing have become mainstream topics in the patched up G-D marketing management model. However, they became mainstream concepts not because the traditional G-D logic model is inherently customer and relationally focused but rather because it treats the customer as exogenous to the enterprise's value-creation efforts; therefore, the enterprise must be *instructed* to be customer oriented. Likewise, G-D logic is focused on transactional exchange and thus enterprises have to be encouraged to take a "relational," long-term, customer perspective. This long-term perspective has been facilitated by the development of various customer relationship management (CRM) software and is often used to estimate customer lifetime value (CLV).[24] Importantly and unfortunately, the CRM and CLV approach to customer and relationship management continues the G-D logic approach by treating the beneficiary actor as an operand resource. The CRM and CLV technologies move the enterprise away from singular transactions to multiple transactions over time, in order to profit from the lifetime value of a customer. Importantly, the result is a "patch" to the shortfalls and limitations of G-D logic, rather than an inherently relational and customer (re)orientation.

Another key problem with G-D logic has been its continued need (and difficulty) to be modified in order to be applicable to "special cases." Thus, it brought about the proliferation of subdisciplines in marketing and management. Two such subdisciplines are B2B marketing and service marketing. Service marketing largely focused on interactivity, based partly on the "inseparability" characteristic that was used to differentiate service(s) from goods.[25] Normatively, if interactivity is dominant in exchange and service provision, then relationships with actors should be fostered and developed.[26] On the other hand, with the B2B marketing orientation the notion of relationship was somewhat more focused on the *embeddedness* of value creation in networks of actors. Also, in B2B the exchange between actors in the network is based on close association, bi-lateral communication, relational norms, and solidarity that become "domesticated markets."[27]

An S-D logic perspective on relationship[28] is grounded in value cocreation by actors instead of the G-D logic, output-producing orientation, in which value is assumed to be added and embedded in the production (and distribution/marketing) of the output. Value is seen as emerging and unfolding over time, rather than as a discrete, production–consumption event. This unfolding, cocreational (directly or through goods) nature of value is relational in the sense that the activities of exchange actors as well as those of other actors interactively and interdependently combine, over time, to cocreate value. From the S-D logic perspective, relationship is not optional. Cocreation of value and service exchange implies a complex web of value-creating relationships. And it may or may not mean repeated economic transactions. A singular economic transaction between actors adopting a service-orientation implies relationship.

The service-centered view is also inherently customer or beneficiary oriented. This is because it focuses the firm on doing things, not just for the beneficiary but also in concert with the beneficiary. It is a model of inseparability of the actor who offers a service and the beneficiary of the service. It is fostered by a continuing dialog between network actors (the firm, suppliers, customers, and stakeholders), in which the voice of each and the voice of the market and society become more clearly heard and understood. From this perspective, the criticism of services as being inferior because they were produced inseparably, with the customer, and heterogeneously becomes a strength and advantage, and not a weakness or liability. Producers of goods and goods-centered enterprises should not so much strive to produce a product but to create a valued relationship.

In closing the discussion of FP8, it should be mentioned that, as presented in FP3, goods might be important to exchange and hence to relationships. However, inanimate items of exchange cannot have relationships; people have relationships. In general, actors do not need goods. They need to perform mental and physical activities for their own benefit, to have others perform mental and physical activities for them, or to have goods that assist them with these activities. An effective way for this to occur is for actors to be relational and oriented to the beneficiary actors to whom they provide service.

Finally, it should be noted that service is inherently customer oriented because, in S-D logic, service is defined as the application of knowledge and skills for the benefit of another; that "other" is what we often call a customer. Service orientation is thus always inherently directed at the beneficiary of the service.

Axiom 3 and foundational premise 9: all economic and social actors are resource integrators

Building on FP8 and the inherent relational and customer orientation that is essential to a service orientation, which in turn suggests that relationship is the joint, interactive, collaborative, unfolding of reciprocal roles in value cocreation, requires zooming out to get a broader, value-creation perspective, as portrayed in Exhibit 3.4. In this illustration there are two resource-integrating generic actors that are not labeled as either producer or consumer. They are generic and each is a beneficiary of what they obtain in exchange with another actor; in Exhibit 3.4 the

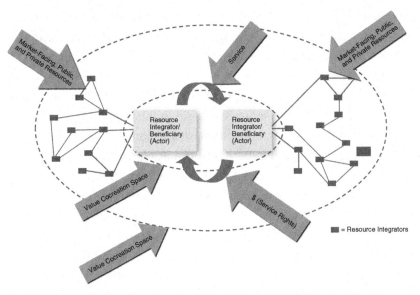

Exhibit 3.4 Exchange through resource integration and value cocreation

exchange of service-for-service rights is shown. However, this is a narrow or zoomed-in focus and in the exhibit actors are also identified as resource integrators, providing a zoomed-out perspective. Resource integrators are actors that create resources by combining other resources. The other resources are market, private, and public resources. Market resources are those that can be acquired in the marketplace. Private non-market-facing resources are primarily the tangible and intangible resources that are exchanged via social exchange networks – for example, lending a friend a car, providing advice to a family member, or asking and receiving a favor. Finally, public non-market-facing resources are tangible and intangible resources that government or quasi-government entities provide to certain individuals or groups – for instance, national defense, roadways, and the laws that regulate traffic. These resources are provided through the exchange of public currency that is also popularly known as payment of taxes. Payment of taxes involves giving up service rights, which are then reallocated or redistributed to other actors or communities of actors for the public good. Overall, S-D logic views the generic actors as attempting to increase the viability of a system through exchange and resource integration; in brief, they are cocreating value.

This zooming out and viewing actors beyond the immediate exchange of service and service rights and seeing them more realistically as actors embedded in and creating networks and resources is well beyond what Levitt advocated in

"Marketing myopia."[29] In fact, it suggests enterprises should also not be "market" myopic – that is, it suggests that they need to recognize that market exchange provides only part of the sources of resources and the institutional framework[30] necessary for value cocreation.

Not surprisingly, however, because business enterprises face the constant need to sell output and increase revenue, managers begin to think that the beneficiary actor is primarily concerned with making purchase decisions related to the firm's output. In fact, a whole area of study has developed around consumer decision-making and choice, much of it concerned with brand choice. However, as much as managers are concerned with consumer choice and decisions, this is not the preoccupation or primary focus of buyers. Buyers are engaged in something much bigger, and understanding this allows firms to transform their organization to better serve these actors, as well as its other stakeholders, including society.

Consider the example of a family purchasing cereal or other foodstuffs for breakfast. To set the context, assume this is a married pair with two children, one of whom is 3 years old and the other 11 years old. Cereal and breakfast food companies are probably trying to understand how households select their break-fast food and perhaps a cereal brand. However, what the parents are more concerned with is integrating resources around the parenting and childrearing experience. From this perspective, there are quite a few resources in each of the three prior categories of resources. Certainly there are market resources that the family previously acquired such as kitchen and information appliances, furni-ture, and the physical space of the house. There are also market resources that it can acquire such as the cereals offered by packaged food firms. But there are also other breakfast offerings, places to eat other than at home through a vast network of restaurants and other eating and dining venues. Also, there is the possibility of growing vegetables or other ingredients in a home garden and to do so usually requires some market resources. This cannot be separated from the integration of private resources. The parents might ask the 11-year-old to help prepare the breakfast for the 3-year-old. Perhaps a grandparent is also living in the home and provides this service. Or perhaps the husband is a stay-at-home dad and provides this service. One could not ignore public resources. Perhaps the public school the 11-year-old child attends has breakfast provisioning programs. Or perhaps the state or federal government increases the income tax deduction for school-age children, and this provides more resources to feed and care for them. Certainly government-mandated nutritional guidelines play into the parenting experience. The details of this example are not elaborated but the message should be clear; the household is trying to integrate resources for something much bigger than the service offerings that firms are trying to sell. Predictably, the same is true of the business enterprise. It is not simply acquiring services (resources) from suppliers but rather integrating these services (resources) with internal resources and public resources to create a market offering that reflects a compelling value proposition to other actors.

Resource integration can also be used to describe the process of innovation. To do so requires three interrelated sets of simple ideas: (1) all social and economic actors are resource integrators, (2) resource integration results in resource creation, and (3) as new resources are created they are integrated with other resources and the process of resource integration and resource creation repeats. The preceding process forms the basis of what Brian Arthur describes as the nature of technology and its evolution. He suggests:

Early technologies form using existing primitive technologies as components. These new technologies in time become possible components – building blocks – for the construction of further new technologies. Some of these in turn go on to become possible building blocks for the creation of yet newer technologies. In this way, slowly over time, many technologies form from an initial few, and more complex ones form using simpler ones as components. The overall collection of technologies bootstraps itself upward from the few to the many and from the simple to the complex. We can say that technology creates out of itself.[31]

In other words, essentially resources and resource integration beget additional resources. These additional resources are often incremental innovations but occasionally they are radical innovations that result in new markets. Stated alternatively, markets are not static or fixed but are unbounded. They are unbounded because the extent of resource integration by human actors is unlimited and, in fact, ever-expanding because the more resources that are integrated the more resources there are to integrate.

The process of innovation cannot be rationally planned. As we have stated before, human actors are not very good at calculating, planning, and coordinating. As described in Chapter 1, human actors are more effectual than rational. Effectuation takes the view that resource-integrating actors operate under uncertainty and cannot predict the future but can take actions that produce effects; but these actions are only one or two steps at a time. The effectual actor makes adjustments as the resource-integration and resource-creation process unfolds and this is always done incrementally, with limited master planning or at least limited successful master planning. Consequently, the results of resource integration and resource creation and, more broadly, the development and evolution of innovative technology are always uncertain and surprising. S-D logic helps actors to navigate uncertainty and capitalize on serendipity.

Axiom 4 and foundational premise 10: value is always uniquely and phenomenologically determined by the beneficiary

The fourth and final axiom (and FP10) simply states that every incidence of service exchange creates a different experience and unique (to the beneficiary) instance and assessment of value. This is because each instance takes place in a different context, involving the availability, integration, and use of a different combination of resources and actors. This results in differential impact on viability of a system (actor), which in turn is uniquely assessed by the beneficiary. Other actors, such as business enterprises or government agencies, might try to impose evaluation of the value but it is done from the perspective of their own goals, objectives, and contexts and thus likely to always be at variance with the assessment of beneficiaries. They might be able to measure surrogates such as economic efficiency or productivity but they cannot assess actual value.

Consider being on vacation and visiting an art museum with three family members and/or friends. You stop by a famous sculpture and gaze at it for a while and then move on to the next exhibit. That evening, over dinner, the conversation turns to the afternoon's museum visit and the viewing of the particular piece of art mentioned above. What you learn from the conversation is that each of your friends viewed the sculpture differently than yourself and had a different experience. Since the physical piece of art was, so to speak, set in stone and thus homogeneous, a goods-dominant paradigm would suggest the value being delivered is hence identical. However, the dinner conversation revealed otherwise.

Contrasting logics

The mindset that develops when guided by S-D logic is quite different from that guided by G-D logic. In Exhibit 3.5 several core differences derived from the axioms and foundational premises of S-D logic are summarized. First, the primary unit or basis of exchange under the traditional, goods-centered logic is the goods that actors exchange. On the other hand, the service-centered dominant

Alternative Views	G-D Logic	S-D Logic
Basis of Exchange	Goods	Service
Role of Goods	End Products	Appliances (means)
Customer	Operand Resource	Operant Resource
Value	Embedded in Offering (good)	Beneficiary Determined
Firm–Customer Interaction	Transactional	Relational
Economic Growth	Surplus Tangible Resources	Application of Specialized Skills & Knowledge

Exhibit 3.5 Contrasting perspectives

logic views actors as exchanging to acquire the benefits of specialized competences (knowledge and skills), or services.

Second, the role of goods under the traditional logic is as operand resources and "end products." Under S-D logic, goods are transmitters of operant resources (embodied knowledge); they are intermediate "products" that are used by other operant resources (beneficiary actors or customers) as appliances in value-creation processes.

A third contrast is the role of the customer or beneficiary of the offering. According to the traditional logic, the beneficiary (customer) is the recipient of goods. To get the potential customer to purchase the goods, the actor is treated as an operand resource or someone requiring *market-ing to*. The beneficiary under S-D logic is a cocreator of value. Here marketing is viewed as a process of doing things in interaction with the customer; or as *market-ing with*. The beneficiary is an actor that is primarily an operant resource.

Value, using a G-D lens, is determined by the producer. It is embedded in the operand resources (goods) and defined as "value-in-exchange." With an S-D lens, value is perceived and determined by the beneficiary (customer) on the basis of "value-in-use," which is always contextual. Value results from the beneficial application of operant resources, occasionally transmitted through operand resources. Consequently, enterprises can only make value propositions.

A fifth distinction relates to firm–customer interaction. From a G-D perspective, the firm acts upon the customer-actor to create transactions. On the other hand, from an S-D perspective, all actors are bound up in relations and these relations are occasionally punctuated by transactions. Furthermore, the customer-actor is not passive or an operand resource but is an active participant (i.e., an operant resource) in relational exchanges and the cocreation of value.

Finally, a sixth distinction relates to the primary source of economic growth. In the traditional G-D logic, wealth is obtained from surplus tangible resources and goods. Wealth is represented and obtained through owning, controlling, and producing operand resources. In contrast, with S-D logic well-being takes precedence over wealth and is obtained through the application and exchange of specialized knowledge and skills.

Concluding comments

Axioms and premises are statements that are assumed to be true. They form a basis for deeper explanations and knowledge development. Predictably, the premises should be sensical but at the same time they should not be overly precise. The role of the axioms and foundational premises of S-D logic is to provide a framework or lens for viewing all actors in the process of exchange. Actors are viewed as becoming more specialized and thus needing to more intensively and extensively exchange service, integrate resources, and create and use resources to enhance the viability of the relevant system(s) within which they are embedded. As such, all actors can be viewed as value centric, effectual, enterprising, resource-integrating actors.

NOTES

1. There are other ways to organize the FPs. For instance, often in presentations we organize as follows: FP1: 4, 5; FP6: 3, 7; FP9: 2; FP10: 8.
2. The lexicon of S-D logic is continuing to develop and includes many other emerging terms such as service ecosystems to be discussed in Chapter 9.
3. It could also be argued that actors are not only to some extent controlled by social institutions and structures but also from below at the microcosm of their genetic makeup. See, e.g., Edward O. Wilson, *Sociobiology: The New Synthesis* (Cambridge, MA: Harvard University Press, 1975).
4. Herbert A. Simon, "Rational decision making in business organizations," *American Economic Review*, 69 (September 1979), 493–512.
5. Adam Smith, *An Inquiry into the Nature and Causes of the Wealth of Nations* (London: Printed for W. Strahan and T. Cadell, 1904 [1776]); Ian Macneil, *The New Social Contract: An Inqury into Modern Contractual Relations* (New Haven, CT: Yale University Press, 1980).
6. Ronald H. Coase, "The nature of the firm," *Economica*, 4 (1937), 386–405; Oliver E. Williamson, *Markets and Hierarchies: Analysis and Antitrust Implications* (New York: Free Press, 1975).

7. William E. Cole and John W. Mogab, *The Economics of Total Quality Management: Clashing Paradigms in the Global Market* (Oxford, UK: Blackwell, 1995).

8. Richard Normann and Rafael Ramirez, "From value chain to value constellation: designing interactive strategy," *Harvard Business Review*, 71 (July–August 1993), 65–77.

9. Ravindranath Madhavan and Rajiv Grover, "From embedded knowledge to embodied knowledge: new product development as knowledge management," *Journal of Marketing* 62 (October 1998), 1–12.

10. Philip Kotler, *Marketing Management: Analysis, Planning, Implementation, and Control*, 3rd edn (Upper Saddle River, NJ: Prentice-Hall, 1977), p. 8.

11. Jeremy Rifkin, *The Age of Access: The New Culture of Hypercapitalism, Where All of Life Is a Paid-For Experience* (New York: Putman, 2000).

12. C. K. Prahalad and Venkatram Ramaswamy, "Co-opting customer competence," *Harvard Business Review*, 78 (January–February 2000), 79–87, p. 83.

13. Jonathan Gutman, "A means-end chain model based on consumer categorization processes," *Journal of Marketing*, 46 (Spring 1982), 60–72.

14. This example is adapted from Erich W. Zimmermann, *World Resources and Industries* (New York: Harper & Row, 1951).

15. The distinction between operand and operant resources comes from ideas expressed in James A. Constantin and Robert F. Lusch, *Understanding Resource Management* (Oxford, OH: The Planning Forum, 1994). Some of these ideas are based on the work of Erich W. Zimmermann, *World Resources and Industries* (New York: Harper & Row, 1951).

16. Bureau of Economic Analysis, Economic Classification Policy Committee, Issues Paper No. 6, "Services classifications" (Washington, DC: US Department of Commerce, September 1993). See also T. P. Hill, "On goods and services," *Review of Income and Wealth*, 23 (December 1977), 315–338.

17. Evert Gummesson, "Implementation requires a relationship marketing paradigm," *Journal of the Academy of Marketing Science*, 26 (Summer 1998), 242–249, p. 247.

18. Christian Grönroos, *Service Management and Marketing: A Customer Relationship Management Approach* (Chichester, UK: John Wiley & Sons, 2000), pp. 24–25, emphasis in original.

19. Donald F. Dixon, "Marketing as production: the development of a concept," *Journal of the Academy of Marketing Science*, 18 (Fall 1990), 337–343.

20. The idea that customers create value and do not destroy value is discussed by Rafael Ramirez, "Value co-production: intellectual origins and implications for practice and research," *Strategic Management Journal*, 20:1, 49–65.

21. Michael Lanning and E. Michaels, *A Business Is a Value Delivery System*, McKinsey Staff Paper No. 41 (July 1988); Michael Lanning and L. Phillips, *Building Market-Focused Organizations*, Gemini Consulting White Paper (1992); Michael Lanning and L. Phillips, *Delivering Profitable Value: A Revolutionary Framework to Accelerate Growth, Generate Wealth and Rediscover the Heart of Business* (New York: Perseus Publishing, 2008); Pennie Frow and Adrian Payne, "The value proposition concept: evolution, development and application in marketing," working paper, Discipline of Marketing, University of Sydney (2008).

22. Lance A. Bettencourt and Anthony W. Ulwick, "The customer-centered innovation map," *Harvard Business Review* 86 (May 2008), 109–114.

23. Roderick J. Brodie, Linda D. Hollebeek, Biljana Juric, and Ana Ilic, "Customer engagement: conceptual domain, fundamental propositions and implications for research," *Journal of Service Research*, 14:3 (2011), 252–271.
24. Sunil Gupta and Donald R. Lehmann, "Customers as assets," *Journal of Interactive Marketing*, 17 (Winter 2003), 9–24; Sunil Gupta, Donald R. Lehmann, and Jennifer Ames Stuart, "Valuing customers," *Journal of Marketing Research*, 41 (February 2004), 7–18; Sunil Gupta and Valarie Zeithaml, "Customer metrics and their impact on financial performance," *Marketing Science*, 25 (November–December 2006), 718–739; Sunil Gupta, Dominique Hanssens, Bruce Hardie, William Kohn, V. Kumar, Nathaniel Lin, Nalini Ravishanker, and S. Siram, "Modeling customer lifetime value," *Journal of Service Research*, 9:2 (2006), 139–155.
25. Valarie A. Zeithaml, A. Parasuraman, and L. Berry, "Problems and strategies in services marketing," *Journal of Marketing*, 49 (Spring 1985), 33–46; Christian Grönroos, *Service Management and Marketing: A Customer Relationship Management Approach* (Chichester, UK: John Wiley & Sons, 2004); Evert Gummesson, "Relationship marketing: its role in the service economy," in W. J. Glynn and J. G. Barnes (eds.), *Understanding Services Management* (New York: John Wiley & Sons, 1995), pp. 244–268.
26. Leonard L. Berry, "Relationship marketing," in L. L. Berry, G. L. Shostack, and G. Upah (eds.), *Emerging Perspectives on Services Marketing* (Chicago, IL: American Marketing Association, 1983), pp. 25–26.
27. Johan Arndt, "Toward a concept of domesticated markets," *Journal of Marketing*, 43:4 (1979), 69–75.
28. Stephen L. Vargo and Robert F. Lusch, "From repeat patronage to value co-creation in service ecosystems: a transcending conceptualization of relationship," *Journal of Business Market Management*, 4:4 (2010): 169–179.
29. Theodore Levitt, "Marketing myopia," *Harvard Business Review*, 38 (July–August 1960), 26–44, 173–181.
30. Some scholars using an institutional perspective to study markets include L. Araujo and M. Spring, "Services, products, and the institutional structure of production," *Industrial Marketing Management*, 35 (2006), 797–805; Michel Callon, "Techno-economic networks and irreversibility," in J. Law (ed.), *A Sociology of Monsters: Essays on Power, Technology, and Domination* (London: Routledge, 1991); A. Venkatesh, L. Penaloza, and A. F. Firat, "The market as a sign system and the logic of the market," in R. F. Lusch and S. L. Vargo (eds.), *The Service-Dominant Logic of Marketing: Dialog, Debate, and Directions* (Armonk, NY: M. E. Sharpe, 2006), pp. 251–265.
31. Brian W. Arthur, *The Nature of Technology: What It Is and How It Evolves* (New York: Free Press, 2009), p. 21.

4 Service as a guiding framework

Customers do not buy goods or services: they buy offerings which render services which create value ... The traditional division between goods and services is long outdated. It is not a matter of redefining services and seeing them from a customer perspective; *activities render services, things render services*. The shift in focus to services is a shift from the means and the producer perspective to the utilization and the customer perspective.

Evert Gummesson (1995)

Introduction

On learning about service-dominant (S-D) logic, some observers say that they agree with its axioms and foundational premises but ask the more fundamental question, "Why 'service'"?[1] That is, they ask whether "service" is the proper designation for and characterization of this "new dominant logic." At times, the question has been explicit and, at others, implicit.

This question of "Why 'service'?" is a potentially critical issue, one that addresses the essential subject matter of markets and marketing and the purpose of business. On a broader level, it also deals with the fundamental nature of human interaction, on which society, markets, and business and marketing practices are built. Language is a form of joint action between actors that helps them coordinate thoughts and meaning and actions.[2] In short, actions are at least partly driven by words and their (shared) meanings. Therefore, how service is conceptualized and the shared meanings we develop around the concept of "service" are crucial to S-D logic and its development and impact.

We have listened carefully to the question "Why 'service'?" and the rationale for alternative labels. Perhaps disquieting to some, we have not relabeled the new logic as they have suggested. We continue to believe and argue that we did not label the new logic prematurely or improperly. Rather, we believe that the term "service" precisely describes what all actors do for each other as they engage in exchange; we also believe that "service" is properly normatively informative and thus is the correct term.

Prior views of services misled

Perhaps the main reason why a few people have opposed the label of "*service-dominant* logic" has to do with prior perspectives and views of "services." Based on that reason, concern about the use of the term is understandable. As we discussed in Chapter 2, Adam Smith's concern about how to increase the wealth of nations formed the basis for how services were eventually perceived. For Smith, the driving concept was "productivity," which he defined in terms of activities that create surplus tangible outputs that could be exported for trade. Other activities, though useful and essential to both individual and national well-being, were not productive by these tangibility and export standards. Over time, the productive versus nonproductive distinction morphed into today's goods (products) versus services distinction, with services being defined as a particular type of "product" (i.e., intangible goods), or what goods are not.

Conceptualizing services as a residual (from goods) led firms to misguided marketing practices. Nonetheless, once on this pathway, the marketing and management professions converged to identify the distinguishing attributes of services in contrast with goods. Doing so created path dependency in the works of services marketing, management scholars, and practitioners who embraced and investigated the fundamental ways in which services were different from goods.

Because marketing and management scholars viewed the distinguishing attributes as a challenge for the marketing of services, the dominant thought led to focusing on making services more goods-like in terms of their characteristics. The characteristics that caused these particular problems for marketers were identified as intangibility, heterogeneity, inseparability, and perishability, or IHIP. Goods were considered superior because they were tangible, which made them relatively imperishable and thus allowed them to be inventoried. This was deemed to contribute to efficiency by supporting constant production cycles in the face of variable demand cycles. Likewise, goods could be produced "separate" from the consumer and thus standardized and controlled for greater manufacturing efficiency. Their ability to be standardized (homogenized) also contributed to production efficiency through economies of scale. Anything that deviated from these ideal characteristics decreased production efficiency and was regarded as a problem to be overcome. Not surprisingly, organizations in the "services" business tried to make their offerings more tangible and homogeneous and to produce as many of them as possible to create superior efficiency.

As Exhibit 4.1 implies, the supposed disadvantages of IHIP vanish from an S-D logic perspective at least as distinguishing characteristics between goods and services as one of the major marketing myths of the past fifty years.[3]

IHIP Characteristic	G-D Logic	S-D Logic
Intangible	Value is embedded into goods during the production and distribution process. Firms can alter natural resources to create new forms, alter the location of goods and the time goods are available, which make them more valuable.	Value is intangible. Value is cocreated by actors. Only in the use and integration of resources is value created. Value is experiential or phenomenologic which is inherently intangible.
Heterogeneous	Products should be made homogeneous to take advantages of standardization and the efficiencies of mass production. Homogeneous products are of higher engineered quality.	Each actor is unique and heterogeneity exists and customized offerings are natural. Efficiency is important but of paramount importance is effectively meeting the actor needs.
Inseparability	Firms and customers should be separated for maximum efficiency.	Actor interaction naturally occurs. Interaction through dialogue and conversation enhances effectiveness of service offerings. It is in the interaction that value is cocreated.
Perishable	Goods are less perishable than services and thus they can be inventoried. Since gaps exist between the time and place where customers need goods, inventory can be used to overcome this challenge.	Experiences are perishable but are remembered and shared. When the offering is tangible, it is the use of the good that is important and this is perishable. Value is perishable.

Exhibit 4.1   The changing logic of value creation

S-D logic shifts the focus from the production of outputs to the cocreation of benefits with and for the customer – that is, from efficiency to effectiveness. When viewed from the perspective of customer value creation, the supposedly negative qualities of services become the realities, if not the ideals or benefits, to be sought. Value is itself intangible and often a function of intangible aspects of the value proposition (e.g., brand, meaning, comfort-in-use). It is idiosyncratic and always involves some degree of customer interaction, within a dynamic context, and thus is inseparable, heterogeneous, and perishable.[4]

None of this shift in perspective should suggest that efficiency is not important. A hallmark of S-D logic is service-for-service exchange, rather than the creation and distribution of value, and the actor-to-actor (A2A) perspective argues that the value-creation process must work for the firm as well, often from the acquisition of surplus service (e.g., money) to efficient operations. But *efficiency without effectiveness* is inherently inefficient: Without effectiveness, there is no basis for service-for-service exchange, and, as such, the efficiency issue is meaningless. The "service" in S-D logic buttresses and emphasizes benefit and, thus, the superordinate nature of effectiveness, with a constraint of relative efficiency (for both the firm and the customer). Exhibit 4.2 illustrates this trade-off between the almost mirror images of value and production.

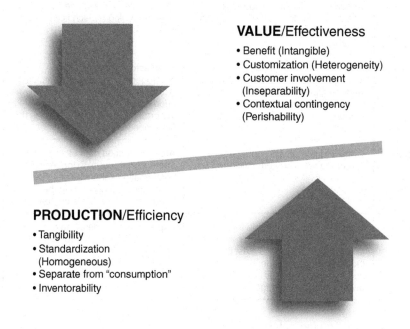

VALUE/Effectiveness
- Benefit (Intangible)
- Customization (Heterogeneity)
- Customer involvement (Inseparability)
- Contextual contingency (Perishability)

PRODUCTION/Efficiency
- Tangibility
- Standardization (Homogeneous)
- Separate from "consumption"
- Inventorability

Exhibit 4.2 The value (effective) versus production (efficient) trade-off

S-D logic argues that what were once considered negative or disadvantageous aspects of services actually represent the realities of all value and value-creation processes, whether directly through service or indirectly through goods. Thus, embracing them can lead to more compelling value propositions. In brief, *intangibility* reflects the experiential nature that occurs in the value-in-use associated with all realized value propositions; *heterogeneity* reflects S-D logic's perspective that value is always unique and beneficiary specific; *inseparability* captures the beneficiary-centered, integrative nature of value creation as implied by the concept of value-in-use (and value-in-context) and points toward more involvement, conversation, dialogue, and adaptation to the beneficiary; and, finally, *perishability*, captures the essential reality of value as always perishable, even (or more likely especially) when provided through a good.

Perishability is not about the entropy of physical matter but rather the perishable nature of value. To suggest that a tangible good is not perishable argues against value being embedded in the good. But if an actor has a good, such as an automobile, but does not have the right to use it (no driver's license), cannot sustain it (no fuel), does not have social connections with other actors (to drive them around), or perhaps does not have service rights (money) to retain another actor to provide this service, the automobile has no value-in-use and thus, in a very real way, is perishable. Or perhaps the actor has a good that he or she no longer uses (e.g., an old computer) that, though it still exists in tangible form and thus, in G-D logic, has not perished, has long perished in terms of use and phenomenologically defined value.

This argument leads us to suggest the concept of "contextual contingency," or the idea that the value of resources is contingent on situational factors, especially the availability (and unavailability) of other resources. Consequently, value is *contextually specific* and thus is *always potentially perishable* because contexts are always changing.

A more comprehensive view of service

In S-D logic, "service" is not defined in contradistinction to goods, nor is it defined in terms of units of output (tangible or intangible). Rather, "service" is identified as a *process* by which one actor applies his or her resources for the benefit of others. Consequently, an S-D orientation begins with a focus on providing benefit for others in return for a reciprocal benefit; it begins with a

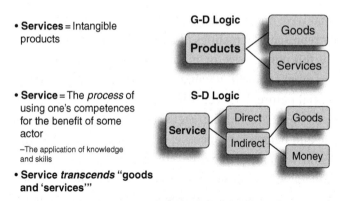

- **Services** = Intangible products

G-D Logic

Products — Goods / Services

- **Service** = The *process* of using one's competences for the benefit of some actor

–The application of knowledge and skills

- **Service** *transcends* "goods and 'services'"

S-D Logic

Service — Direct / Indirect — Goods / Money

Exhibit 4.3 There are no "services" in S-D logic

service-for-service mindset, through which the actors in an exchange are both service providers and service beneficiaries. This mindset is applicable to all actors, including business organizations, government organizations, nonprofit organizations, households, and individuals.

S-D logic uses the singular term "service" to reflect the *process* of doing something beneficial for and in conjunction with another actor, rather than *units of output* – immaterial goods – as the plural "services" implies. This distinction is important because it leads to the conclusion that *there are no "services" in S-D logic* (see Exhibit 4.3). In S-D logic, goods and service are not alternative forms of products. Goods are *appliances* (tools, distribution mechanisms) that often serve as alternatives to direct service provision. Goods as appliances can also enhance service provision – for example, an amplifier can allow the guitarist to enhance the sound – or a good can enable an actor to perform self-service he or she could not otherwise perform – for example, an electron microscope enables humans to see beyond what is possible with their natural eyesight. Money represents service rights, which can also be viewed as an alternative path to direct service provision. Service, then, represents the general and universal case, the common denominator, of the exchange process; *service* is what is *always* exchanged. Goods and money, when employed, aid the service process.

What are the limits, if any, to the premise that *service* is the basis of exchange? Does it apply only to economic exchange, or is it more universal? There are many types of exchange systems, and we cover the more prominent ones in Chapter 5. For now, we consider four institutionalized exchange systems: reciprocity, redistribution, market exchange, and hybrid exchange systems. *Reciprocity* is the giving and receiving of gifts or favors. *Redistribution* involves one actor taking what other actors have and reassigning it to other actors; taxation is a common form of redistribution. *Market exchange* is a process of voluntary exchange, with one actor often using a common medium of exchange (e.g., money, service rights).[5] *Hybrid exchange* combines elements of these exchange systems. Much of the writing and research on S-D logic has focused on hybrid exchange systems, but the axioms and foundational premises of S-D logic are generally applicable to all exchange. That is, service-for-service exchange and S-D logic can be a framework for studying many types of exchange between actors, including voluntary market exchange, gift giving, taxation, welfare payments, joint ventures, and the like.[6]

Implications of "service" thinking

The "service" designation of S-D logic has implications for the development of a more unified theory of markets and marketing and for how actors develop competences and exchange the application of these competences with others. These implications include (1) S-D logic's simplifying nature; (2) the move from value-in-exchange to value-in-use; (3) a learning focus; (4) a resource-centered, redefining, and integrating focus; (5) a normative prescription; and (6) stakeholder unification.

Service-dominant logic's simplifying nature

Before S-D logic, a supposedly complete understanding of markets and marketing required recognizing the differences between goods and services and their different attributes (IHIP characteristics). This led to attempts to understand the market for services versus the market for goods and how to market goods versus services. In other words, because tangible product market-*ing* knowledge was not adequately translatable directly to the market-ing of intangibles, a subdiscipline of services marketing needed to be created to deal with this special class of goods.[7] As such, separate college courses, career tracks, research organizations, journals, conferences, consulting firms, and so on were created, all around the goods versus services distinction. We argue that this separation was misdirected and inherently misinformed because the fundamental basis of all economic activity, if not of society as a whole, is the exchange of service for service. That is, all social and economic actors serve each other, directly and indirectly, through A2A networks.

S-D logic, and its associated concepts of operand and operant resources, cocreation of value, value proposition, and resource integration, offers the means to simplify marketing thought and practice. All actors exchange service for service, and organizations, money, and goods are merely the intermediaries in this process. Thus, organizations, households, and individuals can be viewed as resource integrators that cocreate value with other actors.

S-D logic's approach is to identify – actually, recapture Adam Smith's correct identification of – the exchange of applied specialized skills and knowledge (service) as the heart of exchange. The notion is simple: *service is exchanged for service.* As we mentioned in Chapter 1, service can be provided directly between and among actors with specialized skills and knowledge or provided indirectly by embedding the skill and knowledge in a tangible good – what S-D logic calls an "appliance." Thus, service becomes the unifying focus of exchange, rather than a poor stepchild to a good. Goods still have a central role in S-D logic, but service is the common denominator.

Furthermore, goods-marketing principles are informed and elaborated by and become a subset of S-D logic. Perhaps there is no more entrenched principle than the management of the marketing mix of the four Ps (product, price, promotion, and place) to maximize firm performance. As Exhibit 4.4 illustrates, the traditional marketing mix, which is tactical in focus, becomes more strategic when S-D logic becomes the lens. S-D logic facilitates a move from a product offering to the cocreation of service(s) and experiences, from price to the cocreation of value propositions, from promotion to the cocreation of conversation and dialogue, and from a channel of distribution to the cocreation of value processes and A2A networks, or what we refer to in Chapter 8 as "service ecosystems."

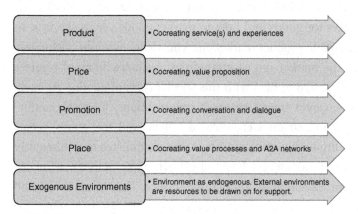

Exhibit 4.4 S-D logic informed G-D principles

Furthermore, S-D logic takes the perspective that what are thought of as external environments, such as the legal, political, social, economic, competitive, technological, and ecological environments, are not exogenous but rather part of the resources that are integrated in the entire value cocreation process.

From value-in-exchange to value-in-use

Providing benefits inherently directs one to *value-in-use* and away from a singular focus on *value-in-exchange* (which is inherently an economics concept). The early philosophers, as we reviewed in Chapter 2, recognized that value-in-use (as opposed to value-in-exchange) was a higher-order concept, and Smith and the other political economists endorsed this relationship. In the subsequent development of economic science, however, value ("utility") came to be understood in terms of value-in-exchange. Marketing, as well as accounting and finance, adopted this embedded, exchange-value meaning and dealt with its role in value creation in similar terms (e.g., "value added"). These activities misdirected the practice of marketing and perhaps, in part, explain the obsessive focus on price, discounts, promotions, and special deals in marketing and on quarterly earnings and daily share price in finance that are such a large part of contemporary business practice. Notably, this focus has become the dominant practice among both goods-producing enterprises and those offering services, such as airlines, hotels, health spas, lawyers, and banks.

Making the term "service" the descriptive core of the new dominant logic makes it superordinate. By shifting service to a superordinate position, value-in-use also takes a superordinate position in relation to value-in-exchange, and the service–goods relationship is clarified. That is, because service is defined in terms of an actor-defined benefit, it is necessarily aligned with value-in-use, whether provided directly or with a good. Value-in-exchange remains important because, in contemporary society, service is often exchanged for service rights (money), and these service rights become the means to further exchange. In addition, when market exchange is the dominant societal institution, an actor can gain some sense of how well he or she is providing service by the financial feedback obtained from the market in terms of service rights and accumulation of service rights over time. Nonetheless, value-in-use is the primary focus of S-D logic, and because this value shift is *inherently beneficiary or customer oriented*, it has both academic and practical implications for approaching value creation. Perhaps most important, it implies that the beneficiary actor is an operant resource and is a central part of the value-creation process.

Learning focus

Service-for-service exchange, the first axiom of S-D logic, is inherently learning- and knowledge-discovery focused. The learning and knowledge focus of S-D logic arises for two reasons. First, in service-for-service exchange, interaction between actors is dominant, and through this interaction the service-providing and service-benefiting actors obtain feedback and learn from each other about the compelling nature of their value propositions. Second, exchange itself involves both actors changing their condition because they obtain something they did not have but give up something they did have; consequently, every exchange involves change – interestingly, the Latin derivative of exchange is "out of change." Service-for-service exchange is thus pro knowledge discovery.[8]

Service exchange is pro knowledge discovery because actors engage in exchange to improve their system viability. Actors have hypotheses or expectations that engaging in agency or action will result in an improvement in their system viability. Actors do not engage in agency to worsen their condition or to deteriorate their system viability. Their hypotheses lead to actions and exchange that result in their experiencing consequences, and thus hypotheses can be falsified. During this process, each actor adjusts his or her phenomenological assessment of value, and thus value itself is dynamic.[9] Consequently, actors serving other actors need to constantly learn how the actors they hope to serve are changing their definition of value.[10]

During the service exchange process, actors learn the relative exchange-value of things. This learning becomes important because knowledge of value-in-exchange enables actors to make more informed decisions about resource integration and about acquiring or giving up service rights. Without service exchange, the actor has little information on exchange-value. In a simple barter exchange system, the actor is able to learn about the units of A that are needed for units of B. Such a system allows the actor to learn the relative exchange-value of various applications of competences and skills (i.e., applied resources), which in turn signals to the actor how to focus efforts and time to enhance system viability. However, barter exchange is quite inefficient in terms of learning relative exchange-value because all the unique combinations of the application of the actor's competences and skills would need to be exchanged to obtain the knowledge of relative economic value of various service offerings. However, with the advent of money, or what in S-D logic is called service rights, exchange-value of various service offerings can be more directly determined. That is, money becomes a common medium of exchange and allows all rights to service to be compared for reciprocal exchange-value on a common metric. When service exchange is indirect and through money, the feedback process is more rapid, and thus actors learn more quickly whether they should continue to do things the same or to be more creative and develop new or adapted skills and knowledge.

On a macro basis, when service-for-service exchange is allowed to unfold across A2A networks, variety increases rather than decreases.[11] In brief, by serving the wants and needs of beneficiary actors, variety expands because actors are heterogeneous in their wants and needs. This variety arises because two actors specializing in serving each other learn from each other and attempt to match each other's offerings with needs and wants of the other beneficiary actor. Thus, across dyads of service-exchanging actors, the offerings are heterogeneous, rather than homogeneous, as assumed in neoclassical economics.

A resource-centered, redefining, and integrating focus

As noted, the "service" in S-D logic is defined in terms of applying resources for the benefit of others. This resource focus and distinction is important for several reasons. First, it ties S-D logic to the continuing movement across a variety of business disciplines toward resource-based views of exchange and theories of the firm[12] and is consistent with viewing the firm as a bundle of resources that can be used to gain advantage.[13] However, it provides an important message, and that is that resource application must be for the benefit of others. Furthermore, the "applied" designation makes operant resources – resources that can act on or in concert with other resources to provide benefit (create value), as distinguished from operand resources – primary. Sometimes these operant resources are referred to as skills, knowledge, capabilities, and competences, but the key message is that the application of resources must be used to benefit other actors. Finally, it views all actors as actual and potential bundles of resources, some of which they use to provide service to others in exchange for service or service rights and in the pursuit of enhanced system viability.

Second, this distinction shifts focus away from units of output – products (goods and services) – toward mutually satisfying interactive processes. Actors are not viewed as separate, with one actor passive and the other active or as one actor operand and the other operant, but as cocreators of value in which the focus moves from taking stuff to market or "market-ing to" other actors to "market-ing with" other actors.[14]

Third, this distinction similarly shifts the focus from static resources, such as plant and equipment (balance-sheet resources), to the employees, the competences of the enterprise, other value-creation actors, and, as noted, beneficiary actors or customers. In brief, the focus is not on balance-sheet resources but on off-balance-sheet resources.[15]

Finally, service points to cocreation of value through resource integration. The cocreation of value redefines the role of the firm and the customer as functionally identical and centered on cooperative value creation to enhance system viability. From this perspective, the role of marketing is quite different from the traditional manufacturing model, in which marketing as well as manufacturing is viewed as combining largely static and operand resources. Thus, the cocreation of value puts marketing and the actor in both service-provider and service-beneficiary roles and at the heart of value creation. This is in contrast with marketing in its more traditional, value-distribution role, with the customer or beneficiary in a receiver role, and the firm in the producing or provider role. It begins to move marketing from a market-ing to customer philosophy to a market-ing *with* philosophy.

Normative prescription

If the purpose of economic exchange is mutual service provision, it follows then that several normative prescriptions are not native to G-D logic. That is, the idea of service being the foundational concept of exchange has some strong and, arguably, very important normative implications for all actors interfacing and in exchange with other actors, but especially for marketing and business in general.[16] It intimates a very different kind of purpose and process for the market and marketing activity and for the business enterprise – namely, to provide service to beneficiary actors, including customers, employees, stockholders, and other stakeholders. It points almost directly to normative notions of investment in people (operant resources), long-term relationships, and quality service flows and "only somewhat less directly" to notions of transparency, ethical approaches to exchange, and sustainability. Arguably, these directions have advantages for both the enterprise and society that cannot be found in G-D logic and are not as well reflected by any other term.

Compared with G-D logic and the neoclassical economic theory of the firm, the service focus of S-D logic has an important advantage related to ethical and normative behavior. In G-D logic and the neoclassical economic theory of the firm, actors need to *import* a theory or code of ethics for the operation of the enterprise, whereas the positive axioms and foundational premises of S-D logic *imply* normative prescriptions, as Laczniak and Santos illustrate with the development of their integrative justice model, which they apply to marketing to the poor.[17] Grounded in positive axioms and foundational premises, S-D logic suggests that actors should do the following: (1) strive for relative transparency and symmetry in information and exchange processes, while appropriately protecting property and other rights of the actor; (2) develop relationships with other actors within the A2A system to enhance the long-term system viability of both themselves and the other actors; (3) recognize other actors (e.g., those serving in the role of employee, customer, and supplier) as valuable operant resources and invest in their skill and knowledge development; and (4) consider offering service flows versus goods *per se*.

Stakeholder unification

The actors in exchange can act and interact to cocreate mutually satisfying value propositions.[18] However, as mentioned in Chapter 1 and as we illustrate further in Chapter 5, most exchange in contemporary society is within complex A2A exchange networks that go well beyond direct one-to-one, restricted exchange. Under these conditions, an actor that is making an offer in terms of a value proposition is also an actor that receives value propositions from other actors and subsequently relies on these other actors for service-providing resources. In turn, these actors are connected with other resource-providing actors. Any actor whose system viability is positively or negatively affected by another actor via his or her activities and service exchanges can be thought of as a stakeholder. Many of these stakeholders through service exchange directly provide tangible and intangible resources to the actor. The value proposition(s) that an actor makes should appeal to stakeholders who provide resources to the enterprise-actor. These stakeholders must see the potential improvement in the viability of their system of resource integration and value creation. Value proposition(s) is communicated whether intended or not. The key is to communicate effectively so that the value proposition(s) is understood by the entire network of resource-providing stakeholders.[19]

Operating under G-D logic, with its focus on value-in-exchange, makes it easy to ignore externalities. Because actors are almost always part of a complex A2A network and web of dependencies and interdependencies, those in the purchase and use of a market offering almost always have positive or negative effects on other actors (i.e., externalities arise). When an enterprise begins to explore the externalities and a more complete service ecosystem, which we discuss in more detail in Chapter 8, it obtains new insights into value-in-use and gains opportunities to cocreate value in novel ways.

Concluding comments

The term "service" is the correct term to capture the process of using resources to benefit actors. Furthermore, the first axiom of the proposed new dominant logic is, *service is the fundamental basis of exchange.* Thus, the use of "service" to characterize a "new dominant logic" is based on a desire for precision more than a default to preference.

Ironically, Adam Smith used the term "service" to convey a meaning very similar to the way intended as the designated focus of S-D logic. This was, of course, before Smith's bifurcated detour (see Chapter 2) toward development of a normative theory of national wealth creation based on making surplus tangible goods for export, which eventually led to G-D logic. In a real sense, then, a return to service as a central concept of exchange is a return to a more foundational, positive economic philosophy than the normative one employed in the development of economic science. Therefore, rather than S-D logic attaching new meaning to service, as some have argued, it actually recaptures an old meaning and amplifies the call for understanding its centrality in economic and social exchange.

Simple ideas can be powerful and can transform industries and nations. Ideas such as democracy, freedom, and justice are simple yet powerful and multi-faceted. So is the idea of service. Service is also the correct designation not only to characterize emerging and converging marketing thought but also to accurately guide and motivate the associated research, practice, and public policy that are missing through a G-D lens. Therein lies the answer to "Why 'service'?" – the answer is in its precision and its power to guide.

NOTES

1. Stephen L. Vargo and Robert F. Lusch, "Why 'service'?," *Journal of the Academy of Marketing Science*, 36 (Spring 2008), 25–38.
2. Herbert H. Clark, *Using Language* (Cambridge University Press, 1996).
3. Stephen L. Vargo and Robert F. Lusch, "The four services marketing myths: remnants from a manufacturing model," *Journal of Service Research*, 6 (May 2004), 324–335.
4. Vargo and Lusch, "The four services marketing myth."

5. Market exchange could occur not through a medium of exchange but via barter. People could go to a marketplace and develop a market in exchange for their service offerings. Some of this is now occurring on the Internet.

6. For an example of expanding S-D logic to study exchange systems, see Anthony Pecotich, Don R. Rahtz, and Clifford J. Shultz II, "Systemic and services dominant socio-economic development: legal, judicial and market capacity building in Bangladesh," *Australasian Marketing Journal*, 18: (2014), 248–255.

7. Raymond P. Fisk, Stephen W. Brown, and Mary Jo Bitner, "Tracking the evolution of the services marketing literature," *Journal of Retailing*, 69 (Spring 1993), 61–103.

8. Robert F. Lusch and Stephen L. Vargo, "Service-dominant logic as a foundation for a general theory," in Robert F. Lusch and Stephen L. Vargo (eds.), *The Service Dominant Logic of Marketing: Dialog, Debate, and Directions* (Armonk, NY: M. E. Sharpe, 2006), pp. 406–420.

9. Robert F. Lusch and Frederick E. Webster, Jr., "A stakeholder-unifying, co-creation philosophy for marketing," *Journal of Macromarketing*, 31:2 (2011), 129–134.

10. Robert F. Lusch, Stephen Vargo, and Mohan Tanniru, "Service, value networks and learning," *Journal of the Academy of Marketing Science*, 38 (February 2010), 19–31.

11. Lusch and Vargo, "Service-dominant logic as a foundation for a general theory," p. 412.

12. Edith Tilton Penrose, *The Theory of the Growth of the Firm* (Oxford: Basil Blackwell, 1959); Jay Barney, "Firm resources and sustained competitive advantage," *Journal of Management*, 17:1 (1991), 99–120; S. A. Lippman and R. P. Rumelt, "Uncertain imitability: an analysis of interfirm differences in efficiency under competition," *Bell Journal of Economics*, 13:2 (1982), 418–438; Birger Wernerfelt, "A resource-based view of the firm," *Strategic Management Journal*, 5:2 (1984), 171–180.

13. Shelby D. Hunt, *A General Theory of Competition: Resources, Competences, Productivity, Economic Growth* (Thousand Oaks, CA: Sage Publications, 2000).

14. Robert F. Lusch, "Marketing's evolving identity: defining our future," *Journal of Public Policy & Marketing*, 26 (Fall 2007), 261–269.

15. Robert F. Lusch and Michael Harvey, "The case for an off-balance-sheet controller," *Sloan Management Review*, 35 (Winter 1994), 101–105.

16. For more insights into the normative and ethical aspects of S-D logic, see Gene R. Laczniak, "Some societal and ethical dimensions of the service-dominant logic perspective of marketing," in Robert F. Lusch and Stephen L. Vargo (eds.), *The Service-Dominant Logic of Marketing: Dialog, Debate, and Directions* (Armonk, NY: M. E. Sharpe, 2006), pp. 279–285; Gene R. Laczniak and Nicholas J. Santos, "The integrative justice model for marketing to the poor: an extension of S-D logic to distributive justice and macromarketing," *Journal of Macromarketing*, 31 (June 2011), 135–147.

17. Laczniak and Santos, "Integrative justice model for marketing to the poor."

18. For more insight into stakeholders, value propositions, and S-D logic, see Pennie Frow and Adrian Payne, "A stakeholder perspective of the value proposition concept," *European Journal of Marketing*, 45;1–2 (2011), 223–240.

19. Lusch and Webster, "A stakeholder-unifying, co-creation philosophy for marketing."

Part II
Perspectives

5   It's all actor-to-actor (A2A)

A state arises, as I conceive, out of the needs of mankind; no one is self-sufficing, but all of us have many wants ... Then, as we have many wants, and many persons are needed to supply them, one takes a helper for one purpose and another for another; and when three parties and helpers are gathered together in one habitation, the body of inhabitants is termed a state ... And they exchange with one another, and one gives and another receives under the idea that exchange will be for their good.

Plato, *The Republic*

Introduction

More than 2,000 years ago, Plato described how actors (e.g., people) rely on one another through the exchange of what service-dominant (S-D) logic refers to as service or applied skills and competences. In the mid-1800s, Bastiat identified this phenomenon as *services-for-services* exchange and argued that it was the basis for understanding economics and economies.[1] As the globally connected network of actors and communities of actors, including business enterprises, governments, and people, become more pervasive, it is easy to believe that more complicated theories, frameworks, concepts, and models are needed to understand the social and economic world. However, S-D logic, as we argued in Chapter 1, is a more abstract, simpler (but broader), more general, and transcending framework for the understanding of human exchange and exchange systems. In a globally interdependent and interconnected world, the simple truth behind Plato's words is too often missed: we are all human beings serving each other, through exchange, for mutual well-being.[2]

Viewing actors generically allows the development of a logic of human exchange systems that includes the economy and society and transcends academic disciplines. We argue that it also allows for an academic discipline that has robust, practical application. However, this has not generally been the case for marketing science and theory. Rather, actors are typically identified in terms of discrete roles and functions. Perhaps the most common of these actors is businesses or producers, often abbreviated as "B," and consumers or customers, often abbreviated as "C." And this simple division of actors actually constrains, limits, and restricts the robustness of theories and other knowledge frameworks.

If we had to select between "B" and "C" for a generic designation, we would argue for "B" because "business" comes closest to capturing the common characteristics of all actors. That is, businesses can be understood in terms of integrating and transforming resources from several sources to create new resources that can be exchanged in the market with other actors (other "Bs" or "Cs"), which do the same. In short, "customers" can also be characterized in terms of resource-integrating, transforming, and exchanging actors. So too can other economic (and social) actors. For example, in a real sense, this is what a household is. The household acquires resources, through exchange with various other actors, and then integrates and transforms these to create new resources that allow it to cocreate value through additional service exchange. In fact, the term "economics" comes from ancient Greek and means to administer or manage the household. Not only do business enterprises and households engage in resource integration, transformation, and exchange of service, but government agencies, schools, and a host of other nonprofit organizations do so as well.

As a broad, abstract perspective, businesses, households, and other organizations engage in the acquisition, integration, and transformation of resources to create new resources and then use these new resources in exchange with other actors to cocreate value. This perspective begins to direct attention to viewing businesses, households, and other organizations, including nonprofits and governments, as essentially and abstractly identical. This insight led us to define exchange and exchange systems in terms of actor-to-actor (A2A) interactions. Importantly, this notion parallels the writing of Bagozzi nearly forty years ago when he discussed marketing as an organized behavioral system of exchange. Bagozzi defined the exchange system as a "set of social actors, their relationships to each other, and the endogenous and exogenous variables affecting the behavior of the social actors in those relationships."[3] Other researchers have also adopted the convention of using "actors" to characterize the diverse set of entities that are part of market exchange systems.[4]

Recognizing that the actors in an A2A exchange are part of an exchange system is vital to understanding S-D logic. As we discussed in Chapter 3, the second axiom of S-D logic is that value is always cocreated. If value is always cocreated, the relationship moves beyond a goods-dominant (G-D) view, which argues that the essence of relationships is the transactions repeated between a producer or firm and a customer. Furthermore, this perspective moves away from the fallacy of the conceptualization of the linear and sequential creation, flow, and destruction of value toward the existence of a much more complex and dynamic exchange system of actors. These actors relationally cocreate value and, at the same time, jointly provide the context through which "value" gains its collective and individual assessment.[5] As we explain when discussing the different types of exchange institutions later in this chapter, this perspective also suggests that relationships cannot be separated from the shared institutions of actors in A2A networks. Essentially, it points to a systems view of generic actors embedded within an institutional structure which is capable of providing richer insights into how a specific actor, such as a business enterprise, can be more effective in serving other actors and society than is possible from a narrower, more micro perspective, alone.

So, does this mean that firm–customer designations are useless in the A2A world? Probably not. They can and should still play a role in dealing with the general perspective from a particular viewpoint – that is, in economic exchange, a "firm" is the actor providing relatively direct service (i.e., directly or through a good), and the "customer" is the actor providing service indirectly to the firm, through an economic instrument (e.g., money), or what has been traditionally referred to as a firm and a customer. Thus, an actor "going to market" with a specific competence with the intention of serving another actor might be considered a firm (also often referred to as a producer), and the actor being served and reciprocating with money would be considered the customer (also referred to as a consumer). It should be clear, however, that from a broader perspective both are resource-integrating actors engaged in the same general activities and that all customers are essentially also producers or firms (i.e., enterprises). The terms "producer" and "consumer" are considerably less useful, probably insufficiently so to warrant their retention in S-D logic. In short, the focal firm is "the firm" only from a particular vantage point. The divide depends on the situation and the relative role of the actor and the perspective of that actor.

Overthrowing divisions

Associated with the rising specialization and division of labor (knowledge and skills) through the evolution of human civilization, actors became more interdependent. As actors became more specialized, and thus increasingly needed to exchange, the tendency arose for one actor to be in a more dominant or controlling position and the other actor to be more passive, similar to the dominant actor being an operant resource and the passive actor being an operand resource. For example, the producer or business enterprise over the customer, the employer over the employee, the physician over the patient, the teacher over the student, and the preacher over the parishioner all helped position the service provider as more expert, knowledgeable, innovative, enterprising, wiser, and leading. In a sense, it is reasonable to understand how this evolved because, with indirect exchange, it is the service provider that is using applied knowledge and skills to make a service offering and the other beneficiary actor (when the exchange is indirect) that is simply receiving the offering and using service rights (economic currency) in exchange for the offering. Thus, the service provider does not observe the applied knowledge and skills the beneficiary used to obtain service rights but only observes the fungible service rights. This traditional view of the service provider as operant and the beneficiary as operand constitutes G-D logic and the linear view of the flow of value from being produced by one actor to being delivered to another actor. But, as we previously argued, the customer is always a cocreator of value.

In S-D logic, a service beneficiary is understood as an enterprising resource integrator that is trying to improve the viability of its own relevant system. That is, a service beneficiary integrates the resources made available through the service providers that offer resource(s) to integrate with other resources to cocreate value. These other resources include the actor's own expertise, knowledge, and creative innovative ability. Traditional studies in B2B have long recognized that the beneficiary of an offering can be a key source of expertise and knowledge to assist the business-actor in developing and refining service offerings. This is because by using and integrating the offerings of the service-providing business-actor, the beneficiary learns of shortcomings and discovers creative ways to adapt and modify offerings for enhanced value cocreation. However, often in the traditional study of B2C, the beneficiary of an offering is not considered a key source of expertise and knowledge. Stated alternatively, the customer is viewed as an operand resource rather than an operant resource.[6]

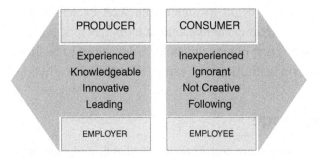

Exhibit 5.1 G-D logic: divisions and separations

In an organizational context, employees under G-D logic are treated (similarly to how the firm treated the customer) as an operand resource. In the field of management, McGregor developed theory X versus theory Y management, which essentially described treating employees as operand versus operant resources.[7] Under theory X, employers take the perspective that employee-actors are inherently lazy and unmotivated to work because they dislike work. Employers thus need to develop systems of supervisions and controls to tightly manage and direct the activities of employee-actors so that they do what they would otherwise not do. In brief, employee-actors are considered operand resources. Diametrically opposed to theory X is theory Y, in which it is assumed that the employee-actor enjoys work, finds it invigorating and rewarding, and thus is self-motivated but also able to exercise self-control or simply manage his or her own service-provisioning activities. These employee-actors are also viewed as having knowledge and skills that include creativity skills that help them solve problems better than if employers superimpose on them the best solution for a particular situation. In brief, employee-actors are operant resources. Exhibit 5.1 illustrates that, with G-D logic, a surprising similarity exists between how human actors in their roles as consumers and employees were treated as operand resources and not as the inherent operant resources they really are. Again, much of this treatment may have been due to the power of language or what these terms meant – another example of performativity.

Generic actor-to-actor exchange

A2A exchange networks actually comprise several general types of exchange, as well as types of exchange institutions. In Chapter 8, we show how these A2A exchange networks assemble themselves into more holistic service ecosystems.

However, for now and as a way to begin to understand A2A exchange, it is helpful to review three general types of exchange among human actors. It is also useful to discuss three institutions that human actors have developed to facilitate exchange, in addition to a fourth institution that can be thought of as a hybrid.

General types of exchange

The three general types of exchange are restricted, generalized, and complex.[8] Each is a way to exchange resources and is related to actor networks. However, not all forms of obtaining resources from other actors come from exchange, as in the case of resource sharing. Examples of resource sharing include household resources being pooled or parenting.[9]

Restricted exchange

Restricted exchange is dyadic exchange in which an actor exchanges with another actor. Actor A gives and receives from actor B, and actor B gives and receives from actor A. Thus, restricted exchange is often referred to as reciprocal exchange. These actors, as discussed previously, take on a variety of labels, such as firm, organization, employer, employee, customer, client, wholesaler, retailer, producer, investor, and shareholder. Exhibit 5.2, part A, illustrates restricted exchange.

Restricted exchange has been the implicit, if not explicit, focus of most research in economics, management, marketing, and business in general.[10] In the marketing discipline are various subdisciplines, including consumer behavior, strategic marketing, services marketing, B2B marketing, and international marketing. One of the commonalities across these various subdisciplines is a general focus on restricted exchange, or what is often referred to as dyadic contexts of exchange.

With restricted exchange, there is a general focus on each actor gaining or being better off from the exchange, which is a form of mutualism. For both parties to be better off and the relationship to develop, the focus is often on concepts such as mutual trust, equality, or equity. However, the focus very much remains G-D in that repeated exchange is equated with repeated economic transactions, which is then anointed as "relationship." However, the S-D logic perspective on relationship transcends restricted exchange. Trust, equity, and equality are not something exclusively evaluated by actors based on their restricted exchange but rather are often in reference to norms, culture, or other shared institutions that are part of larger A2A networks or exchange systems all

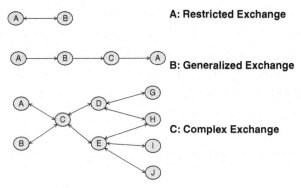

A: Restricted Exchange

B: Generalized Exchange

C: Complex Exchange

Exhibit 5.2 Types of exchange

the way up to societal systems. It is also within these broader systems where value is cocreated, because at least some of the resources integrated into value cocreation are institutions and societal resources.

Generalized exchange

In generalized exchange, at least three actors are implied. The three actors do not directly exchange with one another but do so indirectly through another actor. In this situation, the direct exchange is not symbiotic or mutual, though eventually each actor benefits. In brief, symbiosis is eventual but not mutual. The exchange chain is, actor A gives to actor B and actor B gives to actor C and actor C in turn gives to actor A. Thus, actors do not benefit each other directly but indirectly. Exhibit 5.2, part B, graphically portrays generalized exchange.

Actors often engage in generalized exchange in organizations, but it can also occur in households (a form of organization). Consider, for example, the commonality of generalized exchange in a household. One parent-actor (A) may assist another parent-actor (B) with some household chores he or she normally performs alone for the household. The parent (B) then may take the children-actors (C) to the park for a few hours, and the children-actors (C) may then decide later in the week to surprise parent-actor (A) by cleaning the swimming pool, a service normally provided by actor (A). The concept of generalized exchange regularly occurs in the workplace in organizations. This is because much of the service performed in organizations cannot be efficiently, directly compensated through direct dyadic value-in-exchange transaction. Rather, interdependent actors working together and exchanging service with one another know, as team members, that other team members will not directly compensate them but that the organization will provide the compensation (service rights). Generalized exchange also enables the organization, through its own culture and institutions, to allow workers to do things that are not directly market facing or reciprocal in nature – for example, when a university grants faculty a sabbatical or when a business enterprise allows engineers or scientists to work a certain percentage of their time on their own projects, which often include publishing in scholarly journals. Much of this latter activity actually allows the actors to explore and develop new skills and competences and discover and recognize resource integration and creation possibilities they would not otherwise witness.[11]

Generalized exchange is not unique to internal exchanges within a business or household; it is also found in the marketplace. Consider the case when a local auto dealership (A) provides a charitable gift to the local children's choir (B) and then patrons (C) of a holiday concert put on by the children's choir are touched by the generosity of the car dealer and purchase more autos and auto service from the dealer (A). Here, the symbiosis or reciprocity is not mutual (direct), but is eventual (indirect).

Complex exchange

In complex exchange, at least three actors are also needed. Direct exchange among actors occurs at least once for each actor. Importantly, however, the complex exchange system is "organized by an interconnecting web of relationships."[12] We can illustrate this with what has historically been referred to as distribution channels, marketing channels, or supply chains but what S-D logic refers to as value constellations or service ecosystems (which we discuss more fully in Chapter 8). Consider one actor (A) and another actor (B) as branded component suppliers to a third actor (C), which assembles the components into a system solution and then wholesales this system to actors (D and E), which in turn combine this with credit and a maintenance service agreement and sell it to actors (G, H, I, and J). Exhibit 5.2, part C, illustrates this type of complex exchange.

Actors are almost always part of a complex exchange, especially over time as they and other actors become more specialized. However, that does not mean that they recognize the complexity of the exchange system. This complexity can be observed if the actors are able to zoom out and view where they are in the exchange system in relation to other actors and resources. In Chapter 3 this was illustrated in Exhibit 3.4 with its portrayal of service exchange through resource integration and value cocreation.

Exchange institutions

As they evolved, humans developed at least three primary institutions for exchange: reciprocity, redistribution, and market exchange.[13] Over time, a fourth institution emerged, which can be thought of as a hybrid institution that comprises various combinations of these three pure-form institutions.

Reciprocity

Perhaps the oldest exchange institution is reciprocity, which has its roots in gift giving and potlatch, a gift-giving festival and primary economic system.[14] Reciprocity involves an exchange of obligations between actors. It is based on a belief that helping and assisting another actor is not altruistic but rather, in general, establishes an expectation of immediate and direct help and assistance or indirect help and assistance in the future. In the lexicon of S-D logic, what is exchanged is service, or service obligations.

Not only did forms of reciprocity, such as gift giving, take place in ancient civilizations, but they also occur in contemporary society. Reciprocity regularly occurs in households and organizations. For example, a household actor cooks dinner, and another household actor reciprocates by cleaning the table and dishes. A manager in an organization mentors a recently arrived junior colleague, and this junior colleague reciprocates by helping the manager meet some unexpected client demands. A junior senator in the national government supports a senior senator in passing legislation, and the senior senator reciprocates by putting the junior senator on a key committee. Much of S-D logic, and its view of relationship, is built on the idea that when actors treat each other appropriately, they will reciprocate and the relationship between actors will become one of solidarity and mutuality. Predictably, this is also based on the idea that repeated interactions and exchange occurs among the actors.

Redistribution

Another exchange institution is redistribution, which occurs when an authority or central actor gathers or takes the goods and service capacity of actors and allocates back to actors according to some type of custom, tradition, rule, or simply fiat. In contemporary society, redistribution is most common in the institution of taxation. For example, in the case of a sales tax, or what some nations call a "value-added tax," a portion of each economic exchange (service rights) is taken by the government and then redistributed to other actors either directly or indirectly. However, such service(s) may not be distributed equally to the population of actors in the society but rather based on some other criterion, such as need or vulnerability of actors. For instance, economically disadvantaged actors and children and older individuals may be viewed as having more needs or being more vulnerable and thus deserving of more service or transfer of service rights.

Redistribution is common not only in the institution of government but also in firms and households. For example, it is not uncommon in large corporations for senior management to gather excess cash flow and resources and then redistribute them to the divisions or strategic business units according to strategic plans, capital requirements for growth, or other rationales. Such redistribution also occurs in nonprofit organizations, in which, for example, a public university may collect tuition and other revenue flows and then redistribute them to various colleges and departments. In a family, it could occur when parents pool financial resources, wages, and other income and then redistribute them to family members depending on need. In some households, all the children may work on a farm or in a family business or in the labor market, and then the head of the household takes the resources generated and redistributes them to the household actors and/or other actors.

Market exchange

A final institution that has evolved to address the exchange needs of actors as they become more specialized is market exchange. In market exchange, the actors interface to establish the value-in-exchange for tradable resources. Economists refer to this as the "invisible hand" of the market establishing the prices for resources that then guide exchange. The market is also an institution that has evolved to provide a convenient way for actors to know what to use less of and conserve. For example, as the market price of a resource such as oil or copper rises, the actor is sent a signal to conserve this resource. Prices (value-in-exchange) thus serve an important role in allocating scarce resources. However, what market exchange and prices do not clarify is the integration of non-market-facing private and public resources that are crucial for actors to maintain or improve their system viability.

Markets and market prices also influence exchanges that occur in organizations and households or other aggregates and outsourcing. When managers set salaries or wages, it is difficult to ignore the market worth of the actor. In the household, one actor may have more worth in the market. For example, if that actor works outside the home for service rights (wages or salary), he or she may outsource certain household service to others, such as housecleaning or landscaping. Briefly, as actors become highly specialized and other actors need this applied specialized knowledge and skills, specialists are likely to exchange their skills and competences (service potential) for monetary incentives or service rights that they then use to obtain other needed or desired service(s).

Hybrid exchange systems

Finally, hybrid exchange systems are those that combine two or even all three of the basic systems – reciprocity, redistribution, and market exchange – in various proportions. Indeed, what is described as the market exchange system in many developed economies and in most service ecosystems, which will be discussed in Chapter 8, is a combination of all three of these institutionalized exchange formats. Herbert Simon recognized this when he observed that the United States is not a market economy but a market–organization economy in which organizations are containers for many types of non-market-based exchanges, some of an economic character but others of a social character.[15] Going a step further, the United States and many other nations reflect a market–organization–government economy. There is obviously market exchange, as captured in many of the economic transactions of actors (firms and households) in acquiring service and providing their service to other actors, but within the actor organizations there are also many examples of reciprocity, such as when one actor organization helps another actor organization during a natural disaster or in times of need. Also within these actor organizations, as described previously, is the redistribution of resources or service rights.

Recap

A generic, A2A network perspective offers considerable potential for understanding service-for-service exchange. However, understanding this exchange requires several G-D logic concepts to be replaced because of their constraining nature and also because G-D concepts guide thought and meaning in a manner that results in a limited view of exchange between human actors. At the forefront, this includes viewing one actor as a producer who is the creator of value and the other actor as a consumer who uses up or destroys value. Also at the forefront of the G-D logic is the view of relationship as a repeated, reciprocal economic exchange cast in a market economy. The generic A2A perspective, coupled with the axioms and premises of S-D logic, views all actors as potentially operant resource-integrating cocreators of value. Service exchange is often not reciprocal or direct but indirect. Therefore, it is important also to understand exchange as

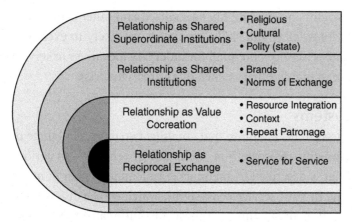

Relationship as Shared Superordinate Institutions	• Religious • Cultural • Polity (state)
Relationship as Shared Institutions	• Brands • Norms of Exchange
Relationship as Value Cocreation	• Resource Integration • Context • Repeat Patronage
Relationship as Reciprocal Exchange	• Service for Service

Exhibit 5.3 Relationship layers

generalized and complex and exchange institutions as reciprocity, redistribution, market, and hybrid. As we will discuss in Chapter 8, the service ecosystem is almost always a hybrid exchange system involving reciprocity, redistribution, and market service exchanges.

Ultimately, then, the concept of "relationship" must be understood in terms of nested levels of meaning (see Exhibit 5.3). Relationship does not arise from transactions; rather, relationship is pervasive in A2A networks, and transactions occasionally punctuate these relationships. Relationship can be viewed as always occurring in an A2A exchange network because of the shared superordinate institutions such as culture, religion, and polity. These superordinate institutions weave themselves through all A2A networks. Nested below this are shared institutions that can include norms of exchange and brands.[16] And further nesting can establish relationship based on value cocreation occurring via resource integration and repeated purchases. Finally, there is relationship as reciprocal exchange of service.

Actor-centric exchange systems

A generic, A2A exchange perspective, as just discussed, begins to support the contention that a focus on any single actor or a dyad of actors is restrictive; rather, actors and exchange dyads are embedded in larger networks of actors exchanging within a service system and within an institutional structure in society. Furthermore, "customer centricity" or "customer orientation" as traditionally employed is redundant, if not vacuous, if one adopts the A2A perspective, along with other central ideas of S-D logic. In G-D logic, only firms have customers – implying and making obvious that it is the firm that needs to be customer centric. Therefore, except from the perspective of the firm adopting G-D logic, there is no customer. The focus on the customer (at least in S-D logic) has a limited purpose – to understand this beneficiary actor sufficiently to make the actor a customer (and, more recently, to keep the actor as customer).

Actor centricity

Firms and their customers are not the basis on which to understand economies, society, and certainly business. Rather, the fundamental basis on which to understand economies, society, and business is service-for-service exchange between actors and within networks of actors, in service systems, and, more broadly, within society. All actors are at the center of their own relevant system for which they are attempting to enhance viability. And all actors are connected directly to other actors and resources and indirectly to a network or system of other actors and networks that are increasingly removed but tied together through an intricate web of relationships or complex exchange (see Exhibit 5.2, part C, and Exhibit 3.2). What this implies is an actor-centric system in which all actors are nodes in one another's relevant system. That is, all actors are at the center of their own system but also at the edge of, though farther away from, other actors' systems.

Because actors are attempting to enhance the viability of their system, the *actor-centric perspective* is, by definition, also a *value-centric perspective*. Importantly, however, actors and resources are connected to each other, and thus it becomes tautological that, when actors act to enhance the viability of their own system, they influence or alter the system of other actors.[17] In other words, the context within which an actor functions influences other actor contexts, and vice versa. Through separate and joint actions, actors cocreate the more macro system or they cocreate their environment. This is somewhat at odds with traditional views of evolution that actors fit into a niche in an environment; rather, through effectuation, they create, at least in part, the environment. It also suggests that institutions, which are such a vital part of a service system and society, are socially constructed.

This is not to suggest that actors are not constrained by institutions and the structured solutions that institutions provide. Institutions can create an "iron cage" that traps, or at least significantly constrains, the action of actors.[18] At the same time, actors do have agency, and part of what these actors help create is the market or marketplace, which has increasingly become the platform for the exchange of service(s).

Generic actors: a behavioral perspective

S-D logic views humans and actors as relational and purposeful but both enabled and constrained by other actors and institutions. Human actors, in general, have a degree of agency or the ability to act in a somewhat unconstrained manner or to act under partial constraints. In their relational and purpose-driven actions, they attempt to pursue paths through non-coercive service exchanges that are intended to make them better off or to improve the viability of their relevant system. Actors, however, are not the fully rational, insightful, maximizing agents that neoclassical economics purports. Actors do not have the capability to see the network or system within which they are embedded clearly enough or to see far enough into the future to be good maximizing actors. However, what they can see is one or a few steps around them and a few steps forward and how to solve the more immediate problems they confront. They are less competent at sophisticated computation than at problem solving. Collectively, actors solve a large number of recurring problems by developing institutions. For instance, one of the oldest human institutions is reciprocity. This forms the basis of relational, cooperative, positive-sum exchange versus coercive and negative-sum exchange. Institutionalized solutions allow actors to reduce the need for recurring problem solving by following certain rules, or what we later refer to as "clever human tricks" for coordinating human activity.

Human actors may not be able to view the complete network or structure, but they can view fairly accurately their context and how to navigate to new positions of system viability. However, this is true more in a static sense than in the crucible of dynamic A2A networks. An actor will often use an institutionalized solution to move forward. However, variety among actors in adopting an institutionalized solution is common since there is mutability in the rules that characterize an institutionalized solution. Furthermore, any improvement in system viability is temporary because, as explained previously, in an A2A network or system the actors are constantly altering not only their context but also the context of other actors and, therefore, their access to resources.

With the central focus on service-for-service exchange, it should be noted that this does not imply that actors are selfish and focus on what is best for them without consideration for others. Generally, as actors strive to enhance the viability of their relevant system, it needs to be recognized that they define for themselves, but influenced by other actors and institutions, their "relevant" system that shapes their frame of reference. Individual actors often define their relevant system as beyond themselves and thus often want to do better at serving a larger community, society, or higher purpose.

Action as exchange

An action by an actor can be viewed as a trade-off between the action taken and the unobserved action(s) foregone. This is the basic notion of opportunity cost that can be traced at least to Friedrich von Wieser, who was a late nineteenth-century Austrian economist.[19]

Furthermore, if actors have some degree of agency in a structurated system, then their actions are a type of exchange. They are exchanging a taken action (assumed to be preferred) over the next best alternative action (less preferred) and hence an opportunity cost is always present whether the actor recognizes it as such or not. This is an important point to recognize and to understand actors in action. Briefly, the meaning of exchange is always intertwined in non-exchange or what was foregone as alternative actions – or what is also often referred to as opportunity costs.

It is easy to observe human action when an actor decides to go to a restaurant or to a movie theater. It is also easy to understand why the actor gives up service rights or created service obligations in exchange for a meal at the restaurant or the entertainment of watching a movie at the theater. Not as visible, however, is that these trade-offs cannot always be phrased in terms of economic opportunity costs, because phenomenological value is often much more complex and cannot be equated to market price or value-in-exchange. For example, if an actor decides he or she needs to work on the weekend and thus must forego a planned trip with a grandchild or other loved one, it is not possible to equate the opportunity foregone to a monetary value. In summary, exchange is involved in all human action in which the actor has some degree of agency,[20] and thus actions also implicitly involve trade-offs.

Actors as density seeking

Resource density, a concept based on the work of Normann, involves mobilizing resources for an actor's value creation at a given time and place.[21] Maximum density is the best combination of resources mobilized for an actor at a given time and place to create the best possible value. Whereas the neoclassical economic model asserts that seller outputs and buyer demands materialize through market exchange to result in prices that allocate resources efficiently in society, an actor-centric view of the economy is quite different. With this view, the enterprising, resource-integrating, specialized actors exchanging with others (i.e., outsourcing) are using their actor and resource networks to gain better density and thus to enhance the viability of their contextual, value-cocreating system.

Concluding comments

To help understand A2A networks and in building a theory of the economy and society around the individual actor versus conventional notions of economies as firm centric, consider the following thought experiment. The setting is the resource density today of a typical human actor compared with that of 200 years ago in a large central place, such as New York City, Paris, Moscow, Tokyo, Lagos, or São Paolo. To put 200 years into a more understandable time frame, consider this as ten generations of human reproduction, an undoubtedly short period. To further contextualize this thought experiment, consider the choices typical actors had in outsourcing meal preparation service. We can most likely conclude that resource density today is relatively greater for the typical actor than 200 years (ten generations) ago. Today, one can leave home and, usually within a few miles, find virtually every type of food service offering with an attractive value proposition. The offering may include Chinese, Mexican, Italian, and Indian cuisine, American burgers and fries, fast-food restaurants, fine-dining restaurants, cafeterias, food courts, family restaurants, supermarkets with home meal replacements, delis, and sit-down cafes. In these outsourcing events, the actor is integrating many other resources, including public roadways and regulations, credit systems, transport systems, and other family or work activities. The actor is constantly acting in an effectual manner to integrate these and other resources to enhance the viability of his or her system.

An alternative result occurs, however, if the context of the thought experiment is changed a bit. Rather than thinking about the choice typical actors face in outsourcing meal preparation, consider the case when actors do not want to acquire service through market exchange. For example, what if they decide they want to grow, prepare, and eat their own food? In this scenario, the contemporary household may have less resource density than in the past because it may not have the knowledge and skills, the time, or the access to soil or other resources to farm. The key point here is that S-D logic and the concepts of resource density and system viability do not impose any type of market solution to problems but rather accommodate other exchange and societal institutions as long as A2A and service-for-service exchange is not "forced" on actors. Forced or involuntary exchange is an interesting area of inquiry but one that S-D logic does not address.

All actors seek resource density to enhance their system viability. Actors integrate resources, cocreate value, and uniquely phenomenologically determine value from their perspective and context. As such, it is well past the time for marketing and other business disciplines to transcend beyond thinking of actors as consumers, producers, firms, and government agencies and to view them in an actor-centric and value-centric framework. Doing so would make it easy to recognize that *resource integration* and *resource density* trump *resource allocation* in helping us to understand the evolution and functioning of economy and society and, thus, business.

NOTES

1. Frédéric Bastiat, *Harmonies of Political Economy*, trans. Patrick S. Sterling (London: J. Murray, 1860).
2. Stephen L. Vargo and Robert F. Lusch, "It's all B2B . . . and beyond: toward a systems perspective of the market," *Industrial Marketing Management*, 40 (2011), 181–187.
3. Richard P. Bagozzi, "Marketing as an organized behavioral system of exchange," *Journal of Marketing*, 38 (October 1974), 77–81, p. 78.
4. E.g., Evert Gummesson, as mentioned in personal conversations with us and in recent presentations, uses the A2A framework. It is also the convention of most Industrial Marketing and Purchasing (IMP) Group scholars, including H. Hankansson and I. Snehota, "The IMP perspective," in Jagdish Sheth and Atul Parvatiyar (eds.), *Handbook of Relationship Marketing* (Thousand Oaks, CA: Sage Publications, 1995), pp. 171–208.
5. Vargo and Lusch, "It's all B2B . . . and beyond"; A. Giddens, *The Constitution of Society* (Berkeley: University of California Press, 1984).
6. The notion of all actors as operant resources is supported in the open innovation literature; i.e., Eric Von Hippel, *Democratizing Innovation* (Cambridge, MA: MIT Press, 2006).
7. Douglas McGregor, *The Human Side of Enterprise* (New York: McGraw-Hill, 1960).
8. For further discussion of the three types of exchange, see Richard P. Bagozzi, "Marketing as exchange," *Journal of Marketing*, 39 (October 1975), 32–39.
9. Russell Belk, "Sharing," *Journal of Consumer Research*, 36 (February 2010), 715–734.
10. Peter Moran and Sumantra Ghoshal, "Markets, firms, and the process of economic development," *Academy of Management Review*, 24:3 (1999), 390–412.
11. Moran and Ghoshal, "Markets, firms, and the process of economic development."
12. Bagozzi, "Marketing as exchange," p. 33.

13. For more discussion and insight, see Karl Polanyi, "The economy as instituted process," in Karl Polanyi, Conrad M. Arensberg, and Harry W. Pearson (eds.), *Trade and Market in the Early Empires* (Glencoe, IL: Free Press, 1957), pp. 243–269.

14. Aldona Jonaitis, *Chiefly Feasts: The Enduring Kwakiutl Potlatch* (Seattle: University of Washington Press, 1991); David J. Cheal, *The Gift Economy* (New York: Routledge, 1988); R. Kranton, "Reciprocal exchange: a self-sustaining system,"*American Economic Review*, 86:4 (1996), 830–851.

15. Herbert Simon, *The Sciences of the Artificial* (Cambridge, MA: MIT Press, 1996).

16. W. Richard Scott, *Institutions and Organizations*, 2nd edn (Thousand Oaks, CA: Sage Publications, 2001). See especially chapters 3 and 4.

17. This is also a key insight from assemblage theory. Manuel DeLanda, *A New Philosophy of Society: Assemblage Theory and Social Complexity* (London: Continuum, 2006).

18. P. J. DiMaggio and W. W. Powell, "The iron cage revisited: institutional isomorphism and collective rationality in organizational fields," *American Sociological Review*, 48:2 (1983), 147–160; E. S. Clemens and J. M. Cook, "Politics and institutionalism: explaining durability and change," *American Review of Sociology*, 25 (1999), 441–466.

19. Israel M. Kirzner, *Subjectivism, Intelligibility and Economic Understanding: Essays in Honor of Ludwig M. Lachmann on His Eightieth Birthday*, illustrated edn (Basingstoke, UK: Macmillan, 1986).

20. In assuming the actor has no agency and is 100 percent structurated, it is not exchanging one action for another that is a foregone action, because that option is not available. The structure controls the actor's actions.

21. Richard Normann, *Reframing Business: When the Map Changes the Landscape* (Chichester, UK: John Wiley & Sons, 2001).

6 The nature, scope, and integration of resources

> Exactly the same resource when used for different purposes or in different ways and in combination with different types or amounts of other resources provides a different service or set of services.
>
> Edith Penrose (1959, p. 25)

Introduction

Resource, as a concept used to discuss economic and social exchange, cuts across many disciplines.[1] Service-dominant (S-D) logic views resources as what actors can draw on for support. Some resources are market facing, but many others are non-market facing; some are tangible, but many are intangible; some are internal to the actor, but many, if not most, are external to the actor; some are operand, but others are operant. Actors themselves are "operant resources" when they apply their resources (primarily knowledge and skills) to provide service to other actors. Service beneficiaries are also operant resources when they use their knowledge and skills to integrate other resources to cocreate value. This view of resources as linked to actors, service provision, and cocreated value offers a systems view of the role of resources in service exchange, actor-to-actor (A2A) networks, and human economic and social progress.

Yet, when resources are discussed, many people revert to thinking of them as primarily tangible (usually natural resources) and often static, or what we refer to as "operand resources." Often these static operand resources are viewed as embedded with "utility" (i.e., value) that a "producer" creates and then delivers to the consumer. This leads to the perspective that these static, valuable things will, in time, be depleted and used up. The purpose of this chapter is to offer a more complete, informed, holistic, and dynamic view of resources, a view that provides the conceptual tools not only to think of economies and enterprises differently but also to begin to develop an actor's (e.g., enterprise's, nation's) strategy that is more appropriately centered on operant resources and resource integration.

Resources explained

As we discussed and illustrated in Chapter 1, resources are not necessarily tangible; that is, they are not necessarily something that someone can hold, possess, or own. They are more than what is reported on an organization's balance sheet or the things that fill up actors' houses, apartments, garages, basements, and offices. They are also more than the natural resources of the earth. But what then are resources?

In Chapter 1, we introduced the example of the farmer and the fisherman, in which the actors exchanged carbohydrate-providing service for protein-providing service. Importantly, the conditions for the service-for-service exchange are based on each of the actors creating, integrating, and applying other resources. A brief, partial inventory of their resources includes (1) mental and physical skills and competences used for fish gathering and grain cultivating and harvesting; (2) tangible artifacts used in fishing and farming, such as boats, nets, plows, wheels, pulleys, and baskets; (3) institutions, such as norms or governance mechanisms, to enable the assignment of roles and sharing and exchange of resources; (4) nutrient-providing soils, seas, and biosphere; and (5) language or other communication and symbol systems to enable interaction and exchange, with and among others.

The preceding set of resources did not exist until humans exercised their agency by learning how to draw on potential resources (tangible or intangible) for support and acting in a manner to cocreate these resources and then use them to improve their system viability or more broadly the human condition. From this perspective, resource scarcity is a function of actor knowledge of and skills in drawing on potential resources, often by integrating them to create new resources. Often, actors are stimulated to search for new, integrable resources to maintain or improve system viability.

This discussion leads us to adopt the view of not what resources are, but rather what they become.[2] This is the essential nature of resources, and so we define them as *anything, tangible or intangible, internal or external, operand or operant, that the actor can draw on for increased viability.* We explain this definition further in the following sections.

Resources and human appraisal

"Resources are not, they become."[3] This is a simple but profound statement and central to understanding the nature of the service-centered view. At the foundation of its meaning is recognizing that some actors' skills and knowledge determine "resourceness." *Resourceness* reflects the quality and realization of potential resources, through the process of human appraisal and action, which then transforms potential resources into realized resources.[4] For example, humans could not draw on timber as a source of energy and building materials unless they developed and applied their physical and mental skills. Humans could not draw on iron ore and other mineral deposits to produce artifacts to leverage human muscle unless they had developed the know-how to do so. Humans could not draw on the potential of unrelated people working together in an organization unless they had developed the concept of the firm and the related management knowledge. Humans could not draw on themselves to rule and govern unless they had developed institutional mechanisms such as norms and laws. Humans could not take many actions today to develop new resources unless they could borrow from others and take the risks associated to create resources. To handle these risks, yet other institutions were developed as resources, such as insurance and the limited-liability organization. There are countless other examples. Humans live in a sea of resource potential,[5] and these potential resources only become resources when appraised and acted on, often through integration with other potential resources.

The preceding paragraph argues that resources are abstractions,[6] since all resources reflect human appraisal of something that can be the source of aid and support. Even a tangible resource is an abstraction because a resource is never a substance or thing. Rather, a resource is a function that the substance contributes in order to achieve a desired end. Consider, for instance, when humans developed knowledge of fire and the skills to handle fire to transform it into a source of support to provide warmth and cooking service, or, more contemporarily, when humans developed knowledge of the electromagnetic spectrum and developed the skills to use the spectrum for A2A transmission of signs and symbols for human communication. In these instances humans uncovered or developed the functional relationship between the latent substance and how it could be used to improve the human condition.

Overcoming resistances

Throughout civilization, humans have demonstrated the ability to develop tools to help them act more efficiently and effectively. These tools have been developed from tangible and intangible potential resources because humans, through their appraisal, assessment, and application, were able to activate the potential resource to become resources when their resourceness is appraised and acted upon. In this activation process, it was necessary to overcome resistances or barriers that prevented or stifled resourceness.

Let us illustrate how overcoming resistances can result in resourceness. We use the example of oceans and their currents. If humans have no knowledge or inadequate knowledge of the ocean current and winds and how to use them to power ships with sails, then the oceans are more a barrier or resistance than a resource. However, even with sailing or steam-powered ships, the oceans were and are treacherous, and many ships have been wrecked when they have encountered severe storms. Few, if any, actors could take the risk of building a ship, loading it with contents, and sailing the seas. However, if these ships could be pooled, actors could calculate from historical data the wreckage rate and, from this, an insurance fee could be charged to protect their investment in the ships. Thus, insurance removed much of the resistance to (risk of) sailing the high seas and thus increased resourceness of the high seas.

Often to remove resistance or activate a potential resource, human actors develop knowledge to accomplish something that at least for some actor(s) is viewed as valuable. In the case of the oceans, knowledge of ship hulls and sails was developed to capture the energy in wind and ocean currents to propel the sailing vessel, and knowledge of risk management was developed from analysis of statistical data and computation to spread the risk by charging each ship's owners a relatively small insurance fee.

Exhibit 6.1 illustrates the linkage among knowledge, potential resources, resourceness, and service. Knowledge, the most critical of all resources, is applied to other potential resources to create resourceness, and when applied can provide service to benefit another actor (or the actor itself). This provides an important insight into how to think of innovation. Innovation is about applied knowledge, used both to create resources and resourceness through integration with other resources and to apply these resources to provide service. Thus, innovation is

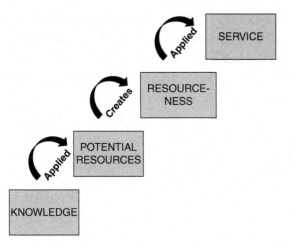

Exhibit 6.1 Applying knowledge to potential resources to create resourceness for service

never about materiality or goods *per se* but fundamentally about human knowledge and skill development to be used in service-for-service exchange.

Resources are operand and operant

As noted, resources can be classified as operand and operant. *Operand resources* are resources that must be acted on by some other resource to create an effect. *Operant resources* are resources that are capable of acting on other resources (operand or operant) to create an effect. This distinction is best illustrated with examples. Keep in mind that operand resources are generally tangible and static and operant resources are generally dynamic and intangible.

Iron ore, petroleum, gold, silver, silica, timber, grain, and water are all things actors must act on to make them useful. However, so are things such as automobiles, computers, apparel, and wine. What they have in common is that humans act on them to create an effect, or often to provide a service. Thus, these resources are operand resources.

As discussed in Chapter 5 (see Exhibit 5.1), the distinction between operand and operant resources can provide an important perspective for understanding how customers and employees are approached and treated by firms. In some enterprises, both historically and today, employees are approached (treated) as not having an interest or desire to work (i.e., not wanting to provide service). Because of this belief, firms tightly manage (supervise) and control them (develop detailed guidelines and make sure they are followed). All of this is done to extract maximum productivity from employees or, at least, the labor productivity that fits with the firm's plan. In brief, the employees are viewed as operand resources.

Some enterprises treat customers in a similar manner. There is a long history to the phrase "buyer beware," but it primarily arose because some and perhaps a relatively small number of enterprises viewed customers as prey the firm needed to capture. Because these firms believed that customers did not want to be captured, they began persuading them to buy, sometimes through misleading advertising programs that largely performed propaganda functions.[7] Salespeople were employed to convince potential customers to purchase what the firm had to sell. All of this was done so that the firm could extract the customer's money. It should be emphasized these practices were probably not dominant; especially if the enterprise expected repeat business.

It is interesting that even today, through firms trying to be customer oriented, customer relationship management (CRM) information systems assume that customers are operand resources. Most CRM systems are based on G-D logic. Customers are treated as something to be targeted, penetrated, and managed for the firm's objective of achieving maximum profit per customer.

The same potential resource, however, can often be an operand or operant resource, depending on human appraisal. Consider again how human actors are treated as employees and customers. If it is recognized that humans have knowledge and skills and can produce effects, they can be viewed and treated as operant resources. In terms of employees, organizations can empower them to make decisions, improve the service they provide to others, and develop innovative ways to serve better. At the same time, organizations can view customers as partners who can be cocreators and help the firm through positive word-of-mouth communication and development of innovative ideas for better service offerings or the development of brand communities. Conceivably, an enterprise could involve customers as cocreators in any aspect of its marketing program, as we discussed in Chapter 4 (see Exhibit 4.4). Regardless, customers are always cocreators of value. Chapter 7 develops the concepts of cocreation more fully. We show that not only can customers be operant resources as cocreators but so too can suppliers, employees, and other stakeholders.

The dynamic nature of resources

Resourceness implies that resources can be dynamic. The dynamic nature of tangible resources occurs when they are combined with other resources that enhance service-providing capability. As mentioned in Chapter 3, "Foundational premise 4," this is primarily what human actors do when they develop knowledge to create resources (i.e., innovate) and then apply these new resources to provide service. The growth of resourceness is generally about the history of human civilization, the growth of human knowledge and skills, and thus the rise in the stockpile of potential resources. Resources are dynamic.[8]

Consider a fleet of trucks in a firm's distribution and transportation division that achieves an average 4.3 miles per gallon of diesel fuel. Then consider the development of knowledge that allows the retrofitting of the trucks with aerodynamic flares, improved tires, and a redesigned engine, resulting in obtaining 6.2 miles per gallon. Essentially, the current stockpile of diesel fuel would effectively be increased by more than 33 percent. Furthermore, the potential stockpile of diesel fuel could continue to grow if, for example, a chemist were to develop a new fuel additive that improves energy efficiency, an engineer were to develop a radically new engine, or a designer were to reduce the weight of the trucks without harming their structural integrity. All these knowledge gains would effectively increase resourceness.

Much of the innovation in tangible products is about enhanced resourceness. Often this occurs by creating tools (i.e., appliances) that can perform functions that, previously, humans had to perform for themselves. In brief, much innovation performs the role of relieving actors of certain self-serving activities. For this to occur, the product engineer, entrepreneur, or inventor needs both to find ways of developing knowledge about how to perform certain functions and to embed this knowledge into some offering. Exhibit 6.2 illustrates seven examples of this phenomenon.

Intangible resources also have resourceness. If a firm educates a worker and is able to retain that worker with the proper incentives, that single employee becomes a better (more useful) resource for the firm. If the firm is able to collaborate better with customers to cocreate value, customer resources expand. Therefore, resources can grow because of their dynamic nature.

In summary, many ideas on resource scarcity are based on a static view of resources. Although natural resources are finite or nearly finite, the use of these materials can be expanded by learning and through the development of human knowledge and skills. Resources are thus increased by human ingenuity that enables civilizations to effectively and efficiently use natural resources to create new resources that when applied and used for the benefit of others provide service. However, human ingenuity can also create nontangible innovations, such as new theories of management, marketing, or child psychology that expand management and marketing resources. These potential intangible resources are unbounded.

Prior Product Form	New Product Form	Service Provided or Relieved
Standard automobile or truck transmission.	Automatic automobile or truck transmission.	Manual shifting of gears and knowledge of when to shift gears.
Manually controlled home or office lighting.	Lighting controlled by presence of humans in the room or area.	Manual turning on and off of lights.
Mechanical windshield wipers.	Rain sensing windshield wipers.	Manual adjusting of wipers in response to changes in rain density.
Word processing software.	Word processing software with automatic spelling correction.	Knowledge of correct spelling of words.
Automatic washing machine.	Automatic washing machine with sensors to adjust water usage.	Knowledge of how much water to put in each load of clothing.
Order entry and tracking software.	Order entry and tracking software that recommends additional products or adjustments in shipping.	Knowledge of what customer might want or need in terms of customer service.
Farm tractor.	Farm tractor with GPS and sensors for soil condition.	Knowledge of how much fertilizer to put on different patches of farmland.

Exhibit 6.2   Evolution of resourceness

Accessness

J. Paul Getty, the oil tycoon, was known for saying that the meek may inherit the earth but not the mineral rights. Again, this view is a throwback to resources being viewed as something tangible but also to the notion that for a thing to be a resource, an actor needs to own it or have property rights to the resource to access it. Consequently, many believe that resources are things that are internal to the economic actor (e.g., individual, household, firm) and to which the actor has property rights[9] or can at least control and possess.

The notion that resources are internal to the enterprise and controlled by it is illustrated in the standard marketing management framework that emerged during the 1950s and became popularized by McCarthy in 1960 with the publication of *Basic Marketing: A Managerial Approach.*[10] In McCarthy's approach and others that followed, the marketing mix reflected the firm's resources that were used to act on the customer. The customer was *exogenous* along with other factors, which became viewed as the *external environment* of marketing. Other external factors (environments) included not only the consumer but also competition and legal, ethical, physical, technological, and social factors.[11]

Resourceness, however, is often about access. Consider again the fisherman and the farmer; neither owns or controls the biosphere, but both have access to the climate it provides, and the knowledge and skills to draw upon it are invaluable resources to both. Similarly, the firm with the trucking fleet uses the interstate highway and local highways as resources – clearly resources that are not internal to or owned by the firm for which access is available. Likewise, consider the legal and justice system in society; consider the educational system that can be a source of support; consider the insurance, banking, and finance markets. All of these enable actors to access resources they would not otherwise be able to access and to use and integrate more resources with other resources; thus, resourceness is enhanced through accessness.

Market, public, and private resources

Another useful way to think of resources is in terms of a market venue. A *market-facing resource* is one that can be exchanged in the marketplace, and thus one to which the actor can gain access by the exchange of service rights.

There are resources that could be obtained via the market but that organizations decide to keep from market exchange. For example, many firms would not be willing to employ a CEO as a day laborer whom they purchase in the market on a regular basis, but rather firms enter into a long-term employment contract that makes the CEO service(s) not subject to daily market exchanges. In general, as they grow in size, organizations increasingly avoid many markets for resource exchanges because of the high transaction costs of market exchange.[12]

In contrast with market-facing resources, there are resources that are not exchanged in the market. Two primary types exist: public and private. A *public resource* is a tangible or intangible resource that government or quasi-government entities provide to general or specifically designated members of society and often includes resources such as fire and police protection, national defense, government legislative and judicial service, education, health care, parks and recreational areas, and many others. A *private resource* is a tangible and intangible resource that is exchanged via social exchange networks and includes such resources as social favors, personal advice, or friendship.

Importantly, it is not the resource *per se* that determines whether it is public or private. For example, many of the public resources identified above can be obtained in the market, such as hiring a security guard or an arbiter to handle a commercial or civil dispute between actors. They could also be obtained as private resources via social exchange. Conversely, some governments may outsource certain service to the market, such as charter schools. But then again, for some actors, this could become a private resource, such as when households decide to home school their children. More likely, what determine whether the resources are public, private, or market facing are social institutions. Thus, in some societies, health care, childhood education, and sometimes a college education are provided by the government, whereas in other countries, they are provided primarily through the market or via social (private) exchange.

In economic theory, one type of public resource is referred to as a "public good." A public good is one that is nonrival and nonexcludable. Nonrivalry means that "consumption" of the good by one actor does not decrease availability of consumption by another actor. Nonexcludable means that no actor can be prevented from access to the good. Actors often take this type of public good and integrate it with other resources. For example, if there is a dramatic sunset one evening and the climate is moderate, an actor might integrate this into a family dinner on the backyard patio.

Note also that public resources, though not provided through the market mechanisms, may involve an indirect service-for-service exchange. Consider an actor who earns a wage by providing service for an organization and pays part of this in taxes, thus giving up some of his or her service rights. In turn, the government uses the tax revenue to provide service(s) for the public or citizens. This is done through government service organizations but also often by the transfer of service rights to another individual, such as the payment of a monthly stipend to a person living in poverty. In national accounting systems, this is often referred to as "transfer" payments, in which cash (service rights) is collected from certain classes of citizens and the service rights are transferred to other citizens. This is also called redistribution, a form of exchange that was discussed in Chapter 5.

Actors as resource integrators

With the possible exception of the idea that economic exchange is primarily concerned with and can be explained in terms of the exchange of output, perhaps no other conceptualization is as detrimental to an understanding of economics and markets as the related notions of "producers" and "consumers." Think about the implications of this conceptualization: one actor creates (produces) value, and the other actor destroys (consumes) it. Thus, the model of the economy becomes one of a continuous cycle of the creation of stuff, the marketing of stuff, the destruction of stuff, and thus the necessity for, and economic growth defined in terms of, the creation, marketing, and destruction of more and more stuff. Is it any wonder that sustainability issues are a central concern and increasing topic of conversation?[13]

Furthermore, this conceptualization implies that economic activity results in something of a consumptive black hole, in which "consumers" are merely benefiting from others' value-creation activities, rather than participating in their own and others' value creation. This is a very restricted view of the economic (and social) world. As we implied in Chapter 5, an entrepreneur, a salesperson, a customer, the head of a household, a carpooling parent, a grocery shopper, and a restaurant patron are not fundamentally different kinds of actors; they are all just people going about the business of their daily lives and trying to improve them through service exchange. Often, quite literally, they are the same person.

As we suggested in Chapter 2, the concept of a production–consumption divide did not occur because some process of scientific, economic discovery identified the true nature of economic exchange; rather, it grew somewhat more incidentally, as an unintended result of the work of Adam Smith in his attempt to define the process through which a nation could increase its wealth in the context of the world of 1776.[14] Given the limitations in communication and travel and the beginning of what later would be called the Industrial Revolution, he identified the essential national-wealth-creation process as the manufacture and export of surplus tangible goods. He labeled the activities that created surplus tangible goods for export "productive," though he fully acknowledged that other activities (e.g., the work of the military, doctors, and lawyers) were just as essential to human and societal well-being as manufacturing; they just did not contribute directly and meaningfully to national wealth creation through international trade, his primary concern.

Also, as we discussed in Chapter 2, the economic philosophers who followed Smith took exception to this limited meaning of "productive" but, having objected, typically acquiesced and accepted Smith's productive protocol.[15] As a result, *products* (goods), the output from this productivity, eventually became the center of economic thought. Smith also talked about "consumers," though not quite in the way they are now conceived as end users. Rather, he used "producer" and "consumer" somewhat casually as abstractions, and the relationship between these two abstracted actors in the "division of labor" was more of a circular one. That is, producers and consumers were not characteristically different kinds of actors with a unidirectional relationship, but rather represented the *joint characterizations of all actors* involved in exchange relationships[16] – in other words, all were, at the same time, "producers" and "consumers." By implication, producers and consumers were distinguishable only from the limited perspective of a particular actor, in terms of a particular benefit provided and obtained through the division of labor.

Resource application

So, if the notion of producers and consumers engaging in selling and buying does not capture the nature of resource allocation and integration, what does? From an S-D logic perspective, it is the common role of *service provider*, but it goes deeper than that. In S-D logic, service is defined in terms of applied resources. Unlike the resources typically associated with goods and neoclassical market logic – relatively fixed properties of usually tangible things, or operand resources – the driving resources in S-D logic are human skills and capabilities, or operant resources, even when operand resources are involved. These resources are *contextual*. That is, their *resourceness* is contingent on the availability of other resources, as well as the purpose at hand – an automobile only becomes a transportation resource in the presence of fuel, a road system, driving ability, maintenance knowledge, and the (at least prospective) need to go somewhere. Resources, as explained previously in this chapter, are also *dynamic*, suggesting that potential resources can be combined with other potential resources in infinite ways to create new resources and, in the process, new contexts. Consider the process of education, which provides foundational life and career resources through the combination of an infinite array of existing knowledge and, in the process, creates new knowledge and abilities. In turn, this dynamic and contextual nature of resources implies that they are created and become useful through integration, and thus, at their core, *all economic and social actors are resource integrators*, as foundational premise 9 of S-D logic suggests.

This resource-integrator conceptualization has several implications for understanding value creation and exchange and thus is foundational to the understanding of other aspects of S-D logic. First, it provides a necessary framework for comprehending the meaning of value *cocreation*. In a G-D logic world, one economic actor creates goods (tangible or intangible) and value simultaneously, and the other consumes both, also simultaneously. In an S-D logic and resource-integration world, the implication is that no one actor has all the necessary resources to create value; rather, value creation is a joint function of the service provision of multiple actors, as integrated by the beneficiary. Thus, resource integration provides the means for the *development of competences* used in service provision, both for the actors themselves and for others.

As discussed, these specialized sources of potential resources are classified as market, public, and private resources. Consider what seems at first to be a simple exchange of money for a new automobile. However, along with ownership and use of the automobile comes the need for other market resources, such as insurance, automobile maintenance, petroleum, and perhaps the purchase of things such as a GPS device, window shades, and so forth. The actor would also need to integrate *private resources*, such as personal driving skills and knowledge of the road and destinations, as well as resources of family and friends, such as suggested destinations and information about traffic conditions. Finally, *public resources*, such as a system of roads, laws governing driving behavior, and a stable monetary system that provides for easy market exchange, would need to be uniquely integrated by the focal actor to create value in a particular value cocreation instance, such as transportation. Thus, all the actors involved become cocreators of value. This is clearly different not only from the idea of a producer creating and delivering value but also from the conceptualization of value cocreation as merely the interaction of two actors (firm or producer and customer).

Dual purposes of resource integration

Broadly speaking, resource integration accomplishes (or at least potentially accomplishes) two related purposes. First, it *cocreates value* for the resource-integrating actor (e.g., individual, organization); that is, it makes possible or enriches life (increases system viability) for the actor. Second, it *creates new potential resources* for use as a form of *currency* (sometimes exchanged for monetary currency) for exchange with other actors. Exhibit 6.3 shows this dual process schematically.

To illustrate, again consider education. A student attends a state university and acquires a full range of potential resources (e.g., knowledge) through service exchange with professors (partly market-facing, partly public resources), facilities (e.g., classroom, library, Internet) utilization (public resources), and dialog

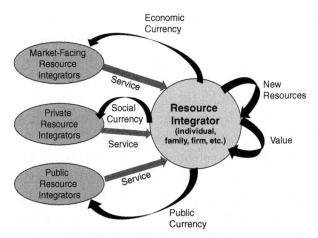

Exhibit 6.3 Resource integration

and other forms of shared learning with fellow students (private resources), as well as his or her own knowledge (private resources). The student then integrates these resources in ways unique to his or her life goals, understanding, available resources, and other contextual-specific conditions to create new potential resources that improve his or her life (i.e., increases system viability) – that is, to make future learning easier, to be used for setting future goals, and so forth. Also created are potential resources the student (1) can use for employment (economic currency), for volunteer work (social currency), or to pay taxes to support public infrastructure, legal institutions, and so forth (economic and public currency); or (2) can use in social exchange with fellow students, friends, and family (social currency). Of course, the university is doing the same thing: integrating resources obtained through market, public, and private service exchange not only to cocreate value for the organization but also to create additional resources to be used in future service exchanges, such as education, service, and research. In short, it is through the process of resource integration that value is cocreated in service exchange and that competences are formed for use in future service exchange and, thus, additional resource acquisition, ad infinitum.

Density

As we discussed in Chapter 4, combined with the notion of resource integration, as shown in Exhibit 6.3, and combined with Exhibit 3.4, the A2A network can actually be viewed as a network between two resource-integrating actors, or RIA2RIA. From this zoomed-out, broadened perspective, the resource-integrating actor (RIA) that is the focal actor (firm) is truly a *focal* actor, in that its role is to integrate resources from a full range of other RIAs to bring the necessary, combined resources to bear (focus them) on another RIA's ("customer's") particular needs through service provision. But this service provision is seldom (if ever) sufficient. The beneficiary must also find other resource integrators, most importantly itself, for the "right" concentration and configuration of resources to address a given problem.

Also, as we discussed in Chapter 5, Richard Normann called this configuration of resources "density"; it reaches a maximum when the *right* combination becomes the *best* possible combination and configuration of resources at a given time and place for a particular actor.[17] Consequently, this might be thought of as a generalized form of what has become customary thinking about the output of production (i.e., a product), but without all the G-D connotations. That is, in general terms, the firm (and other economic and social actors, including the "customer") integrates resources that have resourceness and accessness, to create densities of resources to be used in value cocreation through service provision, thus giving them access to additional resources for other cocreative purposes.

The contextual nature of the density – what we referred to as "value-in-context" – should also be evident. That is, the resources necessary for one RIA (e.g., firm) to create density for another RIA are contingent on the resources available to the second RIA (e.g., customer), as discussed previously. Of course, the second RIA is also creating density for the first RIA. Part of this density is created through the use of money (indirect service provision), but it is also created through activities (e.g., self-service) and participation in brand communities and so on, all of which are contextual. Finally, the cocreative nature of value should also be evident, as noted. This is more than just the interaction of two RIAs (firm–customer); it involves the whole complex network of RIAs (market, public, and private), also as discussed.

At a cost, therefore, this networked and contextual perspective provides a richer picture of exchange than the more traditional perspective. The cost is in the additional complexity, messiness, and fuzziness in the discussion of market activity, such as transactions, exchanges, relationships, and value creation, and even in the meaning of "markets" themselves, to say nothing of the disciplines – such as economics, marketing, and sociology – that study them. The purpose of these disciplines, as well as their core concepts, is to simplify the complex, rather than to complicate what has been treated simply.

Concluding comments

Perspective makes a difference. Logics offer lenses that can reveal quite different world perspectives. We argue that this is the case with S-D logic, and the S-D logic perspective of resources is paramount in this regard. The S-D logic view of resources is that they are a function of human appraisal.

In this chapter, we have expanded the view of resources beyond static tangible matter. We have explained that resources are anything that actors can draw on for support, and thus resources are inherently dynamic as actors obtain the knowledge and skills to convert latent or potential resources into actualized resources. These resources include intangibles and things external to the actor. Resources are central to service-for-service exchange because actors use their applied resources to exchange service with other actors.

To facilitate this exchange, markets were a clever human invention to enable actors to be more specialized in knowledge and skills. However, market exchange does have limits, especially because many resources are not market facing. Furthermore, the use-value of a resource is always in combination, configuration, and integration with other resources. Many of these other resources are non-market facing, both public and private. Resource integration within the A2A network both results in the cocreation of value among and between actors and the creation of new resources. Because this occurs in a dynamic and evolutionary A2A network, actors attempt to be effective and efficient at resourceness and accessness, which can lead to greater density that, in turn, may result in enhanced system viability.

NOTES

1. Eric J. Arnould, "Service-dominant logic and resource theory," *Journal of the Academy of Marketing Science*, 36 (Spring 2008), 21–24.
2. Erich W. Zimmermann, *World Resources and Industries* (New York: Harper & Row, 1951); Thomas R. De Gregori, "Resources are not; they become: an institutional theory," *Journal of Economic Issues* 21:3 (1987), 1241–1263.
3. Zimmermann, *World Resources and Industries*, p. 15.

4. Resourceness is referred to by Zimmermann, *World Resources and Industries*, as resourceship.
5. Zimmermann, *World Resources and Industries*.
6. Zimmermann, *World Resources and Industries*; Constantin and Lusch, *Understanding Resource Management*.
7. Edmund McGarry, "The propaganda function in marketing," *Journal of Marketing*, 23 (October 1958), 131–139.
8. De Gregori, "Resources are not."
9. Michaela Haase and Michael Kleinaltenkamp, "Property rights design and market process: implications for market theory, marketing theory, and S-D logic," *Journal of Macromarketing*, 31:2 (2011), 148–159.
10. Jerome McCarthy, *Basic Marketing: A Managerial Approach* (Homewood, IL: Richard D. Irwin, 1960).
11. Robert Holloway and Robert Hancock, *Marketing in a Changing Environment* (New York: John Wiley & Sons, 1968); Robert J. Holloway and Robert S. Hancock, *The Environment of Marketing Behavior: Selections from the Literature* (New York: John Wiley & Sons, 1964).
12. Ronald H. Coase, "The Nature of the firm," *Economica*, 4:16 (1937), 386–405; Oliver E. Williamson, *Markets and Hierarchies: Analysis and Anti-trust Implications* (New York: Free Press, 1975).
13. For an extended discussion on this topic, see Stephen L. Vargo and Robert F. Lusch, "It's all B2B and beyond ... toward a system perspective on the market," *Industrial Marketing Management*, 4:2 (2011), 181–187.
14. Adam Smith, *An Inquiry into the Nature and Causes of the Wealth of Nations* (London: Printed for W. Strahan and T. Cadell, 1904 [1776]).
15. John Stuart Mill, *Principles of Political Economy* (London: J. P. Parker, 1848); Jean-Baptiste Say, *A Treatise on the Political Economy* (Boston: Wells & Lilly, 1821).
16. G. Gilbert, "Production: classical theories," in John Eatwell, Murray Milgate, and Peter Newman (eds.), *The New Palgrave Dictionary of Economics* (New York: Stockton Press, 1987), p. 991.
17. Richard Normann, *Reframing Business: When the Map Changes the Landscape* (Chichester, UK: John Wiley & Sons, 2001).

7   Collaboration

I'm a great believer that any tool that enhances communication has profound effects in terms of how people can learn from each other, and how they can achieve the kind of freedoms that they're interested in.

Bill Gates

Introduction

The mantra that emerged in the 1950s about firms needing to be customer oriented and the mantra of the past two decades about firms needing to be society oriented are often viewed as signs of the enlightenment of senior executives and managers. They could also be viewed as signs that the traditional model of the firm, or goods-dominant (G-D) logic, was broken and in need of patching and repairing to make it at least resemble a workable model. Think for a moment: to assert that firms need to be customer oriented acknowledges that the customer is something separate and different and requiring special orientation. Similarly, having a special office or senior "C- level" officer of corporate social responsibility acknowledges that the organization is not so oriented. In brief, the customer and society are seen as exogenous or "out there," and the firm needs to reorient toward them. However, in the context of G-D logic, the underlying rationale for this orientation is that the firm can push product and agenda to actors. This push model is based on designing production and distribution systems to be as efficient as possible through standardized processes[1] to supposedly deliver value to customers in containerized packages of multi-attribute bundles of tangible and intangible elements characterized as products. Predictably, with this push model, the firm must use heavy doses of advertising and promotion to convince customers and other stakeholders that its agenda is in their best interests.

With such a firm-centric model, business, primarily over the past 200 years, embraced a perspective that considered itself separate from suppliers and "consumers," as well as from competitors, science, technology, legal and political institutions, culture, economy, and society. However, because these actors and resources were all exogenous to the firm, they needed to be somehow navigated around or managed by the organization. In comparison, service-dominant (S-D) logic has an inherent integration perspective that treats the interaction, exchange, and cocreation with actors as integral. That is, S-D logic recognizes that value creation is a collaborative process.

Actor-to-actor collaboration

How can actors in an A2A network collaborate, coproduce, and cocreate for mutual gain? They do so by developing social practices that contain sets of rules, procedures, and/or methods for meaning making and acting. These practices develop, often over a long time, to enable actors in an A2A network to coordinate their meaning making, actions, and behaviors for mutual gain through service-for-service exchange. They also help us understand how value is cocreated and, more broadly, how markets are cocreated through practices. These practices are representational practices, normalizing practices, and integrative practices, as Exhibit 7.1 displays.[2]

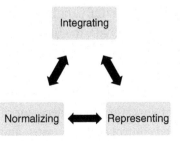

Exhibit 7.1 Cocreation of markets through practices

Representational practices

Communication is the transmission and interpretation of symbols and signs cast in relational statements. One of the cleverest human solutions (innovations) was language. Language helped standardize the relational statements used in communication and thus was an effective and efficient way for relationship between actors to emerge and proliferate, which led to the rise of cocreation practices and systems. Consider, for example, the dictionary or the thesaurus, both of which offer sets of relationships – here, words are equated or made equivalent to sets of other words. Language is a cocreation mechanism because it has no value unless it is used, and when it is used, other actors become involved; hence language is always about cocreation.

Consider, for example, explaining or discussing something with another actor and having that actor ask a series of questions, such as "What do you mean by that word or phrase?" Although dictionaries essentially provide statements of equivalence, when actors use words their meanings might not be clear. The other actor may not know the definition, or the use of the word may mean something different depending on the contextual usage. Thus if language is to be effective the meaning of words (signs) is always cocreated. Essentially, human actors create a resource when they develop and use language. This language becomes an appliance or, more generally, a medium to facilitate service-for-service exchange. As Löbler suggests, signs and practices coordinate service relationships.[3]

Language is therefore a type of innovation, enabling more communication that, in turn, fosters more human collaboration and cocreation. However, throughout history, humans have regularly developed improved communication capabilities and service. Consider briefly the history of the thousands of "clever" communication solutions that human actors have developed over time: between 3500 and 2900 BC, the Phoenicians developed an alphabet, Sumerians developed cuneiform writing, and the Egyptians developed hieroglyphic writing; in 900 BC, the first postal service appeared in China; between 500 and 170 BC, light-weight writing surfaces appeared in the form of papyrus rolls; by 100 AD, the first bound book emerged; 1455 witnessed the Gutenberg Press; in 1855, Samuel Morse developed a wireless code, and Alexander Bain invented the fax machine; in 1925, television signals were transmitted for the first time; 1969 witnessed the ARPANET (Advanced Research Projects Agency Network), or the predecessor of the Internet; and in 1994, the US government released control of the Internet, and the World Wide Web was born. All these inventions were appliances or media that helped human actors develop and use their applied specialized skills and knowledge to provide service to others (or themselves).

The media specifically enhance representational practices that foster collaboration that is vital to service-for-service exchange. Representational practices represent markets and service offerings; you can think of these representations as images of schema that actors develop. These representations influence and/or create service exchange and markets and much of this is via media. As service exchange and markets are fostered, we find, as Marshall McLuhan observed, "all media work us over completely."[4] The media make us who we are as actors because of representational practices or how actors re-present things in terms of images. Kjellberg and Helgesson pay particular attention to how representational practices contribute to how actors depict markets and their workings.[5] The representational practices contribute to form or shape the market and thus are another illustration of performativity. Or consider that "the meaning of a message is the change which it produces in an image,"[6] and because this image is created, it in turn changes the behavior of the actor. This is what McLuhan's insight – that the media work us over completely – conveys. It also suggests the dynamic nature of markets.

Normalizing practices

Many practices are normalizing in that they develop guidelines or parameters for A2A interfacing. Examples include institutions, such as conventions, social norms, and laws. For example, consider the convention of driving on the right- or left-hand side of the street, the norm of reciprocity (provides a guideline that insures repeated exchange), or the laws dealing with contracts or rights (provides guideline for responsibilities and access). In all cases, normalizing practices are a shorthand way to harmoniously coordinate actors for effective and efficient functioning.

Normalizing practices can include public policy about competition, or industry norms of fair competitor behavior, or perhaps voluntary codes of ethics. Normalizing practices can also include the objectives and goals that actors establish.[7] Various models of the firm, business planning, accounting controls, and so forth, all influence these practices.

Normalizing practices often include standardized ways of performing a job (e.g., the procedures a surgeon undertakes to prepare for surgery) or standardized ways of making a product form (e.g., a four-wheel passenger vehicle). Normalizing job practices provide established protocols for performing tasks and processes, which also lower coordination efforts. Standardized parts enable interchangeability of parts, which is something standardized jobs also do because, in both cases, parts or actors can be exchanged and the system will still function similarly. In either case, collaboration is easier.

Modular architecture can be thought of as a normalizing practice. Modularization is a means of parts and job standardization. Within each module, all kinds of arrangements between parts can exist, but the way the integrated system of parts interfaces as a module with other modules or a platform is standardized or normalized. Thus, the interaction between modules is highly fixed or structured (i.e., normalized), in turn lowering coordination effort and costs. Essentially, the higher the modularization, the easier it is for service exchange to occur between actors. The extent of the market is a function not only of the division of labor (specialization of human actors in skills, knowledge, and competences) but also of the extent of modularization.[8]

Integrative practices

As discussed in Chapter 6, human actors constantly integrate market resources with private and public resources to cocreate value. They do so through the exchange of service but also often indirectly through economic, social, and public (taxation) currency. Many integrative practices are hidden from view because they become tightly intertwined with representational and normalizing practices. For example, when traveling to work or to shop, you are integrating resources, including public or private transportation, traffic laws and regulations, driving norms, music or news, conversation with passengers, and public or private parking. Similarly, a meal at home with your family can involve integrating store-purchased food, homegrown food, cooking appliances, tableware, table etiquette, prayer, conversation, or perhaps music, and skills and expertise of different family members in preparing, serving, and cleaning up the food.

A large part of integrative practices is exchange practices,[9] or the concrete activities related to the consummation of individual economic exchange. This broad range of activities includes merchandising, advertising, logistics and distribution, price negotiation, and credit policies. However, these activities also include the exchange practices of actors in their role as customer or buyer, such as saving, shopping, transporting, storing, sharing, negotiating, and so forth.

Finally, specialization, or the unbundling of skills and knowledge by actors, creates more opportunities for density creation. As unbundling occurs the specialized resources can be moved and reintegrated into other resources and hence become a service-exchange offering. Assemblage theory views components or entities as sometimes decoupling from an assemblage and recoupling with a different assemblage.[10] As we will explain next, some of this unbundling and rebundling, or decoupling and recoupling, is being leveraged and enhanced through information technology.

Collaboration and information technology

A significant factor, perhaps a meta-force,[11] in lowering effort and costs associated with collaboration has been the liquefaction of information resources brought about by information technology.[12] Historically, many of the coordination problems with trade and exchange occurred because information was embedded in physical structure and thus could only move at the speed at which the physical matter could be transported. Initially, the physical structures, such as stone, used to embed information were quite heavy, resulting in even more burdensome efforts to transmit or transport information.

As information was embedded in lighter materials (e.g., paper) and then ultimately separated from physical matter, digitized, and transported through the electromagnetic spectrum at the speed of light, the movement of information required less effort, and human collaboration problems decreased. However, this was only a momentary condition, because liquefaction enabled more resources to be unbundled, rebundled, integrated, and created, resulting in additional need for collaboration by humans.

Early on, scholar Roland Rust demonstrated that the advance of information technology was one of the key events accelerating the necessity for a shift to S-D logic from G-D logic.[13] Seven key reasons explain why information technology (IT) growth has enabled the rise of service-provisioning networks – what we refer to in Chapter 8 as service ecosystems – that are consistent with S-D logic principles. These are as follows:

(1) Tangible goods have become embedded within microprocessors and intelligence and thus can become platforms for service provision. This includes digital manufacturing, start/smart parts that embed intelligence, collaborative design through virtual modeling, idea generation through virtual conference rooms, and product life-cycle management to support liquefaction.

(2) The ability of actors to serve themselves increases with advances in IT.

(3) The ability to serve other actors increases with advances in IT.

(4) As the ability to communicate between actors, between goods and actors, and between goods and goods increases, the need for transport declines.

(5) Actors can get to know each other better as the ability to communicate increases.

(6) Actors can interact directly with other actors as many-to-many communication networks rise.

(7) As the ability to communicate at lower cost increases, the collaboration between actors becomes more efficient and effective.[14]

In summary, individually and collectively, these key factors enable resources to be better integrated through improved communication, collaboration, and cocreation.

Information technologies and the digital revolution, including the spread of the Internet, enable more and more actors and resources to be connected and more easily integrated. These increased interactions also stimulate (but do not cause) innovation. Three major factors further drive this trend: open standards, connectivity, and network ubiquity.[15]

Open standards

Open standards, such as in the open source code of LINUX, is not a new phenomenon. Perhaps the first emergence of open standards was language itself. Language enables actors to develop and share rules. As a result of open standards, information is increasingly symmetric as more information and experiences are shared by actors. As open standards increase, collaboration becomes the norm, not the exception, which in turn facilitates innovation.

Connectivity

For most of human civilization, actors did not have much information or knowledge about what other actors could do well and offer as a service. Even when, in principle, actors had this knowledge, large geographic distances between actors could only be overcome by relying on tangible resources being transported at high costs and with long time delays. As connectivity increased, and especially many-to-many communication networks, the exchange system could more quickly respond to actors' needs and capabilities. We have witnessed the market moving from being relatively fixed and static to something highly dynamic and flexible.[16] That is, we can view markets as configurations of market actors engaging in representational, normalizing, and integrative practices. As the actors engage in practices, they do so in a context that influences other actors, thus leading the markets to become perpetually dynamic.[17] Enterprises can use this to their advantage by helping to virtually organize user or beneficiary communities[18] so that they can cocreate the firm's value proposition.

Network ubiquity

A final factor driving collaboration is network ubiquity. Increasingly, all actors and all resources are directly or indirectly connected to one another, and this connection occurs every day and at all times of the day. Network ubiquity is a stimulator and accelerator of open standards and connectivity. In addition, because network ubiquity enables more service-for-service exchange, more specialization is witnessed. And with more specialization markets rise and there are further opportunities for value cocreation.

Because these trends are converging, it is reasonable that actors will be able to increasingly transform everything they do (i.e., all their activities and actions). As such, overcoming physical barriers, though important, may not be what halts or slows down transforming practices; rather, normalizing practices may be the barrier. Norms and societal institutions can define the resistance because of the continuing struggle for their maintenance. Many actors may consciously or unconsciously attempt to protect institutions even though they could benefit over a longer period from the decay of an institution and/or the emergence of a new institution.

The proactive mapping of service processes often reveals opportunities for collaborations for cocreating value among actors. Proactive mapping also makes it more evident where waste in the system is occurring or where waste in one part of the system can become a resource for another part of the system. It is important, however, to emphasize that current service blueprinting paradigms[19] should be expanded beyond the firm to what the beneficiary of the enterprise's service offering does with the offering, because the beneficiary integrates it with other resources to enhance its system viability.

Coproduction and cocreation

Collaboration is the central focus of S-D logic's second axiom: the customer is always a cocreator of value.[20] Cocreation has also become a central part of contemporary business and marketing literature[21] but most of what is thought

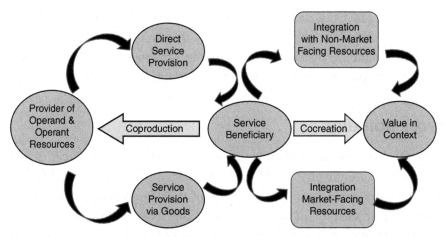

Exhibit 7.2 Coproduction and cocreation

of as cocreation is what is more accurately termed coproduction. Two important, related but conceptually distinct forms of collaboration are the *cocreation of value* and *coproduction*. Cocreation of value is the most encompassing, and nested within it is coproduction. Furthermore, cocreation of value always occurs and thus is not something that actors can opt out of or outsource; conversely, coproduction is optional for the actor. Exhibit 7.2 graphically illustrates these two forms of collaboration, but we expand on them in the remainder of this section to help explain their distinction.

Cocreation of value

The service beneficiary integrates a service offering with other market, private, and public resources and in the process the beneficiary determines value. This value is always value-in-use and occurs in a particular context (the right-hand side of Exhibit 7.2 displays value-in-context). It is important that this contextual value-in-use is always uniquely and phenomenologically *evaluated* by the beneficiary actor and is intertwined with the concept of experience (i.e., customer experience).[22] This is not to suggest that the unique actor is not influenced by others and institutions, but in the end it is the actor that does the evaluation (or assessment) of value.

The fact that beneficiary actors evaluate and experience value should not be confused with the notion that many actors and resources are involved in value cocreation. Value cocreation always resides at the intersection of all the actors and resources that are integrated, including resources and actors from both direct and indirect exchange.

Because value is not something one actor can create and deliver to another actor, a key opportunity for innovation is to identify novel ways to cocreate value. Understanding that the service beneficiary experience is dynamic and interactive can lead to new ideas for more compelling value propositions and service innovation.[23] This experience, or time phased unfolding, involves the service beneficiary integrating various other resources that are part of the experience. From this perspective, an offering involving a tangible good should be viewed in the broader context of resource integration. For example, when an actor picks out one item, such as a microwave oven, from all the other appliances, it becomes evident that the resources and experiences surrounding use of the microwave are a critical part of that actor's experiential value. By zooming out beyond the specific use of the microwave device, other actors and other resources become part of the context of value cocreation. This zooming-out process can provide insights into the beneficiary's experiential value and, in turn, become a source of ideas for innovation.

Coproduction

A second aspect of collaboration is coproduction, as the left-hand side of Exhibit 7.2 illustrates. In this situation, the service beneficiary is an active participant in the development of the value proposition. The service beneficiary can contribute operand and operant resources to help develop direct or indirect (through goods) service offerings. A common example is an actor as a service beneficiary helping to design a new tangible good that will offer more effective or efficient service provisioning. Other, simpler, examples include a service beneficiary advising the hairstylist about a particular hairstyle or a student asking the professor questions that, when answered, also help other students to understand. Many innovations have involved inviting the service beneficiary to be a coproducer. For example, in most supermarkets today, service beneficiaries move a shopping cart around the store, pick out groceries and other items without assistance from store staff, check out through electronic stations, and cart the groceries to their automobile or onto the bus or train to return home. This example can actually be taken a bit further. Most of the goods purchased at the grocery store seventy-five years ago were food ingredients that were then integrated at home to create a meal. However, the shopping bags of today include meals that are fully or significantly prepared and ready to be served. In this example, the home meal is less coproduced than it was seventy-five years ago, but significant aspects of the meal are still coproduced. Thus, actors as beneficiaries involved in coproduction are sometimes referred to as "prosumers",[24] and prosuming has been formally studied.[25] However, in S-D logic, using either a producer or consumer label or some combination is myopic. Actors perform a multitude of roles in their daily efforts at enhancing their system viability.

A variety of models capture the factors that determine how much an actor is engaged in coproduction. For example, Etgar offers a model based heavily on economics and examines the costs of the actor doing internal production versus the costs of exchanging with specialists to do the production.[26] Another, less formal model in terms of mathematics shows how six factors contribute to the extent to which a service beneficiary is an active participant or coproducer in a service offering.[27] A brief description of the six factors follows. To help explain the factors, we detail an example cast in terms of health care provided to an aged parent.

(1) *Expertise.* Actors are more likely to participate in coproduction when they have the requisite expertise. Expertise is an operant resource (see Exhibit 7.2). In the case of an aged parent who needs special medical assistance, you will be more inclined to provide the service if you have the needed expertise.

(2) *Control.* Coproduction is more common when actors want to exercise control over the service's process – that is, when the service beneficiary wants to codirect outcomes. Thus, when caring for an aged parent, you may want more direct control over his or her care and treatment and opt for home health care where you can provide the service.

(3) *Tangible capital.* Coproduction is more likely if actors have the requisite tangible capital to perform activities that contribute to the service offering. Tangible capital is an operand resource (see Exhibit 7.2). Thus, to care for an aged parent, you need space in your home, special beds, and other handling and treatment devices. Home health care becomes a more feasible option when these elements and devises are already available or can be bought/ rented.

(4) *Risk taking.* Coproduction involves tangible, psychological, and/or social risk taking. Thus, a service beneficiary as a coproducer could either increase risk or lower risk depending on the situation. When providing home health care, psychological effects on yourself or other family members could result. Even operating the equipment incorrectly could physically harm your parent or other caregivers or recipients.

(5) *Psychic benefits.* Actors primarily engage in coproduction for pure enjoyment or the psychic or experiential benefits. Here, precise separation between the cocreation of value and coproduction, as Exhibit 7.2 suggests, does not occur.

More specifically, the act of coproducing, such as assembling furniture or cooking a meal, may be a valued experience. Thus, by engaging family members in collaborating in the care of your aged parent, lifetime experiences having high value for you and your family members may ensue.

(6) *Economic benefits.* Perceived and actual economic benefits play a central role in coproduction. Actors often recognize the value of their time in alternative uses and find that spending time on coproduction compensates them well. The cost of health care for your aged parent is very expensive and could, over ten years, consume his or her entire financial assets. Performing these services yourself could lower estimated costs by 75 percent, leaving financial resources in your parent's estate for other uses or to pass along to your family.

These six factors also come into play when a service enterprise decides how to involve a service beneficiary in part of its value proposition to coproduce the service offering. For example, an enterprise that offers aged adult care could help family members perform some health care services by providing them with training and rental equipment. Involving service beneficiaries in coproduction increases the number of contact, interfaces, or touch points with them, helping form the basis of managing customer experiences.[28] Importantly, such actions can also become part of an integrated marketing communications program.[29]

Enterprise boundaries

The central issue discussed in this chapter is the togetherness versus separation of actors in an A2A network or system. However, if carried to the extreme, what results is an enterprise or actor's system with fewer boundaries. This prompts the question: "What are the boundaries of the enterprise?"

The conventional logic is that enterprise boundaries are determined by the exchange of market resources.[30] On the input side of the enterprise, this means the exchange of a wide variety of services with providers. These providers consist of creditors, shareholders, employees, raw material suppliers, and component and system providers who often exchange their offerings in financial markets, labor markets, material markets, and components and system markets. On the output side of the enterprise, market exchanges occur with intermediaries or, ultimately, service beneficiaries. These are known as intermediary or customer markets, such as wholesale and retail distribution or wholesale and retail markets. An additional service provider is the government, which gives the enterprise the license to operate and, in return, charges a tax on the economic flows of the enterprise, usually sales revenue or net profit. In this illustration, essentially exchange markets and value-in-exchange determine the boundaries of the enterprise. The enterprise thus is bounded by direct service providers and beneficiaries as captured through money, value-in-exchange, or service rights.

This view of the enterprise, as captured by direct economic exchange and flows, is narrow and short. The narrow view refers primarily to dyadic economic exchange (with service providers and service beneficiaries), and the short view focuses on the transaction as a single slice of time in the exchange process. Although value-in-exchange attempts to capture what an actor expects to receive in the future, it is still heavily grounded in the present or what has occurred. In an attempt to address this inadequacy, the area of customer lifetime value (CLV) emerged around a decade ago.[31] The CLV approach estimates economic transactions with service beneficiaries, the size of each transaction, the number of transactions, and for how long into the future they will occur. The net present value of these flows is then computed. Although CLV helps alleviate the short view, it does not alleviate the narrow view because it also focuses on direct economic exchange. In fact, it argues for enterprise value as the economic market capitalization of the enterprise or shareholder value.

In contrast with the narrow and short view, a broad and long view of the enterprise examines all stakeholders of the enterprise, including not only direct economic stakes but also indirect economic and social stakes in the enterprise. These actors include not only direct economic stakeholders but also other actors whose system viability is influenced by the enterprise not only presently but over time. This often occurs, for example, when an enterprise goes bankrupt or relocates from a community, with many actors that have been or will be harmed voicing their concerns. From this broad and long perspective, the enterprise is embedded in a larger system of resource-exchanging actors and resource-integrating activities that in turn argues for the value of the enterprise being much greater than the enterprise economic value (shareholder value).[32]

Another way to show a broad view of the enterprise is to take the direct economic stakeholders, zoom out, and examine the direct economic stakeholders of these stakeholders and then continue zooming out to additional tiers or layers of indirect stakeholders. Consider, for example, an auto assembly plant in a community and its direct economic exchanges. This plant has a supplier of front axles (i.e., wheel hanging service), which also has suppliers of steel (i.e., structural integrity service) and other resources, which also have direct economic stakeholders, and so on and so on. The direct economic effects of this illustration ripple through the economy and society. Exhibit 3.4 visualizes this process; the service-for-service exchange of the focal actors has a ripple effect on the other tiers of actors.

S-D logic examines not only market-facing resources but also non-market-facing resources, which include public and private resources and their exchange. S-D logic also treats all actors as both social and economic actors. Every actor, even those involved in market-facing economic exchanges, engages in an embedded system[33] of social norms and culture (i.e., normative practices). The embedded nature of exchange occurs not only among dyadic actors but also with far-removed tiers of actors. For example, when the auto assembly plant closes in a community, economic flows are not the only thing altered. So too is the way in which actors socially interface with one another, in turn influencing the relationships between actors. All these effects cast a long shadow into the future for the actors and their community.

In summary, the broad and long view of the enterprise defines its boundaries through both economic and social exchange with direct service-for-service actors and actor tiers that extend beyond the direct dyad of exchange. Determining the precise boundaries is a strategic choice by the enterprise. Its boundaries are largely a function of its worldview or systems view and how it tries to develop this view among a network of actors as a shared view. We discuss this in more detail in Chapter 8 on service ecosystems.

The enterprise needs to view service beneficiaries and service providers as a strategic choice. It also needs to engage with suitable service providers and service beneficiaries. Such beneficiaries are loyal and have resource-integrating activities and actor networks that are synergistic with the enterprise; suitable service providers are trustworthy[34] and reliable, have strong brands and reputations, and have resource-integrating activities and synergistic networks.[35] The enterprise must make a compelling value proposition and also must communicate and explain this value proposition to both potential direct service beneficiaries and the entire network of resource-providing stakeholders.[36]

Toward collaborative advantage

Collaborating with other actors by drawing on operant resources and service exchange, thereby obtaining mutualism[37] and positive sum collaborative relationships,[38] provides a collaborative advantage that can lead to competitive

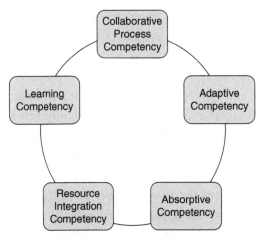

Exhibit 7.3 Sources of collaborative advantage

advantage and improved system viability. Exhibit 7.3 shows the five major sources of collaborative advantage: collaborative process competency, absorptive competency, adaptive competency, resource integration competency, and learning competency. We briefly describe each here.

Collaborative process competency

Collaborative process competency involves selecting the appropriate actors to collaborate with, developing a collaborative relationship, and successfully managing a collaborative process.[39] To accomplish this, the enterprise must have processes in place to monitor initiatives and resolve disagreements when they arise. Selecting actors that have the required operant resources (e.g., expertise, knowledge) and are open to solving problems and pursuing opportunities jointly is an essential aspect of collaborative process competency. This competency is learned and developed over time; it only arises when actors can better facilitate the exchange, synthesize relevant knowledge, resolve conflicts, and take part in joint decision-making.[40]

Absorptive and adaptive competency

Two sources enhance collaborative process competency, especially during times of turbulence and in complex and dynamic environments: absorptive competency and adaptive competency.[41] Absorptive competency[42] refers to how well or capably an actor comprehends trends in the environment and service ecosystem or absorbs new information and knowledge from other actors in the service ecosystem and especially those with whom he or she collaborates. By understanding environmental and service ecosystem trends and discerning information and knowledge about other actors, the actor can better envision ways to turn these trends, information, and knowledge into resources that can be drawn on for support. Often, this involves the ability to detect, comprehend, and then remove resistances to the collaborative process. Two common resistances are prior knowledge and institutions that, because of the dynamic change in the environment, may no longer be relevant or correct. However, actors often stick to what they know and resist change. Thus, developing strategies to overcome this stickiness to prior and outmoded knowledge and institutions is crucial.

Conversely, adaptive competency[43] refers to the actor's ability to adjust to changing circumstances.[44] Specialist actors that try to improve collaboration, coproduction, and cocreation may help expand the extent of service-for-service exchange through markets and networks, but specialized actors have trouble adjusting to change. Whether training a racehorse to run a specific race or refining the skills and capabilities of a specialized actor, as specialization rises, general adaptability is bred out or diminishes. Actors that exploit their specializations by continuing to refine them for improved efficiency and effectiveness do not learn new skills and competences and thus face survival challenges when turbulence and change manifest in the system.[45] For this reason, efficient enterprises develop less specialized work assignments and more collaborative and cross-functional work teams and facilitate these with more IT communication. With greater IT communication intensity, the enterprise becomes more adaptive.[46] This is because IT communication helps actors become more agile and flexible. Actors that are effective collaborators gain the added advantage of partnering with other actors to adapt to change. These other actors then become shock absorbers rather than sources of shock to the system.

Resource-integration competency

Resource-integration competency reflects the skills, knowledge, and expertise needed to integrate and combine resources in a way that increases density. Because an actor never has all the resources in his or her control or domain to obtain maximal density, collaborating with other actors to find synergistic and positive sum or win–win resource-integration opportunities produces advantage for all actors. However, to integrate resources, actors must first detect the possibility of combining resources and then comprehend how doing so can lead to novel service offerings.[47] Actors must also be able to transmit and exchange information, much of which can be tacit and nontransferable.[48]

Learning competency

A final source of collaborative advantage is learning competency. In a networked world (economy and society), learning almost always occurs with other actors, never alone. Part of the learning an actor must acquire is how to be a vital and sustaining part of the service ecosystem.[49] Every time an actor exchanges with other actors, it is bringing to the exchange some unique information and knowledge about how it can gain advantage.[50] Exchanges create changes in both the actor's system and those of other actors. As a result, the actor must always adjust its value propositions to changing circumstances and dynamic conceptions of beneficiary determined value. As the actor offers its value proposition and obtains feedback from other actors, it needs to treat this as a learning experience. Outcomes of economic and social exchange cannot be as anticipated and may be less positive or even negative, but this, too, represents a learning opportunity. If the actor embraces this learning orientation, it will develop better learning about other actors and, at some point, may be able to anticipate other actors and their service requirements. When this occurs, the enterprise will have a stronger collaborative advantage. In the past, knowledge was deemed the key to success; however, knowing is always primarily about what exists today or existed in the past. When the world is complex, dynamic, and turbulent learning becomes more important than knowledge. Learning renews knowledge to make it relevant to contexts today.

Implications for system viability

The focus of S-D logic on collaboration, or what in Chapter 4 we called "marketing with" other actors versus "marketing to" other actors, is a key pathway to improved system viability. The logic flow is straightforward[51] and is illustrated in Exhibit 7.4.

When adopting the market-ing-with (collaborative) philosophy, actors can better learn from one another. A key part of collaboration is collaborative communication or dialogue, which connotes learning together. Learning together allows for more effective and efficient accessness and resourceness.

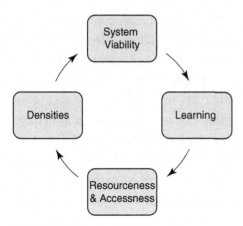

Exhibit 7.4 System viability

First, when actors collaborate with one another for mutual service exchange and benefit, (a) they can remove barriers and find opportunities for accessness and resourceness by better understanding how to integrate resources to create new resources and better serve one another, and (b) errors in service creation and provisioning decline. Learning together about increased opportunities for accessness and resourceness tends to increase effectiveness of the system. Furthermore, when errors decline, waste is reduced and effort or costs decline; in short, the system is more efficient. As a result of increased accessness and resourcesness coupled with reduced errors, resource "density" (see Chapter 5) increases and thus the viability of the system rises.

Concluding comments

When social and economic actors increase their specialization, they become more dependent on other actors for service. This service-for-service exchange results in a mutualism that helps create an interacting network of actors that, in turn, become society. During this process, actors have access to more resources but consequently need to engage in more resource integration. Actors living in this sea of other actors and resources spend a considerable amount of effort on collaboration for coproduction and cocreation of value, which is facilitated through representing, normalizing, and integrative practices.

Collaboration helps actors work together for mutual or non-zero-sum gain. Throughout the history of civilization, but especially with the relatively recent growth of powerful computational devices and the global Internet, collaboration between actors has risen. Such collaboration has enabled more coproduction and enhanced cocreation experiences. However, as more actors interact with one another through many-to-many networks, their actions and interactions change the context of other actors, increasing the dynamics and turbulence in the system. This makes the world more unpredictable for all actors. By taking an extended enterprise view of the system, actors can at least begin to anticipate change and control change. They can become more effectual actors. Being more effectual also involves leveraging connections with other actors and developing collaborative advantage by enhancing collaborative process competency, absorptive competency, adaptive competency, resource-integration competency, and learning competency.

Finally, collaboration enhances system viability. This occurs because collaborative communication and dialogue enhance learning. In turn, learning reduces service errors (creates more efficiency) and promotes better detection of resource integration and creation possibilities (rise in effectiveness). Essentially, collaboration leads to more accessness and resourceness. The interactive and cumulative result of all this is enhanced system viability.

NOTES

1. John Hagel III, John Seely Brown, and Lang Davison, *How Small Moves, Smartly Made, Can Set Big Things in Motion* (New York: Basic Books, 2010).
2. The first two practices were identified by Hans Kjellberg and Claes-Fredrik Helgesson, "On the nature of markets and practices," *Marketing Theory*, 7:2 (2007), 137–162.
3. Helge Löbler, "Signs and practices: coordinating service and relationships," *Journal of Business Market Management*, 4 (December 2010), 217–230; Helge Löbler and Robert F. Lusch, "Signs and practices as resources in IT-related service innovation," working paper, University of Arizona (2013).
4. Marshall McLuhan, *Understanding Media: The Extensions of Man*, critical edition, ed. W. Terrence Gordon (Berkeley, CA: Gingko Press, 2003, [1964]), p. 16.
5. Hans Kjellberg and Claes-Fredrik Helgesson, "On the nature of markets and practices," *Marketing Theory*, 7:2 (2007), 137–162.
6. Marshall McLuhan, *Understanding Media: The Extensions of Man*, critical edition, ed. W. Terrence Gordon (Berkeley, CA: Gingko Press, 2003 [1964]), p. 43.
7. Kjellberg and Helgesson, "On the nature of markets and practices."
8. Robert F. Lusch and Satish Nambisan, "Service innovation: a service-dominant (S-D) logic perspective," *Management Information Systems Quarterly* (forthcoming).
9. Kjellberg and Helgesson, "On the nature of markets and practices."
10. Manuel Delanda, *A New Philosophy of Society: Assemblage Theory and Social Complexity* (London: Continuum, 2006).

11. Yochai Benkler, *The Wealth of Networks: How Social Production Transforms Markets and Freedom* (New Haven, CT: Yale University Press, 2006).

12. Richard Normann, *Reframing Business: When the Map Changes the Landscape* (Chichester, UK: John Wiley & Sons, 2001); Robert F. Lusch, Stephen Vargo, and Matthew O'Brien, "Competing through service: insights from service-dominant logic," *Journal of Retailing*, 83:1 (2007), 5–18.

13. Roland T. Rust, "If everything is service, why is this happening now and what difference does it make?" *Journal of Marketing*, 68 (January 2004), 23–24.

14. Robert F. Lusch, Stephen Vargo, and Mohan Tanniru, "Service, value networks and learning," *Journal of the Academy of Marketing Science*, 38 (February 2010), 19–31.

15. Lusch, Vargo, and O'Brien, "Competing through service," p. 10.

16. Robert F. Lusch, Yong Liu, and Yubo Chen, "Evolving concepts of markets and organizations: the new intelligence and entrepreneurial frontier," *IEEE: Intelligent Systems*, Special Issue on Market and Business Intelligence, 25 (January–February 2010), 71–74.

17. Kaj Storbacka and Suvi Nenonen, "Markets as configurations," *European Journal of Marketing*, 45:1–2 (2011), 241–258.

18. Satish Nambisan, "Designing virtual customer environments for new product development: toward a theory," *Academy of Management Review*, 27:3 (2002), 392–413; Satish Nambisan and Robert A. Baron, "Different roles, different strokes: organizing virtual customer environments to promote two types of customer contributions," *Organization Science*, 21:2 (2009), 554–572.

19. Valarie Zeithaml, Mary Jo Bitner, and Dwayne D. Gremler, *Services Marketing*, 4th edn (New York: Irwin/McGraw-Hill, 2006).

20. A treatment of the historical roots of value co-creation (under the co-production label) is found in Rafael Ramirez, "Value co-production: intellectual origins and implications for practice and research," *Strategic Management Journal*, 20:1 (1999), 49–65.

21. Neeli Bendapudi and Robert Leone, "Psychological implications of customer participation in co-production," *Journal of Marketing*, 67 (January 2003), 14–28; C. K. Prahalad and Venkat Ramaswamy, *The Future of Competition: Creating Unique Value with Customers* (Boston: Harvard Business School Press, 2004); Venkat Ramaswamy and Francis Gouillart, *The Power of Co-Creation* (New York: Free Press, 2010).

22. Joseph B. Pine and James H. Gilmore, *The Experience Economy: Work Is Theater and Every Business a Stage* (Boston: Harvard Business School Press, 1999); Shaun Smith and Joe Wheeler, *Managing the Customer Experience: Turning Customers into Advocates* (Harlow, UK: FT Prentice Hall, 2002).

23. Adrian F. Payne, Kaj Storbacka, and Pennie Frow, "Managing the co-creation of value," *Journal of the Academy of Marketing Science*, 36 (Spring 2008), 83–96.

24. Philip Kotler, "Prosumers: a new type of consumer," *The Futurist*, 20 (September–October 1986), 24–28.

25. Chunyan Xie, Richard P. Bagozzi, and Siguard V. Troye, "Trying to prosume: toward a theory of consumers as o-creators of value," *Journal of the Academy of Marketing Science*, 36 (Spring 2008), 109–122.

26. Michael Etgar, "Co-production of services: a managerial extension," in Robert F. Lusch and Stephen L. Vargo (eds.), *The Service-Dominant Logic of Marketing: Dialog, Debate, and Directions* (Armonk, NY: M. E. Sharpe, 2006), pp. 128–138.

27. Robert F. Lusch, Stephen W. Brown, and Gary J. Brunswick, "A general framework for explaining internal vs. external exchange," *Journal of the Academy of Marketing Science*, 20 (Spring 1992), 119–134.

28. Smith and Wheeler, *Managing the Customer Experience*; Bernd H. Schmitt, *Customer Experience Management: A Revolutionary Approach to Connecting with Your Customers* (Hoboken, NJ: John Wiley & Sons, 2003).

29. Tom Duncan and Sandra Moriarty, "How integrated marketing communication's 'TouchPoints' can operationalize the service-dominant logic," in Robert F. Lusch and Stephen L. Vargo (eds.), *The Service-Dominant Logic of Marketing: Dialog, Debate, and Directions* (Armonk, NY: M. E. Sharpe, 2006), pp. 236–243.

30. Ronald Coase, "The nature of the firm," *Economica*, 4 (November 1937), 386–405; Oliver E. Williamson, *Markets and Hierarchies: Analysis and Antitrust Implications* (New York: Free Press, 1975).

31. Rajkumar Venkatesan and V. Kumar, "A customer lifetime value framework for customer selection and resource allocation strategy," *Journal of Marketing*, 68 (October 2004), 106–125.

32. Robert F. Lusch and Frederick E. Webster, Jr., "A stakeholder-unifying, co-creation philosophy for marketing," *Journal of Macromarketing*, 31:2 (2011), 129–134.

33. Mark Granovetter, "Economic action and social structure: the problem of embeddedness," *American Journal of Sociology*, 91:3 (1985), 481–510.

34. To be trustworthy does not imply that an actor is always transparent. Often, to be totally transparent may not represent a compelling value proposition since many actors want to be able to trust another actor but not know every single detail, which a transparent relationship would imply.

35. Lusch and Webster, " A stakeholder-unifying, co-creation philosophy"; Stephen L. Vargo, Paul P. Maglio, and Melisssa Archpru Akaka, "On value and value co-creation: a service systems and service logic perspective," *European Management Journal*, 26 (2008), 145–152; Stephen L. Vargo and Robert F. Lusch, "From repeat patronage to value co-creation in service ecosystems: a transcending conceptualization of relationship," *Journal of Business Market Management*, 4:4 (2010), 169–179.

36. Lusch and Webster, "A stakeholder-unifying, co-creation philosophy"; Vargo, Maglio, and Akaka, "On value and value co-creation"; Vargo and Lusch, "From repeat patronage to value co-creation in service ecosystems."

37. J.L. Bronstein, "Mutualism and symbiosis," in Simon A. Levin (ed.), *The Princeton Guide to Ecology* (Princeton University Press, 2009), pp. 233–238. Also, for a discussion of mutualism and other biological ecosystem concepts and how they apply to organizations see Matthew M. Mars, Judith L. Bronstein, and Robert F. Lusch, "The value of a metaphor: organizations and ecosystems," *Organizational Dynamics*, 41 (December 2012), 271–280.

38. Robert Wright, *Non Zero: The Logic of Human Destiny* (New York: Pantheon Books, 2000).

39. Zach Zacharia, Nancy Nix, and Robert Lusch, "Capabilities that enhance outcomes of a discrete supply chain collaboration," *Journal of Operations Management*, 29 (September 2011), 591–603.

40. Zacharia, Nix, and Lusch, "Capabilities that enhance outcomes of a discrete supply chain collaboration."

41. Lusch, Vargo, and O'Brien, "Competing through service."

42. Absorptive competency is based on the idea of absorptive capacity, in which competency reflects how well an actor can absorb new knowledge and information. For a discussion of absorptive capacity see Wesley M. Cohen and Daniel A. Levinthal, "Absorptive capacity: a new perspective on learning and innovation," *Administrative Science Quarterly*, 35 (March 1990), 128–152.

43. This term is also referred to as adaptation; see, e.g., B. S. Chakravarthy, "Adaptation: a promising metaphor for strategic management," *Academy of Management Review*, 7:1 (1982), 35–44.

44. Lusch, Vargo, and O'Brien, "Competing through service."

45. James March, "Exploration and exploitation in organizational learning," *Organizational Science*, 2:1 (1991), 71–87.

46. Wouter Dessein and Tano Santos, "Adaptive organizations," *Journal of Political Economy*, 114:5 (2006), 956–995.

47. D. Charles Galunic and Simon Rodan, "Resource recombinations in the firm: knowledge structures and the potential for Schumpeterian innovation," *Strategic Management Journal*, 19:12 (1998), 1193–1201.

48. Galunic and Rodan, "Resource recombinations in the firm."

49. Lusch, Vargo, and Tanniru, "Service, value networks and learning."

50. F. A. Hayek, "The use of knowledge in society," *American Economic Review*, 35 (September 1945), 519–530.

51. We obtained this basic insight partly through conversations with Len Berry and by listening to many of his lectures and talks on service experiences and service quality.

8   Service ecosystems

Our competitors aren't taking our market share with devices; they are taking our market share with an entire ecosystem. This means we're going to have to decide how we either build, catalyze or join an ecosystem.

Stephen Elop, chief executive officer of Nokia (2011)

Introduction

In Chapter 5, we introduced a systems view of actors and the cocreation of value to indicate how market exchange and economies function. Although actors exchange directly with one another, they are also part of many indirect and far-removed exchanges involving other actors that are also involved with this system. A systems view also extends to understanding the market. However, markets have historically been characterized as composed of "supply markets" and the movement of resources to customers, receivers, beneficiaries, or "customer markets,"[1] the latter being a source of demand.

Viewing the market as comprising supply and customer or demand markets is misleading and especially so when adopting a generic actor-to-actor (A2A) view of the economy. A supply market is only a supply market when viewing an actor as a seller (supply source or service provider), and a customer market is only a customer market when viewing another actor as a buyer (demand source or service beneficiary). As we have noted, however, all actors are both resource-integrating sources of "supply" and resource-integrating sources of "demand" – that is, offering service and taking on the role of service beneficiaries. Service-dominant (S-D) logic offers some useful conceptual tools for enhancing this macro lens.

Networks

The past couple of decades have witnessed the increased use of the network concept to describe the organization of economic (and social) activity across actors.[2] As we described in Chapter 5, all networks are created at the most elemental level by dyads of actors[3] that are linked together, though not necessarily through vertical or horizontal chains. This is because a network also includes triads of actors that G-D logic ignores. For example, in goods-dominant (G-D) logic, a vertical dyad would involve stages that link raw material and component suppliers to a manufacturer with a wholesaler or a wholesaler with a retailer, similar to links in a chain. Or it might involve a horizontal link, in which economic actors at the same business level in the supply chain (marketing channel) interact with each other, such as a local department store competing with another local department store. In S-D logic, *dyads* exist, but *embedded in triads* of actors that form a network.

Networks of actors are especially apparent as we move from a simple dyad of two actors to a triad of actors. In a triad, the beginning of a complex exchange network emerges. A triad exists when actor A exchanges with actor B and actor B exchanges with actor C, but C may also exchange with actor A. Consider, for example, a food wholesaler selling to a local chain of restaurants in which both the wholesaler and the chain of restaurants purchase accounting and business software from another firm. With an extended enterprise perspective, which zooms out to the second, third, and additional tiers of dyads and triads of actors and resources, a broader and more realistic perspective of the service exchange system emerges. The idea of zooming out from the dyadic exchange and chains of dyadic exchange to a service system offers a unifying perspective of markets, service, and exchange systems in general and hence in society.[4] Alderson recognized the importance of moving beyond a transaction as captured in a simple dyad and introduced the concept of a "transvection". He defined a transvection as "the unit of action for the system by which a single end product such as a pair of shoes is placed in the hands of the consumer after moving through all the intermediate sorts and transformations from the original raw materials in the state of nature."[5] Dixon and Wilkinson also recognized and contributed to a systems view of marketing and argued that marketing should be viewed in terms of a significant part of society.[6] S-D logic goes further and argues that the exchange of service(s) and all of its manifestations and emergent structures that result actually is society.

A manageable way to move beyond the dyad, but yet avoid the complexities of dealing with systems thinking, is to use the network concept. Predictably, the network concept is not new to either marketing[7] or supply chain management.[8] A supply network structure involves tiers of service providers from first-tier direct interactions to second-tier and beyond indirect interaction and similarly multiple tiers of service beneficiaries. Keep in mind that what is considered first and second tier and beyond is a function of the focal actor. For example, for a provider of apparel selling jeans to a department store, the department store would be a first-tier service beneficiary and the service beneficiary (customer) of the department store would be a second-tier beneficiary. In terms of the service network, the provider (manufacturing firm) would view the cloth provider as first tier, but if the cloth is purchased and already dyed, it would consider the firm that provides the dyes to be a second-tier service provider. However, if the focal actor is the dye provider, it has its own tiers of service (resource) providers and service beneficiaries, which in turn can reach forward to the actor who purchases the jeans from the department store. This example reveals that the actors making up a service network are all dependent on the context and the entity identified as the focal actor of the network in question.

Making the service network even more complex are the internal processes embedded in the tiers of service providers and service beneficiaries with which the focal actor is in an exchange (either directly or indirectly). For example, the inventory management process in the jeans scenario not only includes the fabricated jeans as they are produced, stored, and then shipped to tiers of beneficiaries but also the inventory of dyes, threads, cloth, zippers, buttons, and so on, that must be combined, configured, and integrated to create the jeans. Because S-D logic strongly emphasizes value-in-use and context, this process would also include the inventory of jeans in the closet or of the jeans' beneficiary.

In networks, many of the linkages or ties are weak,[9] which enable relatively unrelated actor networks to form a larger macro structure that can be more fluid, agile, and adaptable. Weak ties are also important in networks because they enhance opportunities that may not otherwise be evident; this is especially true when there is more open collaboration between actors,[10] which becomes an important pathway to innovation.

Ecosystems

The network concept captures much of the complexity of value cocreation but is still somewhat static. A network of actors, when mapped, informs us about connections and ties but not much about flows and exchanges between actors. We have found the systems concept is more amenable to the dynamic service exchanges that are so central to S-D logic. This increased dynamism and realism comes at the expense of an additional layer of complexity. However, this should not be avoided because systems are more reflective of human exchange, markets, and society and S-D logic strives for isomorphism. The concept of an "ecosystem" has begun to emerge in discussions of business, organizations, and economies and is quite useful to S-D logic thinking.[11] The concept comes from biology and zoology. Biological, or natural, ecosystems consist of loosely interconnected actors that are dependent on one another for survival; however, the dependency may not be direct or one-to-one but rather indirect. Each actor in the system cannot evolve in a vacuum because each must obtain resources from and, in so doing, shape the local environment of other actors.[12] Although competition for resources almost always occurs, cooperation in the sharing of resources is also common, as are other forms of win–win resource exchanges.[13] Coevolution is thus central in natural ecosystems.

Service (as defined in S-D logic), when coupled with the concept of an ecosystem, is very powerful. What, then, is a service ecosystem? A *service ecosystem is a relatively self-contained, self-adjusting system of resource-integrating actors that are connected by shared institutional logics and mutual value creation through service exchange.* Four elements (see Exhibit 8.1) help define a service ecosystem: (1) relatively self-contained, (2) self-adjusting system of resource-integrating actors, (3) shared institutional logics, and (4) mutual value creation through service exchange. Exhibit 8.2 also illustrates a service ecosystem but leaves shared institutional logics for subsequent discussion.

Relatively self-contained

In the biological world, all ecosystems emerge from the ground up through the interaction of individual species. These interactions tend to drop off quickly, and thus the ecosystem becomes relatively self-contained. These systems are not master planned, but rather each species focuses on solving a local survival

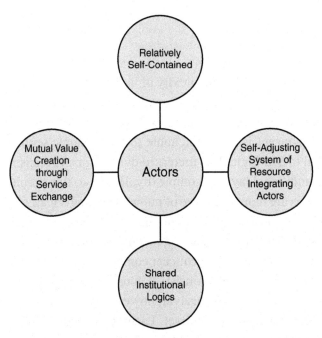

Exhibit 8.1 Key service ecosystem concepts

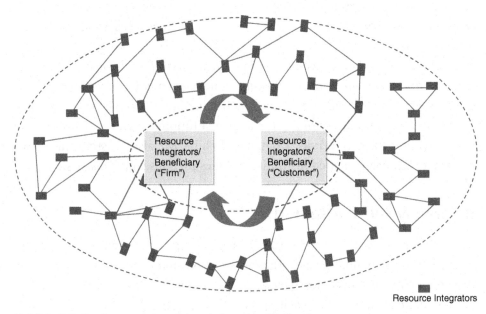

■ Resource Integrators

Exhibit 8.2 Service ecosystem (absent shared institutions)

problem. They do not attempt to determine an optimal solution but merely one that allows them to adequately solve the problem of survival. Stated alternatively, they regularly, if not continually, take action to adapt to the situation rather than trying to optimize their position in the system.

Similarly, if one maps a service ecosystem it appears complex and elegant, as if designed by a master planner, though this is most often not the case. As with biological ecosystems, most exchanges between actors in a service ecosystem are done to solve a local problem or pursue a local opportunity but tend to be repeated when successful. Over time, these A2A exchanges and interactions ripple through tiers of actors, resulting in the emergence of what is a relatively self-contained structure.

Service ecosystems are, however, also often nested within or are part of another, larger service ecosystem. For example, consider a household in which each family member, though part of the household service ecosystem, is also part of other, and often more divergent, service ecosystems. The same would be true of a business enterprise that is also nested in industry and extra-industry service ecosystems. The term "nested" actually confers (but does not guarantee) resiliency, and thus nested service ecosystems are slower to collapse from the removal of actors than other types of ecosystems.

The notion that these systems are relatively self-contained does not mean that they are healthy or functional or that they will persist and survive. Healthiness, functionality, and persistence under one set of circumstances (context) may not translate to another. A family, as a service ecosystem, may be healthy when it experiences high service-for-service exchange and service rights in the domestic habitat, but when the family moves to a foreign habitat (perhaps from a job transfer to another country), the functionality of the service system may dramatically change. In brief, the health of a service ecosystem is context dependent.[14] Furthermore, sometimes actors may not perform optimally even when the ecosystem is resilient. Consider again the family as a service ecosystem in which each family member is not optimizing his or her own individual well-being due to being constrained through representational, normalizing, and integrative practices as discussed in Chapter 7.

Self-adjusting system of resource-integrating actors

The actors in a service ecosystem are resource integrating. As we discussed in Chapter 6, actors integrate both market-facing and non-market-facing (public and private) resources. When integrating resources, actors often obtain resources from nested subsystems or overlapping systems, and thus they have an effect on at least part of these systems. Actors have some degree of agency, and this agency allows them to take actions that shape the ecosystem that others inhabit. Yet actors are also constrained to some degree by the ecosystem's existing structure, which is an important feature of these systems, as we discussed in Chapter 1.

A service ecosystem has a built-in ability to regulate itself through self-adjusting processes. An exchange between actors A and B not only changes actors A and B but also influences the other actors they connect with in other exchanges. This exchange ripples through the service ecosystem and allows actors to adjust to each other. In a service ecosystem, actors that have acute perception, learn relatively quickly, evolve more rapidly, and respond effectively to other actors are more viable.[15] It needs to be recognized, however, that in a service ecosystem that is not highly dynamic, such as one governed by dominant institutions, attempting to evolve too much in the direction of destabilizing the dominant institutions could be detrimental to the actor.

As with natural or biological ecosystems, service ecosystems have a spatial–temporal network structure. Actors are spread over space but also interact over time. Space can be both geographic and relational. For example, actors could occupy the same geographic space but be connected through relationships that form the structure of the system. However, when information requires little physical matter and when physical transport becomes quicker, the space and time dimensions begin to collapse. Actors can increasingly be at a time and a place where they are not physically present through, for example, advanced information technologies, such as virtual worlds. In addition, as simulations become more sophisticated, they enable actors to experience anticipated worlds – similar to modeling aircraft or automobiles on a computer and then crashing them virtually before the tangible product is produced.

An advantage of collapsing time and geographic space into a single dimension is that outsourcing opportunities expand for the typical actor. This means that actors can now be a part of a new or expanded service ecosystem. When transportation and communication were slow and costly, the economics of travel and communication ruled out many outsourcing options. Now consider the case of call center operators in India handling customer service for a firm in Dallas, Texas. Furthermore, telecommunication and transportation revolutions have led to the outsourcing of a host of other services, including engineering, architectural, medical screening, and accounting, to individuals or enterprises throughout the world. This has profound implications for the development of service ecosystems. As more specialized services are outsourced, opportunities emerge for niche actors to become vital, coevolving, and coproducing parts of a healthy service ecosystem.

In summary, the world is becoming increasingly smaller because all actors and things are now linked through advanced communication and transportation technologies. However, the world stays large because actors need to exchange with actors not only at close physical proximity but also at great geographic distances. Thus, most service ecosystems are part of a global village, which allows more density to be created. Increasingly, resources move to the time and geographic space of actors that can best take advantage of and use them. Nonetheless, density is always temporary, and thus both actors and service ecosystems must self-adjust or face lower system viability or extinction.

Resource-integrating actors can self-adjust because they are often loosely coupled with other actors and thus loosely connected with a service ecosystem that allows them relative freedom to exit and form exchanges with other actors and become part of other service ecosystems. When actors are loosely coupled, the speed of adaptation to changing circumstances increases. Actors that are agile and adaptable are better positioned for both survival and growth in the ecosystem. Consequently, actors must constantly learn how to better develop and use their resources for the benefit of other actors that also have changing needs and dynamic and changing perceptions of value. Actors tend to have difficultly adapting to changing value dynamics when the actors they exchange service with are constantly reevaluating and redefining value. Furthermore, as these service ecosystems become global and more complex, acute perception, agility, adaptability, and learning become even more critical to survival and growth.[16]

This logic applies not only to business enterprises but also to individuals or households. In many situations, individuals are no longer tightly coupled with enterprises at which for decades they were employed. On the contrary, individual human actors must view themselves as enterprises with unique and specialized competences that they can offer as compelling value propositions to other actors (individuals or enterprises). In addition, they can no longer rely on public resources (i.e., government) to provide all the education or training they may require to develop skills and competences. Continual learning is just as important for individuals as it is for the business enterprise.

Shared institutional logics

Service ecosystems need shared institutions (rules) to coordinate activities among actors and to function effectively. One such shared institution is language, which, historically, helped coordinate and facilitate exchange and interaction among human actors and later business transactions. Many of the operational problems in service ecosystems arise from basic breakdowns in natural language systems and the failure of actors to communicate with clarity and precision.

Representational practices as discussed in Chapter 7 play a key role in communication because they reflect shared schemas for viewing parts of the world. Consider that product forms and styles, as depicted through a set of related images, legitimize the market. They furthermore represent the market as an institutionalized solution to a problem. For instance, the US health care market is represented by physicians draped in white coats and holding medical instruments and removed from the patient whereas nurses are interfacing and caring for patients. This represents the health care market as an institutionalized solution that involves curing (doctors) and caring (nurses).

Many normalizing practices, as we discussed in Chapter 7, are important components of shared institutional logics of service ecosystems. These include values, norms, and governing principles that guide exchange transactions. Just as language differs, so too institutions can vary by geopolitical area and industry. For example, some countries and cultures highly value integrity and trust even when dealing with relative strangers, but, in other countries, integrity and trust are bound to a tighter network of friends and family. In some countries and cultures, the norm is to negotiate on price and terms of trade, but, in other countries, these terms are more fixed; this can also vary by industry. For example, it is common in the US market to negotiate aggressively for the best price on a new automobile, but this practice is not acceptable when purchasing clothes from a designer apparel store.

Governing principles can also vary. In some cultures and countries, virtually all agreements are codified in a written contract, whereas in other settings, the contract is a "soft" or implicit contract. The key challenge arising from global service ecosystems is that many cultures and industries are mixed, and thus discordant values, norms, and governing principles may be common.

As discussed in Chapter 7, actors in markets also have integrative practices that include tacit and explicit integration as well as exchange practices. Many of these are highly institutionalized and often invisible or taken for granted. For instance, teaching as a practice almost always draws upon a textbook or other books either in tangible form or online. These learning resources are actually the integration of many knowledge resources as they have developed over time and within an academic discipline. Exchanging practices may also involve resource integration. For example, in most countries the sale of a new automobile and many other market offerings is accompanied by a written or explicit warranty but also warranties of merchantability and fitness.

Because actors are part of different service ecosystems, often due to the different roles performed, they can face overlapping and sometimes conflicting practices and institutional logics. In some cases, this can create deleterious behavior, such as when a member of an organization is engaged in institutional logics resulting in normative goals that create actions that harm other actors in other service ecosystems. Consider, for example, the institutional logics that actors may confront working for a large US law firm and trying to make partner but at the same time being a single parent confronting the institutional logics of parenting. Conversely, being part of service ecosystems with different normalizing practices can also be a source of innovation as actors recognize novel ways to reframe practices. Consider, for example, the institutional logics that are part of hobbies (e.g., listening to jazz, gardening, mountain climbing, painting) and how these logics can stimulate creative ways of approaching various work practices.

Exhibit 8.3 illustrates a service ecosystem with shared institutional logics. This, for example, could be an institutional logic that characterizes the overall society within which the service ecosystem exists – perhaps the institution of individual freedom or a common religion. Recall that we introduced the concept of relational layers in Exhibit 5.3. When institutions are shared at a superordinate level, the actors that make up that system have a relationship. However, also note that some shared institutional logics may be shared just by a dyad of resource-integrating actors exchanging service. In addition, other shared institutional logics may be common, in which other actors are not necessarily directly involved in the service exchange, but share a common institutional logic.

Mutual value creation through service exchange

Because actors are loosely coupled and nested within service ecosystems, they must continually invite other actors to engage with and exchange service. They do this by making compelling value propositions that result in transactions. Thus, relationships precede transactions rather than vice versa, as commonly argued in most management and marketing thought.

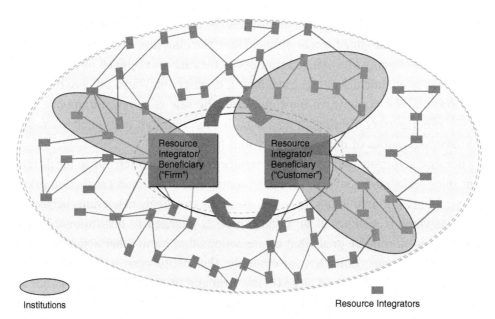

Exhibit 8.3 Service ecosystem

With the rise of global Internet communications, invitations to engage and exchange have few or no geographic limits and increasingly come from actors outside what has historically been viewed as the markets in which they operate. Virtually all actors are being challenged to develop more compelling value propositions of their service offering not only for service beneficiaries but also for the actors and other stakeholders from which they obtain service. Because value is beneficiary determined, and because this value is cocreated and involves the integration of many resources beyond what any single actor can provide, the challenge is difficult and complex. Furthermore, the outcomes of actor offerings and exchanges are never fully predictable because, in A2A networks, other actors are also shaping the context and environment. As we discussed previously, the service ecosystem is "structurated."

Although mutual value creation through service exchange is vital, invitations to engage in service exchange may be quite subtle and indirect. Normann, for instance, suggests "the fundamental process of leadership is that of interpreting a (continually evolving) context, formulating our notions of our own identity and the emerging new contextual logic into a set of 'dominating ideas' that are both descriptive and normative, and then translate these dominating ideas into various realms of action."[17] Consider, for example, the formal leader of an organization in a time of turbulence and perhaps chaos. The leader offers a compelling

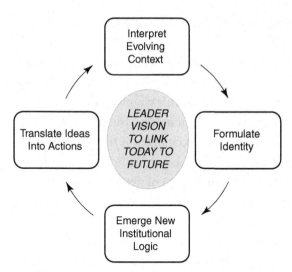

Exhibit 8.4 Leader vision linking today to future

vision of the organization that requires substantial change to its current institutional logic. This vision, if accepted, will help workers interpret their evolving role and formulate a new or modified identity for themselves around a new institutional logic. When this occurs for a large number of workers, the new institutional logic becomes shared, and the workers can provide service that aligns their skills and capabilities with the needs of the organization. As a result, the organization can make more compelling value propositions to potential beneficiaries of its market offering. If potential beneficiaries reciprocate by exchanging their service rights with the firm, the firm, in turn, can reward its workers with more service rights. This process is illustrated in Exhibit 8.4.

Micro, meso, and macro systems

Service ecosystems should not be viewed as one-dimensional or flat, micro-level structures of interacting and service-exchanging actors. Rather, service ecosystems are multi-level in nature. From the micro system a meso system emerges and from the meso system a macro system emerges. In turn, the macro system filters its way down to meso and micro systems and hence influences the actors in these systems.[18] All of this occurs over a time and geographic scale that will vary depending on the context and circumstances. The preceding processes also occur in a sea of change, making all of the systems inherently dynamic. We will now elaborate on the above description.

Service ecosystems begin with A2A interactions and service exchange or what comprises the micro level of the service system.[19] These interactions and exchanges are what we have primarily described in this chapter, with the exception of shared institutional logics, such as meso and macro structures, as we will discuss shortly. The A2A interactions and service exchanges as they cumulatively occur result in emergent structures at the meso level. For instance, emerging out of A2A service exchange at the micro level can be a set of actors that provide the service of market makers such as brokers and wholesalers or service rights intermediaries such as bankers and financial institutions or arbiters of disputes such as lawyers and courts. Also emerging may be a common place where the interactions and service exchange occur. These can be central cities or markets, districts within cities, or bazaars or trade fairs.

The meso level system in turn – as it functions over time – creates yet higher-level emergent structures, referred to as the macro system. The macro-level system is much more rigid, more stabilizing, and less subject to fluctuation. Stated alternatively, it self-adjusts but very slowly. Some of the structures that characterize the macro structure are common knowledge, long-standing and durable institutions, and rules (often tacit and implicit) for how the actors at the micro and macro level assemble into communities.

As we have illustrated, the micro helps to create the meso and the meso the macro but once the macro is structured it has a downward influence on the meso and micro levels. Consider, for instance, if the macro system consists of a common cultural system comprised of things like language, governance, and values. These then constrain micro-actors[20] as they exchange their applied resources (skills and knowledge) with other actors. In short, this is the structuration process we discussed in Chapter 1. Exhibit 8.5 illustrates the above concepts.

The service ecosystem as a system of processes

Service is the fundamental basis of exchange, as axiom 1 of S-D logic states (see Chapter 1). However, before and after each exchange of service are processes. In the service ecosystem all actors are part of many processes, but rarely do these processes start or end with a single actor. Processes actually weave through actors

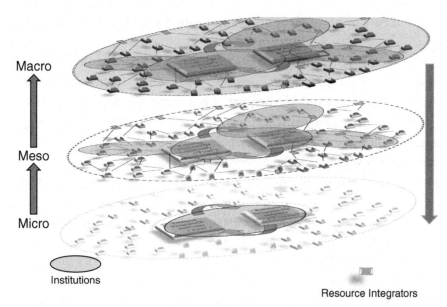

Macro

Meso

Micro

Institutions

Resource Integrators

Exhibit 8.5 Structuration of service ecosystems

and nested service systems. This is because every input, action, or service exchange sets the stage for a continuing process of cocreation. Indeed, environments can be conceptualized in general as a series of processes.[21] By adopting a lens that identifies service ecosystems as a system of processes, external or exogenous environments can also be viewed as endogenous or internal.

Many processes, comprising a set of interrelated actions, are intended to produce a favorable result. However, the result is not the same for every actor involved in the process because they each interpret the resulting value uniquely. Processes produce results or effects, and thus they are operant resources. Actions often occur over time rather than simultaneously and usually require multiple resources and actors to be integrated. These resources can be tangible, such as a factory robot or a computer, or intangible, such as a codified set of rules for performing the process and managing it. Almost always, human actors are part of the processes either in a performance role or as a beneficiary of the process. For example, employees manage service complaints with the goal of satisfying service beneficiaries.

Processes can be resources, but when an actor can package the performance of a process, a service offering can be made. However, virtually all processes extend beyond the enterprise. Thus, most processes in the firm should be viewed as a part of larger and longer processes that stretch to resource-providing actors and resource-using actors. Hagel and Brown call these "process networks" and explain how they can be used to access specialized capabilities on a global scale.[22]

A common problem in managing service processes is that enterprises design work-around functions that actors perform rather than service that other actors receive. In a manufacturing enterprise, it is not unusual to have the following departments with senior managers in leadership positions: manufacturing, purchasing, logistics, research and development, marketing and sales, finance, and human resources. However, the processes performed cut across many, if not all, departments and include the following: customer relationship management, customer service management, demand management, order fulfillment, manufacturing flow management, supplier relationship management, product development and commercialization, and returns management.[23] These processes also tie back to the first, second, and third tier, and potentially more removed service providers. This is especially the case with the global growth in outsourcing. Predictably, these processes also tie forward to first, second, and potentially other tiers of service beneficiaries. Consider, for example, the tiers of actors both backward and forward in the case of a US toy manufacturer subcontracting with a firm in China to produce a toy, which contracts with another firm for the toy's mechanical part, which contracts with yet another firm for the wiring harness. Furthermore, the toys are shipped on an ocean freighter from Hong Kong to a San Francisco seaport. The US toy manufacturer sells the toy directly to large retailers and also indirectly through wholesale distributors. Now suppose that children get an electrical shock when using the toy, and thus the US manufacturer must recall the toy. The problem is traced back to the second-tier Chinese manufacturer that produced the wiring harness. Here, an issue of returns management coupled with customer service management arises. Within the silos of the firm with the previously mentioned departments (purchasing, production, logistics, research and development, marketing and sales, and finance), no single department is responsible for the returns management and customer service management processes.

With the emergence and growth of service science, interest has arisen in studying major service systems in society, often a geopolitical area such as a city. Some of these service systems include governing, water, energy, waste disposal, nutrition, safety, transport, communication, education, entertainment, and health. With any of these systems, it is evident that a series of processes are weaved throughout them. For example, education includes processes that deal with governing, nutrition, transport, communication, safety, entertainment, and likely most other service systems. Here, again, threads and strings weave complex service ecosystems together.

From service ecosystems to ecosystem services

When we previously introduced service ecosystems, we mentioned that the natural ecosystem serves as a metaphor. However, the natural ecosystem is perhaps more than a metaphor because it is the most important service provider to humans and other species.[24] The natural ecosystem provides water, climate, pollination of crops, and often what can be thought of as cultural services, such as a place for hiking, bird watching, camping, or meditating.

We mentioned that environments were essentially a series of processes. Similarly, the natural ecosystem is a set of nested systems or environments that have processes running through them and interacting with other processes. The growth and death of forests, sea life, insects, and so forth, and the development of soil nutrients, weather storms, and so on, are all parts of processes that create environment. As humans interfere with these processes, they change and create new environments. Such behavior is natural for humans and has occurred for millions of years and will likely continue for millions more. In the future, however, new institutional logics – often brought about by institutional entrepreneurs – will make this interference more informed and perhaps more of a win–win and collaboration with nature.

Ecosystem service is becoming a more important part of planning not only by local, regional, and country governments but also by global organizations, such as the United Nations. This is especially important as humans transform more nature into artificial or manufactured built environments. As this occurs, natural ecosystems are often harmed. However, changes in institutional logics can also allow the natural ecosystem to provide needed service. For example, planting trees near a building can provide shade and help reduce energy consumption, and rain draining from the roof can provide water to the tree. Or properly planning natural parks in cities can provide a cultural service and also help improve air quality.

Ecosystem service is also part of the resource pool that actors draw on in their resource-integration efforts. Often, with proper planning, an ecosystem service can be obtained at little or no cost. For example, in the design of a hospital, windows can be placed in recovery rooms to enable patients to see the natural environment and to allow sunlight to beam into the room. Or a restaurant can be properly situated on a plot of land to take advantage of the natural ecosystem. Or natural breezes can help cool or warm a building if windows are designed to open to take advantage of these service flows.

Concluding comments

The movement and exchange of goods in terms of supply chains and marketing channels give way to networks and systems of resource-integrating actors in service-for-service exchange. S-D logic is made more complete by incorporating a service ecosystem perspective. With this perspective, processes never originate or end with a single enterprising actor but rather extend through nested service ecosystems. Human actors, however, inhabit the earth with many other species that are also part of the natural ecosystem that provides service(s). Increasingly, humans are designing ways to interface more effectively with the natural ecosystem and be a beneficiary of the many services it provides. Consequently, all actors can benefit by understanding how they fit into current service ecosystems, how ecosystem service(s) can benefit them, and how win-win collaborative relationships with the natural environment can become standard practice.

NOTES

1. Robert F. Lusch, Stephen Vargo, and Mohan Tanniru, "Service, value networks and learning," *Journal of the Academy of Marketing Science*, 38 (February 2010), 19–31.
2. R. S. Achrol, "Changes in the theory of interorganizational relations in marketing: toward a network paradigm," *Journal of the Academy of Marketing Science*, 25:1 (1997), 56–71; R. S. Achrol and Philip Kotler, "Marketing in a network economy," *Journal of Marketing*, 63 (special issue) (1999), 146–163; Jan Johanson and Jan-Erik Vahlne, "Markets as networks: implications for strategy-making," *Journal of the Academy of Marketing Science*, 39:4 (2011), 484–491.
3. Some organizational actors, such as firms and governments, have attempted to orchestrate or design networks from a top-down or hierarchical master-planned system.
4. Roger A. Layton, "Towards a theory of marketing systems," *European Journal of Marketing*, 45:1–2 (2011), 259–276.
5. Wroe Alderson, *Dynamic Marketing Behavior: A Functionalist Theory of Marketing* (Homewood, IL: Richard D. Irwin, 1965), p. 86.
6. D. F. Dixon and I. F. Wilkinson, *The Marketing System* (Melbourne, Australia: Longman Cheshire, 1982).
7. Ravi S. Achrol, "Evolution of the marketing organization: new frontiers for turbulent environments," *Journal of Marketing*, 55 (October 1991), 77–93; Frederick E. Webster, Jr., "The changing role of marketing in the corporation," *Journal of Marketing*, 56 (October 1992), 1–17; Achrol and Kotler, "Marketing in a network economy."

8. Douglas M. Lambert, Martha C. Cooper, and Janus D. Pagh, "Supply chain management: implementation issues and research opportunities," *International Journal of Logistics Management*, 9:2 (1998), 1–20.

9. M. S. Granovetter, "The strength of weak ties," *American Journal of Sociology*, 78 (May 1973), 1360–1380; M. S. Granovetter, "The strength of weak ties: a network theory revisited," *Sociological Theory*, 1 (1983), 201–233.

10. Bo Edvardsson, Anders Gustafsson, Per Kristensson, and Lars Witell, "Service innovation and customer co-development," in Paul Maglio, Cheryl A. Kieliszewski, and James C. Spohrer (eds.), *Handbook of Service Science* (New York: Springer, 2010), pp. 561–577.

11. Marco Iansiti and Roy Levien, *The Keystone Advantage* (Boston: Harvard Business School Publishing, 2004); R. Adner, "Match your innovation strategy to your innovation ecosystem," *Harvard Business Review*, 84:4 (2006), 98–107.

12. James F. Moore, "Predators and prey: a new ecology of competition," *Harvard Business Review*, 71 (May–June 1993), 75–86.

13. Robert Wright, *Non Zero: The Logic of Human Destiny* (New York: Pantheon Books, 2000).

14. J. L. Bronstein, "Mutualism and symbiosis," in Simon A. Levin (ed.), *The Princeton Guide to Ecology* (Princeton University Press, 2009), pp. 233–238; Matthew M. Mars, Judith L. Bronstein, and Robert F. Lusch, "The value of a metaphor: organizational ecosystems," *Organizational Dynamics*, 42 (2012), 271–280.

15. Moore, "Predators and prey"; Peter R. Dickson, "Toward a general theory of competitive rationality," *Journal of Marketing*, 56 (January 1992), 69–83.

16. Achrol and Kotler, "Marketing in a network economy"; Daniel J. Flint and John T. Mentzer, "Striving for integrated value chain management given a service-dominant logic for marketing," in Robert F. Lusch and Stephen L. Vargo (eds.), *The Service Dominant Logic: Dialogue, Debate, and Directions* (Armonk, NY: M. E. Sharpe, 2006), pp. 139–149; George Day, Samantha Howland, and Roch Parayre, "Looking into marketing's future," *Marketing Management*, 18 (September–October 2009), 12–17.

17. Richard Normann, *Reframing Business: When the Map Changes the Landscape* (Chichester, UK: John Wiley & Sons, 2001), p. 3.

18. Manuel DeLanda, *A New Philosophy of Society: Assemblage Theory and Social Complexity* (London: Continuum, 2006).

19. It can be argued that there is an ecosystem that is more micro than the A2A micro activities of human actors. This can be thought of as the genetic structure of the human actor and the living organisms that are both within and on the skin of a human actor. In a sense, then, the human is controlled from both below by these structures and above by the meso and macro structures of the service ecosystem.

20. DeLanda, *A New Philosophy of Society*.

21. Marshall McLuhan and Quentin Fiore, *The Medium Is the Message* (Berkeley, CA: Gingko Press, 1996 [1967]).

22. John Hagel, III, and John Seely Brown, *The Only Sustainable Edge: Why Business Strategy Depends on Productive Friction and Dynamic Specialization* (Boston: Harvard Business School Press, 2005).

23. Douglas M. Lambert and Sebastian J. Garcia-Dastugue, "Cross-functional business processes for the implementation of service-dominant logic," in Robert F. Lusch and

Stephen L. Vargo (eds.), *The Service Dominant Logic: Dialogue, Debate, and Directions* (Armonk, NY: M. E. Sharpe, 2006), pp. 150–165.

24. Millennium Ecosystem Assessment, *Ecosystems and Human Well-Being: Synthesis* (Washington, DC: Island Press, 2005), p. 155; G. C. Daily, *Nature's Services: Societal Dependence on Natural Ecosystems* (Washington, DC: Island Press, 1997), p. 392.

Part III
Possibilities

9 Strategic thinking

The best way to predict the future is to design it.

Buckminster Fuller

Introduction

Understandably, when introduced to a somewhat radically different perspective of business, such as service-dominant (S-D) logic, there is a natural tendency to ask: "How can I apply S-D logic to make more money for my firm?" Our response might be disappointing to some: in a truly prescriptive sense, S-D logic cannot be applied, at least directly. This does not mean that there are no normative implications arising from S-D logic. In fact, there are, and they have the potential to provide increased firm viability, including increased profits. They just are neither tactical nor prescriptive but rather strategic and abductive and provided indirectly. As we will discuss, these are provided through the additional insights into what actors can do to shape their destiny and the role and importance of agency that S-D logic offers.

The strategic implications for the application of S-D logic have to do with *innovation* and market creation, the ongoing (re)creation and institutionalization of value propositions that assist in the value-creation processes of other actors. Thus, S-D logic cannot so much prescribe as it can suggest a perspective for the approach to and the considerations of *possibilities*. It implies that innovation is achieved through asking the question: "What can I see from an S-D logic perspective that I cannot see from a G-D logic perspective in terms of opportunities for combining and applying available resources to offer value propositions for some other actor?" Arguably, then, the most important endeavor is to step back and examine the landscape.

Zooming out versus zoming in: seeing the bigger picture

The natural tendency in looking for application is to zoom in on micro-level activities – for example, the activities of the firm. One of the hallmarks of S-D logic, however, is context, which implies the necessity of zooming out to a macro (e.g., societal), or at least a meso (e.g., the "industry," brand community), level. More precisely, it implies *alternating* the perspective among micro, meso, and macro levels. The principle is simple: it is not possible to understand what is happening at one level without viewing it from another level.[1]

S-D strategy focuses on increasing the effectiveness of the firm's roles as an integrator of resources and a cocreator of value, through service exchange, in complex, dynamic systems. As we pointed out in Chapter 3 and elaborated in Chapter 6, all social and economic actors integrate resources in their value-creation processes. However, it is not just the resources themselves and the creation of value that are important to service-oriented enterprises, because an economic and social actor rarely, if ever, applies a single resource in isolation. Rather, value creation involves the integration of multiple resources by multiple actors simultaneously or as part of an integrative process, in the context of structures (e.g., shared, institutionalized ways of doing things). These structures can, in turn, be influenced and modified through the innovation occurring at lower levels.

For example, a restaurant integrates multiple resources, such as food ingredients, tables and chairs, knowledge of cooking, cleaning, and serving, to provide service for customers. At the same time, beneficiaries of the restaurant also integrate multiple resources, such as the present meal, past experience, knowledge of appropriate social behavior, physiological factors, transport systems to arrive at and depart from the restaurant, and in general eating-out practices, to derive and determine value. Because no one actor independently has access to all the resources he or she needs, actors must exchange resources with other actors. These multiple actors are also influenced by shared norms of food service and provision such as the practices that define full-service restaurants. And when innovations occur, such as the drive-through, quick-service and largely self-service restaurant, they influence traditional eating-out practices. These interconnected processes of resource integration and exchange form dynamic networks, which have been recognized as service ecosystems, as discussed in Chapter 8.

S-D logic's focus on operant resources – resources that are capable of acting on other resources – emphasizes the influence of social and economic actors on other resources, including social structures (i.e., service ecosystems). That is, as operant resources, actors such as firms, customers, and other stakeholders are perceived as having agency and thus as capable of influencing their environment, rather than just being influenced by it. This view is in stark contrast with traditional business models, which suggest that firms should segment and target customers in preexisting markets that are constrained by the external environments such as the technological, political, legal, social, ecological, and competitive environment.

It also suggests that, rather than focusing on adapting to their environments and responding to market changes, enterprises can influence change themselves, including institutional change. In some situations, these institutional innovations result in the creation of new markets and, occasionally, new "industries." For example, innovations in food service, replacing the more conventional practices of table side-ordering by wait staff, followed by cooking to order, with the customer ordering precooked food at the counter, led to micro-level success that transformed the restaurant "industry" and created the fast-food market. Other examples of market creation through institutional modification can be seen in self-assembly furniture and coffee shops as "third places."[2]

In many cases, this innovation, through challenging higher-level structures in existing ecosystems, transforms those ecosystems and becomes mainstream. Some transformations are facilitated by higher-level ones, such as the development and commercialization of day-care, which facilitated changes in the institutionalized role of females in US households. Others, such as alternative fuels and modes of transportation, are hindered because of predominant meso-level structures (e.g., the placement and practices of refueling stations), as well as macro-level structures (e.g., suburban living and cultural norms of individual freedom and convenience). *Innovation*, then, is *not* so much a matter of *inventing* new things as it is identifying opportunities to *deinstitutionalize* and *reinstitutionalize practices*. This requires both innovative agency and the continual monitoring of practices and their contexts.

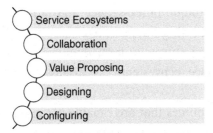

Exhibit 9.1 S-D logic strategic thinking

In the remainder of this chapter we will discuss five ways in which S-D logic shapes strategic thinking (see also Exhibit 9.1). The collective, strategic lens that results enables enterprises to increase the potential of value creation for themselves and for the actors with whom they exchange. As we describe later in the chapter, this can be done by *focusing on dynamic market interactions* and moving from the perspective of the value chain to that of the value network, or *service ecosystem*. From this view, enterprises are capable, to some extent, of (re) configuring and designing their surrounding service systems, both through *collaboration with multiple stakeholders* (e.g., firms, suppliers, customers, employees) and through deliberate efforts to establish long-term, mutually beneficial relationships. Because value is always cocreated in service ecosystems, enterprise strategies focus on *proposing value* throughout the ecosystem, rather than adding value through a sequence of events. Also, the enterprise is not so much viewed as choosing from fixed alternatives but rather as *designing* its future. When this is done, the enterprise is less focused on trying to predict a future than on *configuring and integrating resources* to control its future. The following sections elaborate and contrast these disparate strategic perspectives.

Service ecosystems: developing a systems view of exchange

Traditional models and frameworks of value creation depict a linear sequence of events, or a "value chain."[3] This view suggests that value is created in an engineered and predictable way and that sequential, value-adding activities contribute to the creation and distribution of value from "producers" to "consumers." For example, it implies that a supplier of raw materials, such as sheet metal, provides its resources to a manufacturing company, such as a car manufacturer; the car manufacturer accumulates costs during this process, which provide "added value" to the sheet metal through the use of the raw materials to build the car; the manufacturer then sends the finished car to the dealership, which promotes and sells the car to the "end user," which accumulates additional costs that are also viewed as added value. This simplified example also reflects a goods-dominant (G-D) model of value creation.

The G-D view on value creation focuses on the production and distribution of tangible offerings and how firm-related activities contribute to the creation of value. Alternatively, S-D logic argues that value is always cocreated in exchange and in the use and integration of what is exchanged. This view proposes that multiple stakeholders contribute to the value-creation process by integrating and applying resources to create value for themselves and for others. Individual resource-integration activities are connected with other resource-integration activities through the exchange of service. The exchange of service is not confined to an actor-to-actor (A2A) dyad (e.g. firm–customer dyad). Even when exchange occurs between two actors (e.g., firm and customer), it takes place in the context of a service ecosystem, comprising other actors that are integrating, applying, and exchanging resources simultaneously. Again, consider all of the resources from market-facing, public, and private sources, beyond the automobile itself, which are integrated and applied in the process of creating individual transportation and other benefits.

As we mentioned in Chapter 8, a service ecosystem is a relatively self-contained, self-adjusting system of resource-integrating actors connected by shared institutional logics and mutual value creation through service exchange. The actors are linked by value propositions,[4] which are essentially invitations to participate in a particular value cocreation process.[5] The service ecosystem mainly functions to enable actors to integrate and apply their resources and the resources of others (accessed through exchange) to improve its own viability as a system.

The size of a service ecosystem can range from an individual person and his or her combination of internal (e.g., knowledge, skills) and external (e.g., money, tools, equipment) resources to a group, such as a family or firm, to the global service ecosystem. Service ecosystems are not isolated systems. In general, a service ecosystem is a system of systems – for example, a family is a system of individual systems and a company is a system of departmental systems. This interconnected systems perspective draws attention to multiple viewpoints and stakeholders, particularly in the determination of value. S-D logic argues that value is phenomenologically determined by the beneficiary system. Often, the service beneficiary is thought of as the customer. However, with a service ecosystems approach, the beneficiary can be any system, including an individual, a family, an organization, or a nation, depending on whose well-being is at stake. The various viewpoints of interconnected systems complicate the issue of value creation because what may be considered valuable to one service ecosystem may not be regarded as such by another.

For example, a traditional measure of value for a firm is profit. Thus, firms often focus their efforts on cutting costs and increasing revenue. However, in some cases, the way firms execute their efforts may be considered as value diluting or creating social costs for others.[6] Evidence of this misalignment of perceptions of value often appears in publicized issues regarding firm labor, environmental consciousness, and even communication practices. These alternative viewpoints are often thought of as externalities, which are exogenous to the firm, create systems turmoil, and lead to resistance or failure in value-creation processes. Recognizing these different viewpoints of value is important because the actions that a service ecosystem undertakes generally reflect what that system considers valuable (or not). That is, the actions of a service ecosystem (e.g., a customer, a firm, a nation) are driven by that system's effort to create value (based on what it believes is valuable) for itself and for others. These actions drive dynamic interaction among interconnected service ecosystems.

Some enterprises, recognizing that wealth and value are more than something captured by value-in-exchange, such as profit or shareholder value, focus on a broadened view of value. With what is often referred to as "triple bottom line," these enterprises include social well-being and environmental sustainability in their conceptualizations of value.[7] However, although there are established conventions to measure value-in-exchange, or economic value, there are no established conventions to measure social well-being and environmental sustainability. Therefore, a key challenge is developing an understanding of what these concepts mean from the perspective of other actors versus the enterprises' definition or meaning.

Collaboration: designing for density and relationships

G-D strategic frameworks concentrate on competition for market share among firms and competing for scarce operand resources, such as natural resources. Alternatively, the success of S-D strategy lies in an enterprise's ability to effectively develop cooperative relationships, which in turn provides access to and integration of resources to create new resources that can be used in service provision. As we mentioned, this optimal or "right concentration and configuration" of resources is termed "density."[8] Briefly, density is a measure of the amount of information, knowledge, and other resources to which an actor has access at a given time and place to solve a particular problem. The creation of density occurs through the "unbundling" and "rebundling" of resources – a generalized version of the division of labor.[9] Thus, to create or increase density for a particular situation, enterprises can separate and recombine available resources.

As described, resources do not need to be owned by an enterprise to be integrated. Rather, an enterprise can coordinate the resources and roles of other social and economic actors (e.g., other firms or customers) to help shape and design a service ecosystem that focuses on *creating density for customers*. It is important to emphasize that in the same way that firms unbundle and rebundle resources to create density in the market, *customers create their own density* through unbundling and rebundling resources and resource integration as well. It is recognition of these common, fundamental activities (together with service provision) that underlies our advocacy of the A2A framework as we described in Chapter 5. Thus, S-D strategy focuses on the enterprise's ability to unbundle and rebundle resources in a variety of ways through relationships with social and economic actors, and it enables customers to do the same.

Although S-D enterprises may be capable of driving change and influencing the evolution of their associated service ecosystems, the stability of relationships enables service ecosystems, and the value created among them, to last over time. Good relationships are based on a mutuality of benefit. Dynamic stabilization of these relationships is important for maintaining density and access to resources needed at a given place and time. Service ecosystems depend on ongoing service-for-service (direct and indirect) relationships to increase effectiveness and efficiency and to maintain access to the resources on which they rely. Relationships provide members of service ecosystems with reliable sources of information and access to resources through dedicated channels.

Service-ecosystem members tend to "domesticate" surrounding systems by consciously limiting the number of service ecosystems with which they interact, thus, in effect, creating additional ecosystems. An instance of this type of domestication is evident in the case of brand loyalty. That is, many people repeatedly purchase the same brand of a particular service offering to reduce the time and effort spent in the decision-making process.

Domestication of exchange relationships temporarily stabilizes the interaction among service ecosystems by establishing additional shared protocols (institutions) that provide reliable access to necessary resources.[10] However, it is important to note that the domestication of exchange partners and the development of long-term relationships do not remove all the uncertainty from the market. Long-term relationships may themselves be quite risky. Although the well-developed institutions can increase stability and potentially curb conflict among service ecosystems, they also can be resistant to change and thus can limit adaptability and innovation. Thus, enterprises can benefit from diligently and continually searching for opportunities for value creation related to the deinstitutionalization and reinstitutionalization of types of relationships. These may be initiated by an enterprise (e.g., airline frequent flyer programs) or by other actors (e.g., some instances of brand community built around social networking). In both instances, they provide opportunities for diligent enterprises.

Value proposing: cocreating value with multiple stakeholders

G-D logic suggests that the firm creates value through a series of events that "add value." In this way, firms (and their suppliers and other business partners) create and deliver value to customers. However, S-D logic's notion of value cocreation suggests otherwise. S-D logic focuses on the phenomenological value[11] that is derived and determined through use or the application of resources, in the context of other resources. Because the determinants of value, and thus the reference for context and use, are beneficiaries, beneficiaries should be considered the primary resource integrators.

Value propositions

With the preceding perspective, service providers (e.g., firms) can propose value in the market, but they cannot create it independently of service beneficiaries (e.g., customers). For example, an automobile firm can establish a value proposition that invites potential customers to participate in the value cocreation process that involves driving a particular vehicle, but it cannot force the customers to engage in this process. Thus, the firm will attempt to communicate value by suggesting how this particular vehicle can potentially provide value. Different vehicles or brands of vehicles have different value propositions. For example, the value proposition of a minivan differs from that of a sports car. The minivan's value proposition may include attributes such as space, safety, and convenience, as well as the emotional appeals of family and togetherness. Conversely, the sports car's value proposition may include attributes such as speed and innovative design, as well as the emotional appeals of status and power.

A value proposition is more than a message or communication from the firm. It is also a potential resource (e.g., a vehicle with seven seats and large trunk space) that is appropriated for a particular purpose by the actor proposing its value (e.g., for transporting many people or a lot of things).[12] A value proposition suggests a particular value cocreation process through application of a particular potential resource for a particular purpose. Value propositions may include tangible or intangible offerings and direct or indirect methods of providing service. Essentially, a value proposition represents all the activities and resources necessary for service provision, as identified by the provider. It is an invitation to engage in a particular value cocreation process, such as a driving experience.[13] However, because value is phenomenologically determined, it is up to the service beneficiary to derive and determine value in a particular context, based on access to resources, influence of relationships, and shared institutions.

Value propositions must be compelling, and the enterprise needs to recognize that more traditional market competitors might be simultaneously offering value propositions to attract the enterprise's customers. For example, some value propositions may offer an alternative way to acquire service, perhaps through internal creation (self-service); yet other value propositions may suggest that the actor do without the service. A food processor may thus try to offer tasty desserts to the market; fruit growers may offer an alternative value proposition around tasty and nutritious fruit; and still another enterprise may promote a social movement revolving around eating less.

Suppliers and other stakeholders must view the enterprise as having a compelling value proposition, or they will find alternative sources of value creation. All of this occurs in a dynamic web of relationships, shared institutions, and integrating resource actors that slip into and out of networks and often have more options than they can actualize. The enterprise wants to be in a position within this ecosystem where it has similar options.

The need to develop new value propositions is continual because of the dynamic needs of customers, suppliers, and stakeholders. The dynamics of a service ecosystem necessitate an increased focus on learning rather than knowledge per se. What is known is less important because knowledge will predictably be outdated and not appropriate. Most of the knowledge in science and the social sciences has a half-life of less than a decade and, in some cases, less than 36 months. Similarly, knowledge of the market becomes outdated rapidly. Thus, it is more important to develop the ability to learn. In this regard, both successful and unsuccessful value propositions allow the firm to learn. When the value proposition does not win the business needed, the enterprise must almost instantaneously digest and deconstruct the situation. If the enterprise has been involved in conversation and dialogue with its customers and partners, as we discussed in prior chapters, it should be better prepared to make adjustments or changes in its value proposition.

Proposing value-in-context

The enterprise role of proposing value is an intermediary role in value cocreation. Value propositions connect multiple stakeholders through invitations to participate in particular value cocreation processes. However, as mentioned, value is ultimately derived and determined by the service beneficiary, through use. This conceptualization of value and value creation focuses on value-in-use, or value derived through the use or application of a particular resource.[14] This focus on value-in-use is an alternative to G-D logic's emphasis on value-in-exchange, or the price paid in the market. S-D logic proposes that value propositions driven by value-in-use are more likely to address the real needs of stakeholders than propositions driven by value-in-exchange.[15] This does not mean that price is not an important aspect of a value proposition. On the contrary, S-D logic emphasizes the value-in-use associated with a value proposition. The value proposition includes price, and price often influences value-in-use. For example, people often make decisions to buy more expensive items based on the status and prestige associated with the high price. Alternatively, people may enjoy the feeling of "getting a good deal," the low price of an offering, again influencing value-in-use.

Although this emphasis on value-in-use is in line with the notion of value cocreation, more recently a third conceptualization of value has been introduced in the S-D logic literature: *value-in-context*.[16] The concept of value-in-context suggests that value is determined on the basis of a specific context. In other words, resources are applied and evaluated in the context of other resources, such as time, space, and social surroundings. Thus, value is phenomenologically determined at a particular place and time in a specific circumstance. Consider the previous car example. The price paid for a car is value-in-exchange, and the benefits of the car, such as transportation and status, represent the car's value-in-use. However, the car's value is dependent on the service beneficiary's perspective and the context in which he or she is using the car (e.g., where, when, and how). In addition, the social relationships connected with a service beneficiary also influence his or her determination of value and thus are considered part of the context in which value is determined.[17] For example, passengers in the car or family members benefiting from the car (service appliance) and their social ties to the primary actor also influence the cocreation of value.

The conceptualization of value-in-context highlights the importance of density in service ecosystems. Service ecosystems are like living organisms and thus are constantly learning, evolving, and adapting to changing requirements. Therefore, the structure of the service ecosystem is regularly changing. This adaptive change is always with the intent of seeking greater density, even though the opposite can also occur because all adaptive change is not beneficial. However, if this is the case, the actors in the service ecosystem will make further adjustments to attempt to improve their system viability and density.

Designing: developing value-creating ecosystems

S-D logic reframes competition by refocusing on operant resources and the value cocreated with and derived and determined by the service beneficiary, rather than on competitors. The emphasis on cocreated value suggests that the aim of the enterprise is not to produce and deliver value to customers, but rather to enable customers, and other stakeholders, to integrate resources and cocreate value for themselves and others, based on individual needs and perceptions of value. Contrary to traditional conceptualizations of strategy, which focus on outperforming the competition, enterprises should focus on new ways to create value with their customers and other stakeholders (e.g., suppliers, employees). From this view, problems are solved first by creatively developing organizations and second by guiding the development of the surrounding service ecosystem.[18] Enterprises that recognize the inherent uncertainty of their environment will consider the possibilities of what could happen in the future, rather than focusing on the events that have already happened in the past.

This effectual logic is more abductive than deductive and implies that making strategic decisions in an unpredictable environment is not about selecting among predetermined alternatives, such as deciding which available market to enter.[19]

Rather, an S-D enterprise makes strategic decisions by identifying its own alternatives, possibilities, and potentiality and concurrently assessing the positive and negative aspects of all possible results and processes that help create the results. By focusing on the potential value, as derived and determined by beneficiaries, S-D enterprises do the same. That is, these enterprises focus on understanding the various ways they can create value with the different viewpoints and value perceptions in interconnected service ecosystems. For example, an enterprise that provides the service of helping people prepare their income taxes may consider what is necessary for those with little or no knowledge of filing taxes and offer a direct one-on-one service to assist them. At the same time, the enterprise may also consider how its resources could help create value for people with higher levels of knowledge regarding taxes and instead provide a software package to assist them. This simplified example illustrates how S-D strategy emphasizes the value-creation processes of the enterprise, its customers, and other interconnected stakeholders and attempts to identify and develop new ways (e.g., developing software along with offering one-on-one service) to create value among them.

To employ an S-D strategy, enterprises must constantly be aware of market opportunities for developing new relationships and coproducing new resources, based on the potential value they can create with their customers, suppliers, and other stakeholders. Most important, enterprises can benefit from understanding how customers access and integrate internal and external resources (both operant and operand) and develop relationships within and across service ecosystems. However, enterprises also need to be aware of how other stakeholders and exchange partners access and integrate resources. For example, much of Walmart's early success was based on its ability to provide information to its suppliers through an interconnected inventory system. This enabled its partners to access necessary information about stock levels and customer demand. By providing access to this invaluable resource, Walmart effectively designed a system that closely connected its suppliers and customer base. This effort to drive interconnectivity increased the value created for Walmart, its suppliers, and its customers.

In addition to understanding how resources are integrated in service ecosystems, enterprises must be aware of the institutionalized roles and responsibilities of each social and economic actor and also consider the potential of cocreating and institutionalizing new roles and responsibilities.[20] If the roles of each actor are not understood, the responsibilities in the value-creation process become vague. In the case of a car, for example, the customer is generally responsible for the maintenance of the vehicle after purchase. However, if the customer is unaware of his or her responsibilities in maintaining the vehicle, the value-creation process may not reach its full potential. Likewise, even if the customer is diligent about taking the vehicle in for routine maintenance, if the firm providing the maintenance is not familiar with the specifications for maintaining a particular vehicle, it may not perform certain necessary tasks. Again, the potential for value creation may be hindered. Thus, just as it is important for service-oriented enterprises to know how interconnected actors integrate resources and derive and determine value, it is equally important to understand the institutionalized roles of multiple actors in value-creation processes. By under-standing these roles and responsibilities, the service-oriented enterprise can develop relationships (i.e., design the service ecosystem) with particular partners that have the necessary resources and are capable of enacting specific roles. It may also discover opportunities in enabling actors to take on new roles or reduced roles through innovative service offerings. Thus, roles can be seen as potentially reconfigurable resources.

Configuring: taking advantage of unstable environments

Both the major challenge and the major advantage with strategic planning in complex, evolutionary systems, such as service ecosystems, lie in their volatility and unpredictability. What works today might not work tomorrow. This is problematic in the sense that the traditional models for strategic planning are based on the predictive capabilities of the firm. For example, traditional models for product development suggest that, before market entry, product ideas should be screened and prototypes tested so that the profitability of that product can be predicted.[21] However, even with these predictive measures, the failure rate of new products remains high.[22] This is because, more often than not, additional factors that cannot be accounted for in the prediction process influence the success or failure of a product launch. Thus, the usefulness of predictive models is limited.

In contrast with strategic models that focus on predictive methods, S-D logic's emphasis on operant resources and value cocreation suggests that, as actors interact, they are essentially cocreating markets[23] and thus are envisioning, influencing, and facilitating, rather than just predicting, some aspects of the market or markets in which they wish to provide service. Or, as the quote by

Buckminster Fuller at the chapter opening suggests, the best way to predict the future may be to *design* the future. Enterprises thus move from being "market driven" to "driving markets."[24] Enterprises are able to influence, and to some extent "control," markets when they focus on resources (e.g., knowledge, skills) and phenomenological value and continually search for opportunities to provide new solutions to new or existing problems. In this way, an S-D enterprise focuses on exploring uncharted waters or "blue oceans"[25] to develop new solutions and create new markets.

Recent studies in entrepreneurship call this process of effecting change in markets "effectuation."[26] In particular, effectuation theory argues, "to the extent we can control the future we do not need to predict it."[27] This view aligns with S-D logic's notion that as operant resources, social and economic actors are capable of influencing other resources, including those in the future. Because service ecosystems are continually changing, a firm's predictive efforts are limited to studying what has already occurred in a historical context that no longer exists. Although predictive methods are useful for gauging the future by studying the past, particularly in well-established markets, they also limit understanding of what might happen in the future, particularly in new, emerging, or rapidly changing markets.

Well-established or mature markets can be thought of as "institutionalized solutions," or socially constructed, normative solutions nested or embedded within a particular service ecosystem. However, because institutions or markets are regularly being translated and recreated, so are the approaches to problem solving (e.g., transportation problems solved by various methods as technology advanced), and even institutionalized solutions over time. Thus, rather than focusing on predicting what will happen in a particular market, S-D strategy (1) envisions service as a solution that benefits people's lives and (2) integrates the necessary resources to provide that service, oftentimes *creating* new markets through the development and institutionalization of new solutions, rather than just making better (or cheaper) versions of existing solutions.

Reconfiguring resources

To participate in the configuration of value-creation service ecosystems, enterprises should consider reconfiguring resources for improved density as a major strategic option.[28] Greater density is achieved by altering the structure of the service ecosystem. In all enterprises and organizations, forms or structures have purposes or functions, and dominant forms and structures emerge and proliferate over time. Tangible examples are automobiles and bicycles, warehouse racks, packaging, office furniture, houses, apparel, and desktop computers. Intangible forms include contracts, policies, and procedures, and business processes. Although dominant forms emerge, it is important to question these forms with the intent of discovering whether they can be altered or reframed to better perform a function(s) – that is, whether they can become a more useful tool or service appliance and increase density.

One aspect of reconfiguring forms, which is often discussed in the context of S-D logic, pertains to the development of standardized, integrable modules and outsourcing that S-D logic encourages the firm to consider. By creating standardized components, especially through the use of modular architecture,[29] such as in componentized software and web services, it is possible to outsource activities that are not core to organization competence. By standardizing component processes, the actors in a service ecosystem are also able to offer more customizable value propositions. Thus, they can also increase effectiveness, while simultaneously increasing efficiency. It is similar to authors using a standardized language of thousands of words that they can then combine into an almost infinite number of narratives. The offering thus can be tailored, even though it consists of an integrated set of standardized components.[30]

The timing of the performance of activities either in an enterprise or by an individual actor in day-to-day affairs is an important determinant of the viability of the service ecosystem. Therefore, a second reconfiguration opportunity pertains to the institutionalized time when various activities are performed. Mapping a set of activities involved in the sourcing of inputs for production, the production of the product, the distribution and sale of the product, and the use of the product by the customer arranges these activities along a time continuum. Certain activities precede others, either by custom or by necessity. For example, in building a site-based house, most contractors use a PERT chart for the process: stake the lot, dig footings, do the rough plumbing, pour the foundation, rough the carpentry, rough-in electrical wiring, and so on. However, again, this does not need to be the exact process. Why? Because this process assumes that the house is built on site. Conversely, it is possible for the walls to be assembled with rough-in electric and optical wiring at a factory while the foundation is being poured and then delivered and installed in a few hours. This illustrates the multiple new configurations that are possible when asking whether the time truly is by custom, by norm, or by necessity.

Other actors (e.g., customers, users) in the service ecosystem should also be considered in this time-reframing of various practices. For example, traditionally furniture makers would craft the completed piece of household furniture before shipping it to the wholesale and retail distribution channel. However, some enterprises have reframed furniture manufacturing to involve the customer doing part of the production after purchase versus the manufacturer doing it in the factory. Furthermore, when evaluating the customer as part of the service ecosystem, no enterprise should overlook the resources available on the Internet and how this technology has altered the time sequence of traditional processes. Many of these resources allow customers to obtain information they traditionally obtained by visiting a store or a service provider. Armed with this information, customers now interface differently with retailers and service providers, which has often resulted in a shift in power from the seller to the buyer. The organization that has not adapted or does not adapt to these changes will face increasing survival challenges.

A third reconfiguring design opportunity is in the place where activities are performed. Digitization and networks have altered the concept of place, where a task is performed, and where resources are delivered. In today's world, in which firms are networked across the globe with customers and suppliers/partners, an order may originate in France, the parts may be ordered from manufacturing sites in Taiwan or Mexico, and the product may be assembled in Ireland. Similarly, a call center service request may be placed in California (or anywhere in the world), processed initially at a location in India, escalated to someone in New York, and then responded to by someone again in India a few minutes later. Personalized web portals can make the "place" from which a "product" is ordered and delivered the consumer's desktop; here, the customer can track the order through the entire service ecosystem, from initial placement to final delivery.

Increasingly, collaborations throughout the service ecosystem are occurring virtually, in which participants meet through the Internet to work on projects. In this way, documents can be shared not only throughout the organization but also with any other relevant actors in the service ecosystem. Actors can work on these documents at their places of business or elsewhere, becoming part of a virtual organization in which work is independent of place. Such collaborations are being done not only with simple, repetitive, and explicit tasks but also with more complex projects, such as new product development.[31]

A fourth reconfiguration opportunity pertains to the institutionalized role of actors (see the prior section) in terms of ownership and possession of material things. However, S-D logic implies that it is the service, including the flow of service from appliances (goods), that matters rather than the necessity of possession of a good *per se*, at least in many instances. This simple idea can be used to reconfigure service ecosystems and improve density because it suggests that firms can lease assets or pay for the use of service flows, rather than selling or purchasing goods – a model that is increasingly used in the software industry.[32] Such reconfiguring occurs when jet engine manufacturers move from selling jet engines to selling thrust service. But this can be taken a step further. Aircraft manufacturers do not need to sell jet airplanes; rather, they can retain possession and take responsibility for the repair, maintenance, and overhaul of the aircraft according to a performance-based contract. Enterprises in the business of plant or office construction can now view themselves as designing, building, operating, maintaining, and protecting infrastructure, as well as performing a host of other related service(s). Furthermore, by retaining possession of the infrastructure and selling the service flows, the enterprise can gain more predictable revenue flows and thus can manage costs and resources more effectively. In brief, they can improve density for themselves and the actors they serve.

Innovations, such as the iPod, the automobile, the printing press, and the World Wide Web, provide evidence that social and economic actors (e.g., firms) often have more control over market creation and development than traditional models of marketing and economics suggest. However, this "control" is not captured by the actions of one actor. Rather, the ability to influence markets and market creation often rests on the ability of an enterprise to integrate the competences of other actors (e.g., other firms and customers) and, thus, to co-design service ecosystems to support the development and spread of a new solution (i.e., innovation). These concepts of the codesign and co-evolution of markets stand in sharp contrast with the more-often espoused goal of gaining market share. In fact, if an enterprise can create a market, its long-term goals will probably include declining market share in markets it has created (and in which it thus initially held 100 percent), rather than entering and fighting for market share in an existing market.

Toward an S-D logic strategy appraisal

Returning to the question at the start of this chapter, "How can I apply S-D logic to make more money for my firm?," whereas specific, prescriptive actions might not be possible, some normative considerations can be suggested. First, it should be noted that, while S-D logic places an emphasis on system viability, for which of course making money, or generating positive cash flow, is crucial, resilience,

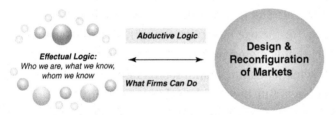

Exhibit 9.2 Toward an S-D logic strategy orientation

adaptability, and similar sources of viability are equally important. Additionally, S-D logic is broadly applicable to all types of organizations – profit and nonprofit and private and government organizations – for which "success" may be defined differently from making money. Regardless of the type of business, our normative suggestions are intended to help a firm to realize its potential to design and (re)configure future markets, rather than be controlled or restricted by them.

In Exhibit 9.2 the central role of effectual and abductive thinking is emphasized. The mindset characterized by this type of thinking has been echoed throughout this book.

A firm should begin by examining four crucial elements of effectual thinking. First, "Who is the firm?" It is easy to provide a superficial answer that adopts the standard industry lexicon and perhaps what the marketing communications staff develop to represent the firm to the public; however, this often does not truly represent the essence of the firm. Second, "What does the firm know?" Again, this is not easy to answer. It probably requires considerable dialogue with employees, customers, and other actors in the service ecosystem. Third, "Whom does the firm know?" Of course, the inclination is to cite specifically who the most senior executives know. Or, to answer in very broad categorical terms, we know our suppliers, labor, or bankers. But to act effectually, the firm needs more precise answers related to accessibility to specific actors (people) through managers, senior executives, and other employees.

Fourth, firms need to know *what they can do* and how they can use abductive thinking to design and reconfigure markets. Abductive thinking can consist, for example, of envisioning some desired future and then constructing a "future history" about how that future would unfold. Then, by applying effectual thinking to the S-D logic axioms, foundational premises, and related frameworks the firm can begin to shape its destiny. This journey will not be smooth and unidirectional but rather an iterative process between effectual and abductive thinking.

How does the firm begin to make the preceding more actionable? We suggest it do so by conducting an S-D logic, strategic appraisal, as illustrated in Exhibit 9.3.

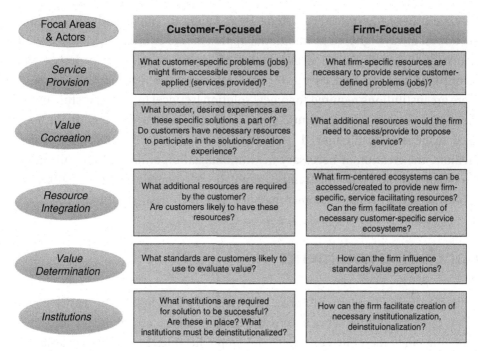

Focal Areas & Actors	Customer-Focused	Firm-Focused
Service Provision	What customer-specific problems (jobs) might firm-accessible resources be applied (services provided)?	What firm-specific resources are necessary to provide service customer-defined problems (jobs)?
Value Cocreation	What broader, desired experiences are these specific solutions a part of? Do customers have necessary resources to participate in the solutions/creation experience?	What additional resources would the firm need to access/provide to propose service?
Resource Integration	What additional resources are required by the customer? Are customers likely to have these resources?	What firm-centered ecosystems can be accessed/created to provide new firm-specific, service facilitating resources? Can the firm facilitate creation of necessary customer-specific service ecosystems?
Value Determination	What standards are customers likely to use to evaluate value?	How can the firm influence standards/value perceptions?
Institutions	What institutions are required for solution to be successful? Are these in place? What institutions must be deinstitutionalized?	How can the firm facilitate creation of necessary institutionalization, deinstituionalization?

Exhibit 9.3 S-D logic strategy appraisal

This appraisal is presented as a matrix, with focal areas as rows and focal actors as columns. Note that the matrix can be easily expanded and/or adjusted to accommodate the context of a particular firm. However, in its basic form, the focal areas include service provision, value cocreation, resource integration, value determination, and institutions. We provide a set of questions to guide the strategic appraisal. The questions are developed around a (potential) customer-focused appraisal as well as a firm-focused appraisal. This is necessary because a firm-focused appraisal, in isolation, will never allow the firm to gain the insights needed to develop compelling service offerings and value propositions that a customer-focused audit will reveal. It also can be the key to developing more innovative service offerings and designing and reconfiguring markets and, potentially, industries. Also it is necessary to design for density, which requires collaboration and relationship that a firm-centric lens does not reveal. As indicated in Figure 9.2, the strategic appraisal process is iterative.

The first four focal areas in the strategy appraisal audit come from the four axioms of S-D logic and reflect service provision, value cocreation, resource integration, and value determination. Institutions are the fifth focal area of the strategy appraisal audit. Although they are not mentioned in the four axioms, they are central to service ecosystems (see Chapter 8). Importantly, institutions are almost always ignored in traditional approaches to firm strategy. However, it is one of the most crucial determinants of a firm being able to design and reconfigure markets and its future. For customers, the firm needs to know if there are institutions required for a new solution (service) to be successful, and, if there are, whether these institutions are in place, and whether any institutions need to be deinstitutionalized. And the firm needs to determine how it can facilitate the creation of necessary institutionalization or deinstitutionalization. If certain institutional constraints cannot be overcome and new institutions formed then the firm or customer may not have their desired future.

Concluding comments

Strategic thinking by an enterprise that embraces S-D logic is primarily about value creation in the service ecosystem. Ecosystems are dynamic and ever changing and, therefore, unstable and unpredictable. In service ecosystems, enterprises need to take an active role in configuring at least a part of their relevant service ecosystem. By doing so, enterprises have more control over their future because they are essentially designing their future. Density needs to be obtained, and often this occurs when enterprises develop relationships that are adaptable and thus allow the reconfiguring of resources through the unbundling and rebundling of resources. Moving beyond dyadic exchanges, engaging with stakeholders other than just customers and shareholders, and developing value propositions that help unify the diverse interests of all these various actors will become more important as networks expand, as markets become more complex, as systems become more dynamic and turbulent, and as resources flowing to, through, and from them become more fluid.

NOTES

1. Jennifer D. Chandler and Stephen L. Vargo, "Contextualization: network intersections, value-in-context, and the co-creation of markets," *Marketing Theory*, 11:1 (2011), 35–49.
2. Mark S. Rosenbaum, "Exploring the social supportive role of third places in consumers' lives," *Journal of Service Research*, 9:1 (2006), 59–72.
3. Michael Porter, "How information gives you a competitive advantage," *Harvard Business Review* (July–August 1985), 149–174.

4. Jim Spohrer, Paul P. Maglio, John Bailey, and Daniel Gruhl, "Steps toward a science of service systems," *Computer*, 40 (2007), 71–77; Jim Spohrer, Stephen L. Vargo, Nathan Caswell, and Paul P. Maglio, "The service systems is the basic abstraction of service science," in *41st Annual HICSS Conference Proceedings* (CD-ROM), Computer Society Press (10 pages).

5. Jennifer Chandler and Robert F. Lusch, "Value propositions," working paper, University of Arizona (2013).

6. Ronald H. Coase, "The problem of social cost," *Journal of Law and Economics*, 3 (October 1960), 1–44; JoNel Mundt, "Externalities: uncalculated outcomes of exchange," *Journal of Macromarketing*, 13 (Fall 1993), 46–53.

7. Lisa Penaloza and Jenny Mish, "The nature and processes of market co-creation in triple bottom line firms: leveraging insights from consumer culture theory and service dominant logic," *Marketing Theory*, 11:1 (2011), 9–34.

8. Richard Normann, *Reframing Business: When the Map Changes the Landscape* (Chichester, UK: John Wiley & Sons, 2001).

9. Adam Smith, *The Wealth of Nations* (New York: The Modern Library, 2000 [1776]).

10. Johan Arndt, "Toward a concept of domesticated markets," *Journal of Marketing*, 43 (Fall 1979), 69–75.

11. Many insights into a phenomenological view of value appear in Morris B. Holbrook (ed.), *Consumer Value: A Framework for Analysis and Research* (London: Routledge, 1999).

12. Melissa Archpru Akaka and Jennifer D. Chandler, "Practices, processes, positions and propositions: a resource-based approach to value co-creation in value networks," paper presented at the Forum on Markets and Marketing, Cambridge, UK (September 2010).

13. Jennifer Chandler and Robert F. Lusch, "Value propositions," working paper, University of Arizona (2013).

14. Smith, *The Wealth of Nations.*

15. Christian Kowalowski, "The service function as a holistic management concept," *Journal of Business and Industrial Marketing*, 26:7 (2011), 484–492.

16. Stephen L. Vargo, Paul P. Maglio, and Melissa Archpru Akaka, "On value and value co-creation: a service systems and service logic perspective," *European Management Journal*, 26:3 (2008), 145–152.

17. Jennifer D. Chandler and Stephen L. Vargo, "Contextualization and value-in-context: how context frames exchange," *Marketing Theory*, 11:1 (2010), 35–49.

18. Saras Sarasvathy, Nicholas Dew, Stuart Read, and Robert Wiltbank, "Designing organizations that design environments: lessons from entrepreneurial expertise," *Organization Studies*, 23:3 (2008), 331–350.

19. Saras Sarasvathy, "Entrepreneurship as a science of the artificial," *Journal of Economic Psychology*, 24:2 (2003), 203–220.

20. Melissa A. Akaka and Jennifer D. Chandler, "Roles as resources: a social roles perspective of change in value networks," *Marketing Theory*, 11:3 (2011), 243–260.

21. Gloria Barczak, Abbie Griffin, and Kenneth B. Kahn, "Trends and drivers of success in NPD practices: results of the 2003 PDMA Best Practices Study," *Journal of Product Innovation Management*, 26 (2009), 3–23.

22. J. T. Gourville, "Eager sellers and stony buyers: understanding the psychology of new-product adoption," *Harvard Business Review*, 84 (June 2006), 98–106.

23. Brian Loasby, "Understanding markets," in *Knowledge, Institutions and Evolution in Economics* (London and New York: Routledge, 1999), Chapter 7.
24. Bernard Jaworski, Ajay K. Kohli, and Arvind Sahay, "Market-driven versus driving markets," *Journal of the Academy of Marketing Science*, 28:1 (2000), 45–54.
25. W. Chan Kim and Renee Mauborgne, *Blue Ocean Strategy: How to Create Uncontested Market Space and Make the Competition Irrelevant* (Boston: Harvard Business School Press, 2005).
26. Sarasvathy, "Entrepreneurship as a science of the artificial"; Stuart Read, Nicholas Dew, Saras Sarasvathy, Michael Song, and Robert Wiltbank, "Marketing under uncertainty: the logic of an effectual approach," *Journal of Marketing*, 73:3 (2009), 1–18.
27. Sarasvathy, "Entrepreneurship as a science of the artificial," p. 208.
28. This section draws heavily from Robert F. Lusch, Stephen L. Vargo, and Mohan Tanniru, "Service, value networks and learning," *Journal of the Academy of Marketing Science*, 38:1 (2010), 19–31.
29. Carliss Baldwin and Kim Clark, "Managing in an age of modularity," *Harvard Business Review*, 75:5 (1997), 84–93.
30. R.M. McCarthy, "Cost-effective supply chains: optimizing product development through integrated design and sourcing," in K. Butner, T. Gilliam, H. Goldstein, J. Kalina, C. Taylor, and M. Witterding (eds.), *Reshaping Supply Chain Management: Vision and Reality* (Boston: Pearson Custom, 2007), pp. 102–135.
31. S. Ganesan, A. J. Malter, and A. Rindfleisch, "Does distance still matter? Geographic proximity and new product development," *Journal of Marketing*, 69:4 (2005), 44–60.
32. C.A. Tormabene and G. Wiederhold, "Software component licensing," *IEEE Software*, 15:5 (1998), 47–53.

10 Conclusions and considerations

Life is what happens to you while you're busy making other plans.

"Beautiful Boy", John Lennon

Introduction

Service-dominant (S-D) logic is a work in progress. With the assistance of academics and practitioners we will continue to refine and develop it to create a stronger, more cohesive research tradition grounded on a core set of axioms. From the outset, we have positioned S-D logic as an evolutionary pathway moving toward a dramatically different perspective and explanation of business. The basic, underlying idea that all humans apply their competences (knowledge and skills) to benefit others and reciprocally benefit from others' competences translates into the simple idea: *service is exchanged for service*. Nonetheless, as we have explored the implications of this simple idea over the past decade, we, along with others, have discovered that it has considerable potential explanatory potency; one not only applicable to micro-level, dyadic exchanges but also applicable to the meso and macro systems that emerge from these service exchanges. Perhaps predictably, we also discovered that this service-for-service exchange is not only relevant to business and economy but to society, more generally.

Convergence

The title of our first article, "Evolving to a new dominant logic for marketing," provided a gateway to discuss a variety of trends occurring in applied business and marketing, as well as in scholarly writing and the trade literature. In Chapter 2, "Roots and heritage," we reviewed the long history of the development of goods-dominant (G-D) logic and discussed how a variety of thoughts were converging around a new dominant logic. From the rapid ascendance and impact of the services marketing and management literature in the 1970s and 1980s, we began to see other currents of change in thinking. As is often the case, when thinking starts to change, it is supplemented or leveraged by the emergence of a new lexicon, which, in turn, further influences thinking and ultimately behavior or action. During the 1990s we witnessed such an explosion of new concepts and ways of thinking, including the following: operand and operant resources, coproduction, cocreation, mass customization, experience economy, network economy, core competency, value constellations, and value propositions. All of these, in one form or another, suggested a shift from logic of separation of "producers" and "consumers" to a logic of much more interaction between many actors in the creation of value – that is, the cocreation of value in a network or system.

A meta-idea

Each year there are scores of business books, both trade and academic, that suggest new, prescriptive insights, frameworks, and tools, if not panacea. Likewise, there are a large number of consultants that present similar value propositions. This book is not intended as a prescriptive solution. As mentioned in the preceding chapter, there is a fundamental fallacy in cookbook expectations, which assume that someone removed from the context of an enterprise can solve problems with standardized solutions, planning canvases, and blueprints. This does not imply that they are useless, however, just that they need a more holistic framework for making sense of the process and context of value creation to allow their selective use in the innovation of cocreated solutions.

Paul Romer refers to a meta-idea as one that helps to support the creation and transfer of other ideas.[1] However, meta-ideas can also provide a transcending worldview, a fertile and robust platform for the creation and application of other, more specific ideas.

We did not begin, nearly two decades ago, with the thought that what now has emerged as S-D logic would become a meta-idea. But today, through continuing development, not only by us but, more importantly, by scholars and consultants worldwide, we find increasing adoption of S-D logic as a transcending and unifying, meta-framework for organizing ideas from diverse disciplines and for thinking innovatively about marketing, business, and the economy in general.

S-D logic provides a lens to look at complex exchange systems in a different light. Virtually all observers of society – for example, journalists, social scientists, historians, and business and government leaders – acknowledge that the world is becoming more complex. We each experience more connections to friends and other actors, augmented by technologies and institutions.[2] The billions of human actors and millions of organizations are parts of many complex and evolving service ecosystems. S-D logic helps us to make sense of these complex systems. Norman, in his book *Understanding Complexity*, differentiates between "complexity" and "complicated": *complexity* describes the state of the world and *complicated* describes a state of mind.[3] Complexity is thus inherent in the system. S-D logic can help unclutter and uncomplicate complex service ecosystems in a manner that provides insights regarding the development of better solutions.

How does S-D logic unclutter and uncomplicate? It does so by helping to focus thinking by providing a compact set of axioms, foundational premises, and core concepts. This provides a brighter, better-focused vision that allows the visualization of more possibilities for innovation and enhanced system viability. It also helps equip leaders with the conceptual framework to better communicate the vision of their enterprise and its value propositions. Similarly, for scholars, it unleashes unbounded possibilities for research, which contributes to cocreating S-D logic.

This does not imply that adopting a true S-D logic perspective is easy – just as with any skill, such as art or surgery, it requires mastery through study and accumulated experience. Similarly, the potential usefulness of S-D logic cannot be realized by adopting only part of the framework. For example, some have found the concepts of cocreation and resource integration to be particularly appealing, but understanding and employing these concepts without the entire S-D logic framework limits their usefulness. S-D logic needs to be understood and adopted in its entirety.

Part of the difficulty of mastering S-D logic is the enduring, strong pull of G-D logic. G-D logic is not only embedded in many organizational routines and practices, it is also embodied in our minds, and practices and institutions of society. In fact, even after nearly two decades of intense work on S-D logic and its associated lexicon, we still find ourselves occasionally slipping back to the G-D logic mindset and lexicon. Be forewarned: it takes work and training to see every firm offering, tangible or intangible, as just an input, something whose value is only realized in its use and in the context of and integration with resources from other sources. It is difficult to emancipate oneself from the restricted perspective of the firm-centric model, which treats customers as operand resources, whose role is to be captured for the net present value of their flow of financial resources to the enterprise – what, in G-D logic terms, is referred to as lifetime value of the customer, which is inappropriately paraded as "relationship" marketing. It is difficult not to think about the firm as the center of the wealth creation or as the producer and provider of value. It can be equally difficult to divorce oneself from that view that customers consume and destroy value. It is difficult not to think about innovation as something that primarily occurs in the laboratories and offices of the enterprise, as opposed to something that occurs throughout the service ecosystem, through the social and economic processes of resource integration and service exchange.[4] The pervasive influence of G-D logical lexicon and frameworks on all of the business and management disciplines is a hard one from which to break free. It is extremely difficult not to think about a profit shortfall as the fault of management and employees but rather as due to the inadequacy of the G-D logic model.

We believe commitment to S-D logic and its premises and lexicon, focusing on and understanding its nuances and fully grasping its transcending nature, will reveal not only new solutions to old problems but also unlimited and unbounded opportunities for market expansion and the creation of new markets. That is a fairly bold value proposition but one that we think is achievable through becoming untethered to G-D logic and mastering S-D logic.

The bigger picture

S-D logic presents a bigger picture of value creation at every level of society – for example, the household, government, the enterprise. But in one sense, that picture is not a picture at all; it is a real-time, unfolding, unrehearsed, non-directed, never-ending video of resource-integrating, service-exchanging actors that span interconnected micro, meso and macro systems. The meta-idea of S-D logic offers a narrative for this video, providing insight into its theme and story-line. An enhanced understanding of S-D logic allows one to become a trained observer of society, something of an ethnographer, with the ability to zoom both in and out to see the actors, (e.g., individuals, households, and firms), not in isolation but in all of their service-exchange relationships with other actors (e.g., employees, suppliers, customers, and other stakeholders). What is revealed is a society that is a very large-scale service ecosystem cocreating value through resource integration and service exchange.

Dependencies and interdependencies, like strands of optical threads, weave through this ecosystem, and reveal more and more mutualistic, symbiotic exchanges, both immediate and eventual. S-D logic reveals not only the value cocreation taking place between two actors (e.g., firm and customer) but also what can be thought of as *massively cocreated* value. This occurs as many actors play microscopic roles of which they are usually unaware, in an accelerating number of large, value-creating service ecosystems. The collective knowledge and skills involved in this massively collaborative value cocreation has been called the "collective"[5] or "global" brain.[6]

This global brain, along with the institutions that enable it to cocreate value, has resulted in accelerating well-being.[7] That is, as actors engage in more and more service exchange, even as each knows less and less about the whole, the overall human condition improves at an accelerating rate. For all of humanity the number of service exchanges follows something similar to Moore's law – the observation that the number of transistors on a microchip doubles every eighteen months – with the number of service exchanges for all of humanity doubling in a relatively short time period. These service exchanges, however, are more and more indirect (see FP2 on indirect exchange in Chapter 3) and leveraged with other resources (see FP9 on resource integration). This implies that the accumulated knowledge of humanity and value creation grows at an accelerated rate, as resources are combined in novel ways to create new resources used in innovations, which, in turn, become the platforms for more innovation.[8] Hence the more we innovate the more the innovation frontier expands.[9] We believe that the S-D logic lens will allow a fuller understanding of this process of accelerating, massive value cocreation, which will have important implications for how firms can more effectively participate.

More inversions

As reviewed in the first few chapters, goods have traditionally been viewed as the dominant market offering. At best, "services" were seen as things added to goods;

at worst, services were viewed as inferior goods, because they were regarded as intangible, heterogeneous, inseparable from "consumption", and perishable. S-D logic inverts that logic by viewing service as the basis of economic (and social) exchange and all economies as service economies. And as we stated in Chapter 1, service can be delivered directly or indirectly, through a good (a service appliance). Service thus transcends goods and "services."

As S-D logic is more fully embraced, it points toward even more, similar inversions, each of which has the benefit of reducing complicated conceptual relationships. These are introduced briefly below.

Entrepreneurship versus management

Management is a relatively young academic discipline, emerging less than 200 years ago and proliferating especially after World War II. Much of management thought has its roots in the Industrial Revolution, the scientific management of large, bureaucratic organizations, neoclassical economics, and an old manufacturing logic. By the 1970s journalists and scholars had begun to refer to a post-industrial society[10] but it was still primarily built on a managerial, economic framework.[11] In both the public and private sector, the five-year strategic plan continued to be the central approach, supported by annual, quarterly, and monthly plans. The pervasive and expanding influence of this old industrial, managerial model was evident in development and growth of business disciplines such as marketing management, services management, human resource management, customer management, financial management, supply chain management, and information systems management. In brief, what observers began to call the post-industrial economy was still a model of central- (within the organization) planning and top-down-management command and control, in which both workers and customers were viewed as operand resources.

In the mid-1980s, Peter Drucker, who was a keen observer of emerging societal change, began to identify a movement toward what he coined *entrepreneurial management*. This is a vision of management in which the economy and organizations were not seen in terms of machines to be fine-tuned and operated through levers and switches for optimal performance, but rather in terms of biological processes, genetically organized through information. In fact, Drucker identified his role as a business academic as that of a "social ecologist."[12]

As stated in Chapter 8, S-D logic defines service ecosystems as relatively self-contained, self-adjusting systems of resource-integrating actors that are connected by shared institutional logics and mutual value creation through service exchange. This implies dynamic systems in which actors both influence and are restricted by the structural context that develops from their collective value (viability, well-being) creating processes through innovative resource integration and service provision. Thus, value creation is an unfolding process, for which there is no end state to optimize or toward which to move; it is an entrepreneurial process.

In Chapter 9, we discussed entrepreneurial management in terms of effectual logic, in which actors take small steps (resource identification and integration, collaboration, and trial) to innovatively develop new value propositions and, eventually, markets. Also, as discussed, these new markets are created through processes of *institutionalization* (widespread acceptance) of generalized value propositions as acceptable solutions to common needs. Thus, perhaps ironically, through *performativity*, they lead to something like the *a priori*, measurable, and predictable markets assumed by managerial marketing.

All of this suggests that the relative roles of management and entrepreneurial approaches might be misconstrued, both in business schools and in practice. That is, we tend to see (marketing) management as primary and entrepreneurial activities as a special case. The above, however, suggests that this logic needs to be inverted: entrepreneurial activities are fundamental to value creation in ecosystems of resource integration and service exchange and management within markets, and traditional marketing activities within the firm are a special case, applicable to the relatively few (temporarily) established markets, resulting from institutionalization. Consistent with S-D logic, we suggest that inverting the relative role of management and entrepreneurial activity brings innovation into sharper focus.

Market-ing versus manufacturing

As discussed in Chapter 2, the centrality of the idea of being "productive" (and thus the "product") became the focal concept in economic exchange, at least in large part, because of the work of Adam Smith, whose central concern was not economics at all but rather how to foster national wealth creation in the context of the beginning of the Industrial Revolution. As the Industrial Revolution progressed, and production moved out of the cottage and into the factory, and as goods became standardized and efficiently mass produced, more businesses and governments became convinced that the key to prosperity was manufactur-ing – the production of products. As discussed in Chapter 1, this view impacted how we thought of "services "in terms of the production of intangible units of output. Even early marketing thought was hijacked and led in this direction, as marketing was thought of as the movement (i.e., distribution) of initial sources of goods from producers to consumers. Manufacturing was seen as the use of labor and capital to shape and reform matter to embed it with utility (i.e., form utility) and then marketing was seen as adding time, place, and possession utility, through distribution. Marketing was considered secondary and played a supporting role to manufacturing.

S-D logic inverts this logic by seeing market-ing as primary and manufacturing (and other production processes) in a support role. Market-ing, in this sense, is not limited to the activities of the marketing department, what is captured in traditional marketing management as segmenting existing markets for the purpose of targeting one or more segments and positioning firm offerings through manipulation of the marketing mix. Rather, it involves the creation and recreation of markets by finding innovative approaches to resource integration and service provision; it represents the *purpose of the firm*. Drucker once noted that the firm has only two functions: marketing and innovation.[13] In S-D logic, they are the same.

However, it is important to understand that this removes the firm from the primary, central role in value creation to the role of a participant in the value-creation process of and for others in the context of service ecosystems. Manufacturing, when involved, plays a supportive role, one that can often be outsourced. As Levitt once noted, "we habitually celebrate Ford for all the wrong reasons . . . his real genius was marketing. Actually, he invented the assembly line because he concluded that at $500 he could sell millions of cars. Mass production was the result, not the cause, of low prices."[14]

Market-ing is a transcending function. Unlike manufacturing, it cannot be outsourced. Again, we believe that understanding this central, but non-centric, role by inverting the manufacturing–marketing relationship reveals new opportunities in innovation.

Innovating versus inventing

We have been taught that humanity progresses because of the great inventors throughout history. However, invention is not the pathway to prosperity. Inventions are isolated devices that, unless they are connected to actors in service ecosystems, are neutral artifacts and unrealized, if not wasted, resources. In fact, the great inventors we often refer to, such as Guttenberg, Newcomen, Edison, and Ford, were more than inventors of devices or process improvements; they were market visionaries and creators (actually cocreators), through innovative solutions to human problems, through resource integration, and they were able to gain institutionalization of their innovations. This typically required innovative participation in the development of ecosystems that supported their innovation. That is, it took the innovation of a host of actors, as well as innovation in the coordination of these actors. In this sense, innovation is more of a design, visionary, and entrepreneurial task than invention, which is more of an engineering task. Thus, in S-D logic, just as marketing becomes superordinate to manufacturing, innovation becomes superordinate to invention. It is here that the real risk taking is found, in social and economic processes of innovation[15] and, likewise, most of the potential reward.[16]

Effectiveness versus efficiency

The Industrial Revolution involved many converging and integrating technologies, not only around manufacturing, but also around transportation and communication. In all of these technologies, the unending pursuit was for efficiency or productivity, the doing of more and more with fewer and fewer resources, and the elimination of "waste." It was at the very core of industrialization and the central focus of essentially every activity. Efficiency was captured in value-in-exchange that translated into low cost. To be efficient, firms focused on managing and controlling costs. It is inherently producer-centric.

Effectiveness, on the other hand, is a user-centric concept and was typically only considered important if the organization or system was first efficient. Effectiveness, as a user-centric concept, is captured in "value-in-use" and "value-in-context." Thus, not surprisingly, S-D logic inverts the efficiency–effectiveness order, with the latter being primary. That is, without effectiveness, efficiency becomes a mute issue. Moreover, effectiveness can be considered an essential route to efficiency, at least in the long run. Once again, understanding this relationship is critical to innovation and value cocreation and, thus, effectiveness for the firm.

Next steps

S-D logic is very much a work in progress. Its development needs to be continued on all fronts; however, below we note a few areas that we feel need particular attention.

Role of institutions in value co-creation

In service ecosystems, actors are held together not only by reciprocal service exchange but also by institutions. These institutions are shared meanings and normative standards for evaluation and behavior that provide clever human shortcuts for communication and coordination and decision-making in the face of the very limited computational abilities of humans. They can be found not only at the micro level, such as between actors (e.g., a firm and a customer) but also at meso levels (e.g., brand and market cultures) and macro levels (e.g., society or pan-society).

They have been studied under various names in a variety of business and related disciplines; yet we know relatively little about their role in value cocreation. Some institutions constitute markets (institutionalized solutions), such as the tacit agreement, at least for a period of time, to provide for personal-transportation needs with a four-wheeled vehicle approximately 3 meters long, holding four to five individuals, and powered by an internal combustion engine. Other, structural institutions further institutionalize market institutions, such as the development of road systems, the standardization of fueling stations and processes, and cocreated rules of the road. Yet other, more meta institutions, such as intellectual and other property rights, distributed justice, and open market systems, facilitate the development of these market-related institutions. Some institutions, such as democracy, are recreated, with modification and translation, across other institutions, such as national and ethnic cultures. Still others, like rules about the sanctity of life and contractual agreements, develop organically and independently, but with great similarity, more or less simultaneously in different cultures.

Of particular interest is the role of institutions in the facilitation of the massively cooperative value cocreation in large-scale systems, as evidenced by the increasing returns to scale in global (macro-level) human well-being that is occurring through billions of loosely and remotely linked, micro-level exchanges taking place around the world, even as the population increases. This no doubt involves the interplay of institutions at all levels, creating overlapping and nested ecosystems, but we know relatively little about how this complex interplay works. However, if we can understand it, we should be able to provide normative insights for actors at all levels (e.g., individuals, firms, governments) that might allow them to contribute to their own viability through contributing to the viability of others.

Bridging theory and practice with midrange theory

As discussed, S-D logic is a meta-idea. It was developed as a framework at a high level of abstraction so that it could provide a transcending perspective and, in time, perhaps serve as a foundation for a general theory, initially for markets and marketing and, later, more generally for social and economic value cocreation. It also was intended to be enduring and robust and thus to transcend time and space. Thus, as discussed in Chapter 9, it is not intended to be a toolbox filled with specific instruments (actions) that will increase the profits of the firm.

Nonetheless, while it is still a work in progress, the framework is sufficiently in place to begin to connect the meta-framework with compatible, more action-able tools. We believe this can be done through the identification of compatible mid-range theories[17] and frameworks. Many of these, such as "blue-ocean strategy," "jobs to be done," "lean consumption," and "experience innovation," already have a presence in the practitioner literature. They are not always prescriptive in an absolute sense but they do often at least provide specific, near-actionable guidelines. What remains is the need for organizing these around the core concepts of S-D logic, probably through the axioms. Since much of this literature provided input into the development of S-D logic, we think that, taken together, these mid-range theories will not only bridge S-D logic and practice, but also provide a bottom-up support for S-D logic at the same time.

Concluding comments

Possibilities for S-D logic are not fixed, but rather are mostly a function of where the S-D logic community wants to take it. There is no end in sight, nor should there be one. As more individuals from the business disciplines, computer and information science, service science, and other social sciences become engaged, it will likely unfold in ways we could not now imagine. Thus, this introductory book is intended as much as an invitation to participate in S-D logic's advancement as it is an explanation of its core concepts and a statement of its status. We welcome all interested parties, both academics and practitioners, in this cocreative unfolding of the possibilities of S-D logic.

NOTES

1. Russell Roberts, "An interview with Paul Romer on economic growth," Library of Economics and Liberty (November 5). Accessed on February 2, 2013 at www.econlib.org/library/Columns/y2007/Romergrowth.html

2. Robert F. Lusch and James C. Spohrer, "Evolving service for a complex, resilient, and sustainable world," *Journal of Marketing Management*, 28:13–14 (2012), 1491–1503.

3. Donald A. Norman, *Living with Complexity* (Cambridge, MA: MIT Press, 2011).

4. W. Bernard Carlson, *Innovation as a Social Process: Elihu Thomson and the Rise of General Electric, 1870–1900* (Cambridge University Press, 1991); Henry Chesbrough, *Open Business Models: How to Thrive in the New Innovation Landscape* (Boston: Harvard Business School Press, 2006)); Eric Von Hippel, *Democratizing Innovation* (Cambridge, MA: MIT Press, 2006).

5. Matt Ridley *The Rational Optimist: How Prosperity Evolves* (New York: HarperCollins, 2010).

6. Satish Nambisan and Mohanbir Sawhney, *The Global Brain* (Upper Saddle River, NJ: Pearson Education, Inc., publishing as Wharton School Publishing, 2008).

7. Some of these ideas share an affinity with new growth theory: Paul M. Romer, "Increasing returns and long-run growth," *The Journal of Political Economy*, 94:5 (1986), 1002–1037; Paul M. Romer, "The origins of endogenous growth," *The Journal of Economic Perspectives*, 8:1 (1994), 3–22. Also, for a good summary of related ideas see David Warsh, *Knowledge and the Wealth of Nations* (New York: W. W. Norton & Company, 2006).

8. W. Brian Arthur, *The Nature of Technology: What It Is and How It Evolves* (New York: Free Press, 2009).

9. Arthur, *The Nature of Technology*. Arthur attributes the source of this idea to William F. Ogburn, *Social Change*, reprint (New York: Dell, 1966 [1922]).

10. Daniel Bell, *The Coming of Post-Industrial Society: A Venture in Social Forecasting* (New York: Basic Books, 1976).

11. Peter F. Drucker, *Innovation and Entrepreneurship* (New York: Harper & Row, 1985).

12. Barnaby J. Feder, "Peter F. Drucker, a pioneer in social management theory, is dead at 95," *New York Times* (November 12, 2005). Accessed on July 7, 2014 at www.nytimes.com/2005/11/12/business/12drucker.html?pagewanted=all&_r=0

13. Peter F. Drucker, *The Practice of Management* (New York: Harper & Row, 1954).

14. Theodore Levitt, "Marketing myopia," *Harvard Business Review* (July–August 1960), 45–56.

15. Amar Bhide, *The Venturesome Economy* (Princeton University Press, 2008).

16. Robert F. Lusch, Yong Liu, Yubo Chen, and Jurui Zhang, "The emergence of innovation: a social cultural perspective," working paper, McGuire Center for Entrepreneurship, University of Arizona (2013).

17. Roderick J. Brodie, Michael Saren, and Jaqueline Pels, "Theorizing about the service dominant logic: the bridging role of middle range theory," *Marketing Theory*, 11 (March 2011), 75–91.

APPENDIX

Reflection and dialogue

Chapter 1: The service-dominant mindset

1. Why do actors specialize? Can you design a society that would function with generalists and no specialists? Would this world or society approach nirvana?
2. If specialization produces benefits to individuals, organizations, and nations is there a limit to these benefits as actors become more and more specialized?
3. Can a society of specialists exist without markets and if so how might this occur?
4. If service is exchanged for service and service is the fundamental basis of exchange then it could be argued that the essence of society is service exchange. Agree or disagree and defend your position.
5. Do you agree that things cannot have intrinsic value? Can a flower garden or a single flower have intrinsic value?
6. Consider the four axioms of S-D logic and provide an example in a household setting that illustrates each axiom.
7. Consider what you and others around you view as your most important competences. Discuss how the concepts of performativity, structuration, and effectuation relate to these competences.
8. If your home was on fire or was flooding and you had to evacuate within two minutes and could only take a few items, what would you take with you? Try to analyze why you would take the items you have identified.
9. Identify an enterprise that is known predominantly for the tangible market offerings it makes and suggest how a service-dominant mindset could assist in developing innovative ideas for new market offerings.

10. Identify examples of how performativity influences the way in which the organization you work for or lead thinks strategically.

11. What do structuration and effectuation imply in terms of how a firm should organize?

Chapter 2: Roots and heritage

1. Besides goods-dominant and service-dominant logic, what other dominant logics can you identify? How do they influence your thinking?

2. We suggest that economic science was patterned after Newtonian Mechanics model of science. Besides economics, what other scientific fields has the Newtonian Mechanics model influenced? Can you identify alternatives to this model?

3. Bastiat argued that "services are exchanged for services" represents the "beginning, the middle, and the end of economic science." How would you evaluate this statement? Is it too strong? Not strong enough?

4. Smith's "productive–unproductive" distinction has led to the often-cited view that manufacturing jobs are the "real" jobs – the "good jobs" and service jobs are less desirable. Evaluate this view.

5. Similarly, Fisher's differentiation between primary (agriculture), secondary (manufacturing), and tertiary stages has been interpreted to mean that "services" characterize the latter and has led to the suggestion that advanced economies have entered a "new services economy." Evaluate this notion. Has service just now become important?

6. Some have suggested that the difference between G-D logic and S-D logic is just a switch from seeing goods as most important to seeing services as most important in economic exchange. Is this a correct view? If so, why? If not, why not?

7. How might marketing thought in the twentieth century have developed differently if S-D logic had emerged as the dominant thinking following Bastiat's insight that the beginning and end of economic science is services exchanged for services?

8. If Adam Smith were alive today, how might he recast his *Wealth of Nations* treatise? In brief, is there a new *Wealth of Nations*?

Chapter 3: Axioms and foundational premises

1. In Exhibit 3.1 the foundational premises (FPs) of S-D logic were classified under four central FPs or what were called axioms. Can you suggest an alternative classification? Explain.

2. Do you believe the axioms and foundational premises are equally applicable for an early stage developing economy as for a more mature economy? For example, is S-D logic just as applicable in Bolivia as it would be in Sweden? Is it as applicable for explaining Europe during the fifth century BC as it is today?

3. If you were 18 years old and had a choice between (a) receiving $2,000,000 (US dollars) and not being able to either gain additional knowledge and skills or exchange your skills and competences with other actors or (b) being able to continue your education, learning, and knowledge enhancement through-out life and exchange your skills and competences with other actors, which would you select? Discuss.

4. Can a legal economic transaction occur in a market economy without relationship? Explain your reasons.

5. List the operant resources of a business enterprise you are familiar with. Which do you think are the most important to developing strategic advantage? Explain the type or nature of the strategic advantage that is gained.

6. How can a business enterprise understand value from the perspective of the beneficiary of a market offering?

7. How can a government enterprise understand value from the perspective of the citizen beneficiaries of government-provided service(s)?

8. Who in the business firm should be responsible for making the firm's value proposition? Explain why.

9. Would the data that a nation would need or find helpful for understanding the economy be different under G-D logic and S-D logic? If you see a need for change, what new measures would you suggest and why?

10. Brian Arthur, as mentioned in this chapter, essentially argues that resour-ces and resource integration begets additional resources. We suggested that this means that markets are unbounded. Do you agree or disagree and why?

Chapter 4: Service as a guiding framework

1. Identify some of the activities or habits of an enterprise known for its service nature (e.g., airline, health care, education, finance) that characterize a G-D or output orientation. Suggest ways that this enterprise could become more S-D oriented.
2. Are the IHIP characteristics of services desirable or even possible for goods? Explain your reasons.
3. Are there markets where efficiency is more paramount in importance than effectiveness?
4. An S-D orientation begins with a focus on providing benefits to others. It begins with a desire to help others in return for service or help; it begins with a service-for-service mindset. Is this mindset consistent with an entrepreneurial spirit for enterprise? Why or why not?
5. S-D logic argues that service represents the general case, or the common denominator, of the voluntary exchange process among humans and that this occurs across time and space. Service is what is *always* exchanged. Goods, when employed, are aids to the service process. Critics have argued that this universal perspective goes against pluralism or a willingness to accept alternative views of the world. Do you agree or disagree? Explain your position.
6. The S-D logic-informed G-D principles (see Exhibit 4.4) appear to suggest that a firm's traditional marketing mix should be cocreated. Agree or disagree and provide examples to support your answer.
7. Discuss the normative prescriptions that result from S-D logic. Do these prescriptions apply in all situations or contexts?
8. Can an enterprise make a value proposition that is compelling or appealing to all direct stakeholders? Give an example.

Chapter 5: It's all actor-to-actor (A2A)

1. If all actors are generic, what is the purpose of people in management or executive education taking part in role-playing exercises?
2. Discuss whether the organization you work for (or have worked for in the past) is more a G-D or S-D organization.

3. Generalized exchange is less common in market society than in premarket or non-market society. Do you agree or disagree? Discuss.

4. Develop examples of redistribution as an exchange institution as you have experienced it in an organization. Explain why this redistribution occurred.

5. How much agency do you have in your life? What are the constraints on your agency?

6. Think of some of the major actions you have taken over the past twelve months. What was the trade-off or implicit exchange that occurred? Express these as opportunity costs.

7. Why do actors in a high-level market economy have more access to offerings and more tangible things but also often experience frustration and a scarcity of time? Explain the following concepts in this situation: cocreating value, resource integration, density, system viability.

8. Can society change without the exchange of service(s)? Explain your position.

Chapter 6: The nature, scope, and integration of resources

1. We suggest that tangible resources and natural resources are not the most important resources for human advancement. Yet humans need natural resources and other tangible resources for survival. Can you explain this apparent contradiction? Do you agree or disagree with us? Explain.

2. The conventional wisdom is that when people are put in prison for whatever reason, they are no longer useful and in fact are often viewed as a liability and not a resource. Using the ideas presented in this chapter, how might prisoners become resources?

3. Consider a household that is living in a community of 40,000 people and contemplating moving to a city of 2 million people that is 1,000 miles away and in which it has no family ties. With this move, what are the (a) market-facing resources, (b) public resources, and (c) private resources the household should consider? Which of these resources might be lost or foregone, and which might be gained. What are the implications for the service(s) the family will be able to access?

4. Select a firm you are familiar with and identify what you think its ten most valuable resources are and then classify them as market-facing, private, and public resources.

5. One could view the management of resources as driven by the state of the wants and needs of actors and the state of science and technology. Should innovation to develop new resources be driven more by the "pull" of the state of wants and needs of actors or by the "push" of current science and technology?

6. Do humans invent tools to become more efficient and effective but at the cost of the inefficient use of natural resources? How can the concepts and ideas of S-D logic, and especially those related to resource integration and system viability, shed light on this issue?

7. Develop a set of ideas for increasing density with your existing resources (market and non-market facing). Discuss what you believe is the top idea you come up with and how it would influence the viability of your system.

8. If you were head of new product innovation for a large publicly traded firm what ideas for managing new product innovation could be derived by concepts in this chapter?

Chapter 7: Collaboration

1. Consider the organization you work for and your current job. What efforts do you engage in to do your job that is normalizing practice? Discuss how representational practices also influence your job.

2. Can you think of examples in which you have used IT to coproduce and/or collaborate with other actors? Describe these examples and what went well and not so well.

3. Is it desirable for a firm to develop market offerings that minimize cocreation processes? Generate a few ideas for offerings that minimize cocreation processes. Can you imagine an offering that has no cocreation processes?

4. Six factors drive how much coproduction an actor engages in and these are: expertise, control, tangible capital, risk taking, psychic benefits, and economic benefits. Use these to explain how much your family or household engages in home-based production activities (cooking, cleaning, home schooling, etc.).

5. Are there limits to the division of labor in society? Elaborate and discuss.

6. If you were mayor of your city, how would you engage the citizens to be coproducers of various services? Can these activities also enhance cocreation of value for the citizens?

7. Consider your experiences in general with children under the age of six versus adults over the age of twenty. Reflect on the five key sources of collaborative advantage, and discuss whether children or adults are more inherently competent at collaboration.

8. We discussed an extended view of the enterprise. Apply this thinking to your household. What are the implications for system viability?

Chapter 8: Service ecosystems

1. What is the relationship between outsourcing and the concepts of markets, supply chains, and marketing channels?

2. Four key elements define a service ecosystem: (1) relatively self-contained, (2) self-adjusting system of resource-integrating actors, (3) shared institutional logics, and (4) mutual value creation through service exchange. In your opinion, which of these key elements is the most important? Explain your reasoning.

3. How can a service ecosystem become more resilient?

4. How are the ten foundational premises of S-D logic related to service ecosystems?

5. Take the concept of a service ecosystem and develop a graphical representation of your own personal service ecosystem.

6. Service systems in a city include governing, water, energy, waste disposal, nutrition, safety, transport, communication, education, entertainment, and health. The mayor recently appointed you as the first chief innovation officer for the city. Using at least one of these service systems, apply the concepts in this chapter and prior chapters to develop a list of at least three innovative service offerings.

7. Service systems mentioned in this chapter were part of a typical city. Identify and discuss whether a country would entail different service systems.

8. What is the role of a leader such as a CEO in a service ecosystem?

9. Consider your home or place of business and identify ecosystem services that could benefit you.

Chapter 9: Strategic thinking

1. Consider an enterprise you have worked for and describe the service it offers.
2. For the service described above, what is the enterprise's value proposition? Is it compelling to potential service beneficiaries (customers)? Would it also resonate with employees and customers? Why or why not?
3. Next describe how service beneficiaries use the service. How is it integrated with other resources? How does use change under different contexts?
4. Using the situation above identify several key suppliers to the enterprise and describe the service they provide. How is each service integrated with other resources? How does this change under different contexts?
5. Enterprises also perform many service(s) within the enterprise. Identify one or two of these and discuss the service and how it is provided. Why is this service provided within the firm rather than via market exchange?
6. Identify one of the enterprise's most important resources. Try to be fairly specific – for instance, if you identify human resources, you might specify the product engineering staff or the salesforce. Do this for both a key resource within the enterprise and one outside (i.e., in the service ecosystem).
7. Map the service ecosystem of either the firm or a key department such as the information systems department or the corporate social responsibility department. What are the shared institutions in this service ecosystem? Develop ideas for the redesign of the service ecosystem. Are shared institutions a barrier to change or do they motivate change?
8. Agriculture is one of the oldest industries. Develop some innovative ideas reconfiguring for improved density. Specifically consider reconfiguring around form, time, place, and ownership.

Chapter 10: Conclusions and considerations

1. Do you agree that S-D logic is a meta-idea? Explain your reasons.
2. Describe how S-D logic has helped you to understand a complex service ecosystem you are familiar with.
3. S-D logic needs to be understood and adopted in its entirety. Is this possible? Why or why not?

4. Do you agree that society is a very large-scale service ecosystem, with the sole purpose of value cocreation through resource integration and service exchange? Explain why you agree or disagree.
5. The more we innovate the more the innovation frontier expands. Do you agree or disagree? Give your reasons.
6. Why is entrepreneurial management aligned with S-D logic?
7. Why is market-ing and innovation essentially the same business function?
8. What is more superordinate, invention or innovation? Give your reasons.
9. Discuss the need to better understand institutions in order to apply S-D logic.
10. Where do you see the biggest needs for mid-range theory in S-D logic?

INDEX